D1142307

SING
WHEN YOU'RE
WINNING

First published in Great Britain in 2006 by

André Deutsch
an imprint of the
Carlton Publishing Group
20 Mortimer Street
London W1T 3JW

Text copyright © Colin Irwin 2006
Design copyright © Carlton Publishing Group 2006

ISBN-13 978-0-23300-184-5
ISBN-10 0-233-00184-0

Grateful acknowledgement is made to Billy Bragg and Pete Boyle for
their kind permission to reproduce their song lyrics.

The publishers would like to thank the following sources for their kind
permission to reproduce the pictures in this book.

ACTION IMAGES: 7 (bottom); /MSI: 1 (centre); /John Sibley: 3 (top);
/Sporting Pictures/Peter Stack: 7t. EMPICS: /S&G/Alpha : 2b.
GETTY IMAGES: /Graham Chadwick: 3b; /Phil Cole: 8tl; /A.R.Coster: 2t;
/Express/Victor Drees: 1t; /Laurence Griffiths: 6b, 6t; /Keystone: 1b;
/Keystone/Douglas Miller: 7c; /PNA Rota: 2c; /Ian Walton: 5t.
AUTHOR'S OWN: 4t, 4b; 8tr, 8b. PETE BOYLE: 5b

Every effort has been made to acknowledge correctly and contact the
source and/or copyright holder of each picture and Carlton Books
Limited apologises for any unintentional errors or omissions which
will be corrected in future editions of this book.

Typeset by E-Type, Liverpool
Printed and bound in Great Britain by Mackays

SING
WHEN YOU'RE
WINNING

FOOTBALL FANS, TERRACE SONGS AND A
SEARCH FOR THE SOUL OF SOCCER

COLIN IRWIN

André Deutsch

In loving memory of my mum, Gwen Irwin
A Swindon Town fan

Feb 2, 1924 – Feb 17, 2006

Acknowledgements

Grateful thanks for their valuable assistance to:

My dad, Bill Irwin, for suggestions and unerring knowledge.

Val for unwavering support, understanding and company on long away trips.

Kevin and Christy for enthusiastic assistance and mouthy advice.

Ian 'Walsall' Gittins for moral support and copy-editing. Miranda, Jim and all the other lovely people at André Deutsch.

The players and officials of Wick Academy FC and Total Network Solutions FC.

Billy Bragg, Martin Brown, Rob Mason, Ian Lancashire, Jules Spencer, John Hemmingham, Greg Dyke, Barry Hearn, Bob & Rose Winstanley, Iain McNay (Cherry Red Records), Faye White, Mike Alway, Martin Cooper, Pete Boyle, (copies of Pete's CD at peteboys.co.uk) David Elleray, Mohamed Al Fayed, Boff from Chumbawamba, Jasper Carrott, Dave Burnley, Alan Beecroft, Kjell Skjerven, Derek Elston, Sue Townsend, Phil Fox, Hannah Cawsey, Lee Clarkson, Clive Miers and the Leeds United Ultras (lufcultras.co.uk).

Cheers also to the unfortunates who found themselves sitting next to me at matches or who freely shared their thoughts over a half-time Bovril or a pint at the end of the game.

Thanks to media officials at Sunderland, Leeds United, Swindon Town, Notts County, Bristol City, Torquay United, Everton, Manchester City, Fulham, Orient, Southampton, Middlesbrough,

Hull City, Oxford United, Wolverhampton Wanderers, Stockport County, Burnley and Barnet for their assistance.

A pox on all the other clubs, who were totally unhelpful (and a special raspberry for the Leeds United stewards).

Credit (again) to Alberta the Bold Cavalier, and respect to anybody who goes out on a freezing night in February to sing their hearts out for the lads.

Contents

Introduction

HARRY'S GAME

'Spectators are what professional football is all about. Without them it has no point, no status and no future. I know professionals who see the game as their own property and the fans as people whose part in the ritual is a kind of privilege. The positions should be reversed.'
Alan Hardaker, former secretary of the Football League

Harry Norris was a big man. A big man with an impossibly square jaw, a sleek slither of silver hair largely hidden by a flat cap of indeterminate colour, and the perennially stony expression of someone taking a slow walk to the guillotine in front of a baying crowd. He seemed ancient. But then all adults seem ancient when you're six years old.

He wore a dull grey overcoat and a rather sad shabby red-and-white scarf under cheeks of such glowering ruddiness that they looked set to explode at any second. He was there every Saturday at the bus stop by Chertsey Station, stamping his feet in the cold – even when it wasn't cold. And we'd stand next to him, my dad, my brother and me, stamping our feet in sympathy, peering up the road, wondering why the bus always got stuck on the wrong side of the level-crossing gates. Harry Norris would sniff a bit, glance at us with those strange, menacing eyes, and say, 'Aye aye.' We'd dutifully say 'Aye aye' back in perfect harmony, and hope the bus would come soon.

When the No. 48 did finally arrive we'd clamber up the stairs

and sit a couple of rows behind Harry. For some reason he'd
wait until we passed St Peter's Hospital, just a couple of stops
up the road, and then he'd start. He would shift his bulk
awkwardly to face us and a few other unfortunate apostles
collected *en route*, give us a long, hard stare and say, 'Another
load of rubbish today, I expect …'

The voice of doom would then accompany us all the way to
Woking FC's ground. By The Otter he'd start on the goalkeeper,
who must be Dracula because he's so scared of crosses. As the
rest of us stared out of the window to clock the famous pianist
Russ Conway's house to see if we could catch a glimpse of Russ
playing 'Side Saddle' in the potting shed, Harry would move
on to the defence: 'I've seen milk turn quicker than our full
backs.'

The rest of us would hold our breath as the bus driver
attempted to negotiate the infamously perilous Six Crossroads
where my grandad was an AA man who'd been knocked over
three times trying to direct the traffic; it was so dangerous spectators would come with packed lunches for a day out watching
the crashes. But not Harry. He couldn't give a toss about the evil
Six Crossroads. He would be too busy ranting on about the half
backs: 'useless buggers can't pass wind, let alone a football'.
And by the time the No. 48 trundled into Woking town centre
he would be on to the forward line, who were useless no-marks
not fit to wear the shirt and clearly couldn't score in a brothel.
Whatever that was.

I became fascinated by Harry Norris. We'd stand a few yards
from him on the touchline, close enough to hear him without
anyone thinking we were in any way remotely acquainted with
him. The match had barely started when his booming voice
would echo around the small ground, offering spectacles to the
referee, dissertations on the offside law to the linesman and an
in-depth analysis of the shortcomings of any player unfortunate enough to come within easy earshot. His tirades were
vicious and unrelenting and it scarcely mattered if the player
belonged to them or us, or indeed if there was the remotest

justification in his criticism. Abuse was an end to itself for Harry Norris.

In those days there was a hockey pitch within the Woking ground, and at half-time we'd all turn to watch the women's match going on behind us. Almost immediately a familiar voice would boom out: 'Shoot! Woman, shoot! I hope you're quicker than that in the kitchen!' The hockey players – whose only interaction with the football was normally an occasional visit from the Woking keeper Brian Farris, in pursuit of the ball and perhaps a few phone numbers – would be shell-shocked by this totally unwarranted tirade from someone who clearly had no grasp of the rules of their game whatsoever. The loud running commentary would last for 10 minutes and then suddenly the footballers were on the pitch again and Harry would turn back to watch Woking stumble to another 1-0 defeat against Hendon, oblivious to the appalled faces he'd left behind.

Harry had a long-running feud with Brian Finn, the Woking captain who still holds the club record for most appearances. Finn played much of his career at right back, positioning himself for the kick-off right in front of Harry. As play started, he'd hear a loud voice in his ear: 'Have they picked you again, Finn? Hope you're going to play better than you did last week – you were rubbish …' Finn always did his best to ignore Harry but usually failed, swearing and cursing at him and offering to give him his entrance money back if he'd only go away when he came over to take a throw-in.

On another occasion, Harry maintained a constant barrage directed at an opposing winger from, I dunno, Enfield or Leytonstone or Dulwich Hamlet. Harry was enjoying himself, questioning the guy's parentage, comparing his facial features to a weasel, backing his pet tortoise to beat him in a sprint and helpfully suggesting he'd be better off playing tiddly-winks. Suddenly the guy sprinted over the touchline, stood eyeball to eyeball with Harry and snarled, 'Right – you and me, after the game, we'll sort this out once and for all.' Five minutes from the end of the match we saw Harry do something he never *ever* did – he left early, muttering something about getting home to Mrs Norris. I'm not sure which was more shocking – the fact that he'd left the match early, or that he was married.

For months I assumed the object of football was to give grumpy old men licence to vent their daily frustrations on hapless gladiators stuck on a field solely for their displeasure. It was a while before I took account of the other supporters around me who would shout encouragement, clap and cheer and, on the rare occasions when Woking actually scored a goal, even be moved to jump up and down. I would squeal in delight with them, stealing a sneaky glance along the touchline to see Harry Norris snarling and claiming his next-door neighbour's cat could have scored that goal. *Why did he come*? Masochism? Sense of duty? Cruelty? Habit? Warped loyalty?

Who knows what insanity drags people to see a team, *their* team, every week, when the weather's freezing cold, the money's tight and the entertainment is scant? But come they do. Every club has a Harry Norris. Or rather they did, until grey-suited accountants invaded the game to turn it into a corporate playground and price the Harry Norrises out.

Not that I'm a blind advocate of old football over new. Far from it. The crumbling stadiums of yesteryear were a disgrace – cold, cheerless, unwelcoming places where at the big matches you could hardly see anything anyway. Some of them even proved literally to be death traps. The sophistication of today's football, from its family centres to blanket television coverage, has both glamourised and sanitised it. The football itself is also technically, tactically and physically light years beyond its former incarnation, thanks to mostly sensible new laws protecting the flair players from the thuggish centre backs of old. It's just a shame it's resulted in a new breed of greedy, egotistical, overpaid prima donnas trying to get opponents sent off and executing a series of elaborate dives at the first whiff of an opponent's boot; and attracted odious accountants and oily money men to run the game.

But ask anyone – *anyone* – what it was about going to their first match that got them hooked, and they will tell you it was the atmosphere. And by atmosphere they mean the fans. And by the fans they mean the singing. There is an extraordinary tribal spirit that binds fans together as one solid, fiercely united representation of a community and creates an almost irresistible intensity. At its worst it's violent and plain ugly, but at its best it's thrilling, exhilarating and inspirational. At its *very* best, it creates its own swell of energy that permeates beyond the terraces and almost tangibly lifts the players on the pitch to a higher plane. To be part of it is a deeply emotional, almost spiritual experience. It can even win matches.

The great folk singer and guitarist Martin Carthy once told me that football crowds represent the one true surviving embodiment of an organic living folk tradition; i.e. a network of songs which evolved out of existing songs, sung by the people, adapted to meet the specific needs of geographical identity and seemingly created by spontaneous combustion, the unheralded originators remaining anonymous. I've watched in awe and wonder as, seemingly without warning, a crowd suddenly launches into a chant or a song. Hundreds of people bellow a topical lyric about one of the opposing players and you think, 'How the hell did *that* happen?'

You hear enough about the infamous firms who terrorised football in the 1970s and 1980s, rampaging around Europe with radishes for brains and swastika sneers, and the upgrading of the game over the last decade means it is no longer the property of the proletariat. Yet the fans still maketh a football club. Players, managers and directors come and go at a furious rate. They have their own agenda, usually financial, and however often the club badge gets a kiss in moments of ecstasy, this matter of the heart will seldom override matters of the wallet. 'Don't forget we pay your wages!' my mate Steve used to yell at the players during yet another hapless performance … but they usually did.

Respect to Kevin Keegan, who freely admitted that during

his eventful tenure as Newcastle United manager he would listen to what the fans were chanting, and sometimes made substitutions based on who they were calling to see. When Keegan walked out of his job as England manager at the end of a miserable match against Germany at Wembley in October 2000, his terse explanation was that it was the wish of the fans: 'They got me the job in the first place, and they let me know when it was time to leave.'

This book started out as an exploration of Martin Carthy's theory that football fans represent the new folk tradition, an investigation of terrace anthems, but it quickly developed into a celebration of football fans, the true heroes of the game. Not just the fans that make a racket, either. I know devout supporters who suffer in complete silence throughout the matches, scrunching up their faces in concentration, showing no emotion at any of the drama unfolding in front of them, yet internally kicking every ball and emerging at the end of the game in a state of nervous exhaustion, chattering non-stop about each subtle nuance of play. Others can't bear to be close to the singing because it interferes with their own concentration, and more than one terrace drummer has been offered helpful suggestions as to where exactly he can stick his snare.

Personally I don't mind drummers, but I won't engage in conversation while play is going on. Especially not with annoyingly reasonable fans from the opposition who have somehow nabbed a seat next to you and want to be friends, saying things like 'I get on with everyone, I just want to see a good game, me ...' A poke in the eye usually sorts it out.

Then there's the middle-class, middle-aged blokes behind who spend the entire game talking about their mortgages and plans for early retirement and their holidays in Marbella. You hear them droning on through the whole game, pausing only to sniff in disdain at the bloke with exploding cheeks in front of us who is threatening to hang, draw and quarter the referee, linesman and manager. 'Fancy taking it so seriously, it's only a game,' they say, before starting a discussion about their top-of-the-range new motors. The prat quota has undoubtedly escalated in recent years.

Perhaps worst of all, though, is the network of mainly younger fans with earphones clutching radios tuned to Radio Five Live, giving a running commentary on the breaking scores coming in from other grounds. 'Hull one-up against Crewe!' they shout triumphantly, expecting us all to swivel round and demand to know the name of the Hull scorer and the size of the crowd. You want to know the other scores, mate? Go home and watch them on Teletext.

Some of us still yearn for the days when men in white coats would clamber along the hoardings putting small home-made numbers against even smaller home-made letters to indicate the half-time scores in other matches. You'd peer at them hard trying to decipher it all. A: 2-1. B: 0-0. C: 2-2. You'd then scour your programme to find the tiny print where you could interpret which matches were represented by the various letters. 'Ooh, Bolton beating Middlesbrough 2-1,' you'd say, trying to get excited, before realizing that was 'B' and 'A' was Wolves v. Charlton. Just as you'd get it all sorted the man in the white coat would reappear, decide he'd got it all wrong and change them around again. Then someone would tip Bovril over your programme and you'd be completely buggered.

They've had to withstand a lot lately and they may even be a dying breed, but without hardcore fans showing unconditional love – even if it's tough love – then football is nothing. It's Sheffield United fans chanting 'We hate Wednesday' and Millwall fans responding with 'We don't like Mondays'. It's Watford fans chanting 'Where's your jewellery gone?' at Ozzy and Sharon Osbourne as they were introduced on the pitch at half-time following a recent burglary at their house.

God help the poor misguided fool who decided to propose to his girlfriend at half-time in a Cambridge United match. The romance of the occasion was rather shattered by the ensuing chant of 'We've all had your missus, we've all had your missus'. And when a bride and groom appeared on the pitch during a match between Charlton and Coventry City, they were met with a barrage of 'You don't know what you're doing'.

A male streaker who braved the pitch at Stamford Bridge was greeted with 'Is that all she gets at home?' to the 'Bread Of Heaven' hymn usually reserved to taunt opposing fans with 'Is that all you take away?' And of all the personalised chants enjoyed by favoured players, the one Arsenal fans came up with for their former midfielder Emmanuel Petit is surely the best. 'He's blond, he's quick, his name's a porno flick … Emmanuel, Emmanuel.'

There are some wonderful variants, too, on 'Guantanamera', a 1966 hit single for The Sandpipers that started life as a patriotic poem by Cuban statesman, journalist, painter and nationalist Jose Marti in 1891. At 16, Marti was sentenced to six years in prison by the Spanish authorities (who ruled Cuba at the time) for treason, and suffered debilitating injuries from the chains that manacled his legs. Eventually released but exiled from Cuba, he rallied popular support against Spanish rule among other expatriates throughout Europe and the Americas. While resisting American attempts to annex Cuba, he attempted to lead a nationalist revolution. In 1895 he published the Manifesto of Monticristi, declaring independence for Cuba, and led a rebel invasion, but was killed by Spanish troops at the Battle of Dos Rios. The war ended three years later and today an airport in Havana is named in his honour, but surely his greatest legacy is his poem about a dying man – later set to music by Jose Fernandez Diaz – popularized by Pete Seeger and the American folk movement of the sixties.

There possibly aren't too many aware of such a noble history among those appropriating the tune of the chorus of 'Guantanamera' to bellow 'You only sing when you're winning' at opposing fans at football matches, but that is maybe part of the fascination of terrace culture, and further evidence to support the argument that football anthems represent the one true modern folk tradition.

The first adaptation I remember of 'Guantanamera' came

during a period of intense pressure by Arsenal against Southampton when the crowd started baying, 'Score in a minute, we're gonna score in a minute'. It was then used to hail any hero of the day with enough syllables in his name to fit into the chorus: 'One David Beckham, there's only one David Beckham …' or, in the case of Celtic's Scottish international keeper Andy Goram on being diagnosed with schizophrenia, 'Two Andy Gorams, there's only two Andy Gorams'.

The ditty has been further amended on numerous occasions, with highly mixed results:

'Sing when you're fishing, you only sing when you're fishing …' (to fans of Grimsby Town).

'Sing when it's snowing, you only sing when it's snowing …' (Chelsea fans to supporters of Norwegian side Tromso during a Champions League game played in a blizzard).

'Sing when you're whaling, you only sing when you're whaling …' (to any Scandinavian/Icelandic/Russian team).

'Small town in Poland, you're just a small town in Poland …' (to fans of Walsall, based on the disingenuous 'confusion' of Walsall with Warsaw).

'One team in Tallinn, there's only one team in Tallinn .. ' (Scotland fans in Estonia, when the hosts failed to turn up for an international during confusion over a kick-off time).

As my mate Steve used to say – never trust a man who doesn't drink, never trust a woman with thin lips, and never trust *anyone* who doesn't like football.

The thing is, it's not just the national sport, it's the soul of the nation. Well, the soul of the nation I was raised in. Does it still exist in the moneybags world of Sky saturation TV coverage, foreign imports, all-seater stadiums, prawn sandwiches, executive boxes and directors with double-barrelled names? And do they still sell Bovril and Wagon Wheels at football matches?

So I set off round the country. From the most southerly league team in the country, Plymouth Argyle, to the most northerly senior club, Wick Academy, just the toss of a caber from John

O'Groats. I walked on through the wind, I walked on through the rain, and though my dreams were tossed and blown, I walked on with hope in my heart to find out.

I felt I owed it to Harry Norris.

— CHAPTER 1 —

Who Ate all the Wagon Wheels?

*'The lower middle and the working classes may be divided into two sets:
Fabians and footballers, and 'pon my word it's difficult to say which is
the greater nuisance to the other members of society.'*

Anonymous English gentleman, 1892

'**A**re you a spy?'
     'Beg pardon?'
'A spy? From *Oldham*?'

The portly bloke poking me in the ribs at Brentford FC,
chortling at his own wit while sitting in a stand disconcertingly
known locally as the Wendy House, is a geography teacher. I
know this because he's wearing brown corduroy trousers and
specs held together by Elastoplast. He has spent the first 15
minutes of the match sharing his brilliant tactical acumen
('What they need to be doing is passing the ball to one another
and then kicking it in the net ...') with his blotchy pre-teen
daughter, who has shown her indifference by sticking on head-
phones to listen to the latest Pussycat Dolls album, stopping
only to sneeze all over her dad.

He turns his attention to me as I am scribbling unreadable
gibberish about a Chesterfield player with gushing blond hair
currently receiving an almighty volley of obscenities and hand
gestures from the home fans in front of us because he's ... well,
because he's a Chesterfield player with gushing blond hair, really.
That, and the fact that he looks a bit of a ponce. My geography

friend clocks the notebook and jumps to the obvious conclusion: 'You're a spy from Oldham checking us out before the cup game on Tuesday, aren't you?'

Er … yeah, you've rumbled me, mate, I say with heavy irony. 'I knew it! As soon as I saw you writing notes I thought, "Aye aye, I bet he's from Oldham …"' Delighted to discover that an alternative career as Miss Marple awaits him should he ever give up on geography and errant schoolboys, he shakes my hand vigorously. I smile wanly and retrieve my hand from his grasp to discover it is covered in the contents of his daughter's nose.

'So what do you think of us so far – seen any *weaknesses*?' he asks, with a wink and a nudge. I glance back at the pitch just as the gargantuan home centre half Michael Turner is attempting to deal with a huge hoof from the Chesterfield back line. It's not pretty. Like a drunken lumberjack hacking at a troublesome bough dancing in the wind, he spends ten seconds making several ugly stabs at bringing the errant ball to order before Wayne Allison, Chesterfield's bruising striker, finally trundles into view to put him out of his misery. He barges Turner out of the way, nicks the ball off him and slides it deftly between the legs of baby-faced keeper Nelson into the net. 'Any weaknesses?' I say, looking back at the geography teacher, now staring gloomily into his daughter's crisps. 'That big centre half for a start. Our strikers will be gobbling him up for their supper on Tuesday …'

You can get Bovril at Brentford FC. And Wagon Wheels. *Bovril and Wagon Wheels*, the true spirit of football. Where else would you consider buying *either* but at half-time at a football match? Who else even *sells* Bovril or Wagon Wheels except for that kiosk under the stand? We are talking the snack of gods, the official feast of the beautiful game.

I'm not entirely sure why I picked Brentford to begin my search for the soul of football. Probably because it's the closest professional club to where I live (which obviously means I never go there). My last visit was in another age entirely, in the days before penalty shoot-outs, when men were men and would happily play out five or six pulsating 0-0 draws, plus stamina-sapping extra-times in mud, snow, ice and tempest, with a ball made of concrete, before an FA Cup tie was resolved. Griffin Park, Brentford was the neutral ground chosen as a second replay in a cup match between Barnet and my team, Woking.

Jimmy Greaves, who was then in the, well, not so much the autumn of his career as the last day of winter, was playing for Barnet. We all trooped along to the first tie at Barnet, excited to see the great man in action. Five minutes into the game Barnet were awarded a free kick on the edge of the penalty area. Greaves stepped up to bang a peach of a shot into the net. As he raised his arms in celebration, the ref ordered him to retake the kick because he hadn't blown his whistle.

Greavesy, possibly irked that he'd had to interrupt a five-day bender to be here, didn't take kindly to having his fun spoiled by a jobsworth in black, and offered words to this effect. Suddenly the referee was pointing dramatically to the dressing room (there were no fancy coloured cards in those days) and, spitting venom and possibly the contents of last night's pub crawl, Greavesy trudged off. The match ended 3-3, Jimmy was suspended for the replay at Woking, which also ended 3-3, and he barely got a kick in the second replay at Brentford, which Woking won at a trot. It's a funny old game, Saint …

Armed with warm, if antiquated, memories, I park in a supermarket car park and join the pockets of red-and-white scarves making their way through the small terraced houses lined against the back roads to Griffin Park. It's a reminder of old-school football in the days before executive boxes and purpose-built all-seater stadiums out of town, a time when football was the opium of the masses, a genuine working-class obsession that poshos didn't understand at all.

I actually see an old boy coming out of his terraced house wearing a red bobble hat to walk 50 yards to the match, and I imagine his wife will have his tea on the table for 5 p.m. when he will stomp inside, kick the cat and swear he'll never set foot in that ground again until they get a decent centre half. Sadly, though, he fails to wield one of those huge wooden rattles that were inexplicably a compulsory accessory for the 1950s football fan, and the only songs heard as we turn into Braemar Road are from the telly in the Griffin pub.

But a chirpy Salvation Army band are playing Christmas carols inside the ground with a smattering of children around them mouthing the words while staring with understandable concern at the red-faced tuba player, whose eyes are popping out of his head. It's a charmingly innocent cameo scene interrupted only by the bloke behind me bellowing into his mobile: 'Did you see Gary Neville the other night? Did you *see* him? That bloke is SHIT!' This is one of the incontrovertible facts of modern football. Arsène Wenger always misses the sending-off incident, Jose Mourinho is the king of cool and everyone but Manchester United fans hates Gary Neville.

Not that everything in the Brentford garden is blooming. A man standing forlornly holding a bucket with a sign on it saying 'Bees Utd £1m Appeal Fund' betrays the woes seriously threatening the club's very existence. Ask anyone down here about it all and the name 'Ron Noades' is repeated at you, with a menacing stare and a knowing nod. Noades, or 'That Bastard' as he's more commonly known around these parts, cops most of the fans' blame for the club teetering on the brink of collapse in recent years, with the sale of Griffin Park and a ground-share with non-league clubs like AFC Wimbledon and Woking among the options explored to keep them afloat.

I almost feel sorry for Ron Noades. I mean, he's got a comedy name for a start, with all the attributes of a Monty Python pantomime villain, and the ground is so dated that you almost expect to see Alan 'Fluff' Freeman popping up at the turnstiles to flog you Brentford Nylons. Noades became Brentford's majority shareholder in 1998 and then appointed himself team manager. He even picked up two Manager of the Month awards and won the old Third Division title, and everyone thought he was, well, the Bees' knees.

As things got tough a couple of years later, Noades decided to relieve himself of his duties. Imagine the conversation he must have had with himself in the boardroom: 'Ron, I think we need to make a change ...' He runs round to the other side of the desk. 'But Mr Noades, I can turn it around.' He vaults across the desk again. 'No Ron, I've decided we are going to give that Lewington chappie a crack at it ...' He sprints back round the other side and falls to his knees. 'But I love this job, boss, please don't sack me, I've got a wife and a football club to provide for ...'

Ron doesn't live here any more, having stepped down as chairman in March 2003, and as the lads in red-and-white stripes grapple with the might of Chesterfield, the Bees United Supporters Trust is well on its way to raising the funds to take over the club and its reputed £8 million debt. Still, Brentford's problems are hardly unique. Show me a lower league side and I'll show you a club in some sort of financial peril. Here, in the shadow of the M4 flyover, we're but a stone's throw from Billionaire Central at Chelsea but we could be on another planet. And you know what? There is a lot to be said for this particular planet, with its Salvation Army band and its mufflers and Wagon Wheels and Bees United collection buckets.

'We're banking on Antti Niemi leaving Southampton,' one fan tells me in the convivial Princess Royal pub next to the ground. I look at him blankly but, slopping lager over my toes, he explains his line of reasoning: 'Paul Smith, see. Our ex-goalie. We sold him to Southampton and we get shitloads of money from them based on his appearances for them. But he can't get in their team until Niemi leaves. So we want Niemi to leave Southampton.' Maybe you should buy Niemi off Southampton then, I say. That way you can be sure Smith will get regular games. He looks at me in bewilderment. 'But we'd have to pay more for Niemi than the extra money we'd get for Smith and we've got no money ...' He suddenly realises that I'm joking, guffaws loudly, claps me on the back and tosses the rest of his lager down my trousers.

Weirdly enough, a few weeks later Southampton *do* sell Niemi – to Fulham – and I can imagine the bloke in the Princess Royal dancing on the ceiling shrieking, 'We've been saved, we've been saved!' Unlike many of the shots aimed at Southampton's goal once Smith is installed, unfortunately. Smith plays a couple of games and is then dropped for a Polish teenager with an unpronounceable name. Brentford's extra windfall may be a while coming yet.

Still, they like a laugh at Brentford. They'd have to, with Martin 'Mad Dog' Allen as manager. Now here's a guy who understands the true spirit of the terraces and the importance of a bond between players and fans. The grandson of a Jarrow marcher, he was paying the rent by clearing leaves when he was offered a coaching job at Reading. After taking Barnet to the brink of the Football League, he was offered the job as Brentford manager and, asked what salary he wanted, is reputed to have said, 'a car, and six tickets for every match'.

Now Allen organises matches between the first team and the fans, raised £22,000 on a 25-mile sponsored bike ride from Maidenhead to Brentford to help stave off administration, is celebrated for wearing grotesquely unfashionable tank tops on the touchline, has a dog called Monty that goes to work with him, will occasionally get his players in for training at 7.30 a.m. to give them a reality check, and once famously stripped to his boxers and dived into a freezing cold river in Hartlepool to show his players what he was made of (and took £160 off them in a bet into the bargain). Watching him tearing his hair out and doing a passable impression of a demented dingo along the touchline, it's easy to see why Allen was voted BBC London Sports Personality of 2005. He met England coach Sven Goran Eriksson at an awards do and invited him to visit Brentford. Sven just looked at him blankly, apparently, and Allen stormed off in disgust.

Actor, comedian and never-off-the-telly lovable geezer type Bradley Walsh was also a Brentford winger/full back in the early 1980s. He reduced opposing defenders to tears of laughter with impressions of Worzel Gummidge and Norman Wisdom at corners, and won a place in the first-team squad for entertainment value in the coach and dressing room.

Today, though, they don't have much to laugh or sing about, and the fans grouped behind the goal barely get beyond some fleeting ritual abuse of the small pocket of Chesterfield fans shivering on the uncovered Ealing Road terrace at the other end of the ground and the odd chorus of the Brentford song, 'Hey Jude'. Why 'Hey Jude'? I ask the fans near me. They all shrug their shoulders. Shouldn't you have a Rod Stewart song? He was supposed to have been on Brentford's books at one time, wasn't he? 'Do Ya Think I'm Sexy?' or 'Young Turks' or 'Sailing'? After all, every other football crowd sings a variant on 'Sailing'. 'No,' says a passing Bee, scorning the absurdity of the question, '"Hey Jude" – it's always been "Hey Jude". It's the Brentford song.'

Although the team has been flying high in League One lately, a sense of duty rather than destiny prevails at Griffin Park this bleak Saturday. Yet somehow it still represents an essence of football that may be dying but still rings far truer than the rarefied glory-chasers populating the executive boxes of Old Trafford and Stamford Bridge. It's something the nu-football fraternity will never understand. Why drag yourself to this crumbling old ground in the lower leagues and eat Wagon Wheels when you can pop up the road into a gleaming stadium and dine on steak? These people could never understand why you'd want to do that. They would certainly never understand why Bob and Rose Winstanley are here today.

Bob and Rose have spent 22 hours and about £200 on the dubious privilege of a 1,000-mile round trip to see Brentford take on Chesterfield. It's the same virtually every home game. They get up at silly o'clock on Friday morning in the village of Ardentinny on the banks of Loch Long in Argyll, Scotland, and catch the 7.30 a.m. ferry from Gourock to Dunoon to embark on the epic drive to Griffin Park, stopping overnight with family in Swindon. They eventually arrive back home late on Sunday night – a long haul for a dull 1-1 draw. Roll on the local derby when they play Blackpool away, a short 250-mile hop.

Born in Carshalton, Bob saw his first Bees game in 1964 and met Rose when he moved to Swindon at 17, started coaching the Swindon Spitfires ladies team and fell in love with their star striker. They married 23 years ago and carried on travelling home and away to Bees matches together while Bob set up business selling football memorabilia. They followed the Bees through thick and thin, home and away, amid multifarious promotions and relegations and the disappointment of five losing play-off finals. There was also the pomp, drama and pride they felt when swanning off to Wembley for the 1985 Freight Rover Trophy Final. It's days like that which make it all worthwhile, say Bob and Rose. Shame they lost 3-1 to Wigan Athletic.

Oh yes, Bob Winstanley has seen it all in his 40-odd years of single-minded devotion to Brentford, and can give you chapter and verse on every lower league ground in the country. His speciality subject is bogs. 'Oh God, I've seen some horrible ones, horrible,' he says, getting suddenly animated. 'Workington. What a place that was. You just got there and thought ... God, get me out of here! The old Chester ground had the worst toilets *ever*. Disgusting, it was. Mind you, Lincoln was pretty bad too. I got drenched in Lincoln. Oh, and Colchester had the worst stewards. Organised hooliganism, we called it. They've just got no sense of humour ...'

In 2002, Bob and Rose decided to change their lives and moved to the idyllic remoteness of the Scottish highlands. For even the most devoted among us, that would surely have been that as far as our commitment to a lower league English team went. We'd have listened to the results every Saturday and been delighted with news of a victory or saddened by defeat, kept abreast of events via the club website and still referred to the team as 'we'. But you'd find some little local team to support; you wouldn't battle your way through almost the entire length of England and half of Scotland to go to matches, would you? *Would you*?

'I think,' says Bob, chewing over the question as if it's the first time he's ever heard it, 'that if we actually thought logically about why we make such a long journey to see a football team every week, we wouldn't do it.' So it's best not to think about it then, eh? '*Quite.*' Don't people where you live think you are bonkers? 'Oh yes,' he says cheerily. 'The nearest Scottish teams to us are Dumbarton or, if we take the ferry, Greenock Morton. Oh, there's an amateur team, Dunoon, but we haven't been to any of their games. We'd rather come and watch Brentford.'

The Winstanleys were never tempted by the forbidden fruit of the super-rich brigade up the Thames. The mere mention of Chelsea sends Bob into a rant about 'two-minute wonders', the catastrophic consequences of allowing too many foreign players into our game and the shortcomings of the back-pass law. 'It's just not right, is it?' he grumbles. 'It means the goalkeeper has got to be more than a goalkeeper and teams used to be able to hold it up and play it from the back – they can't do that any more.'

Personally, I think the back-pass rule has improved the game no end, but I decide it's probably best not to engage Bob in a huge debate on the matter. He's had a long journey, after all. Instead, I ask him if there isn't a teeny little piece of him that secretly envies the lot over the road and makes him wish he supported a glamour team rather than Brentford? He practically bites my head off. 'No! See, there's more passion in the lower leagues. And you can have a laugh at matches. You go in the pub before a game and they all know who you are. You don't get that at big clubs. I'm Brentford and proud of it.'

The match ends in a 1-1 draw. I have just finished telling the geography teacher that I'll be reporting back to Oldham that the Bees right back O'Connor is a disaster waiting to happen when O'Connor suddenly jolts forward as if Martin Allen has thrown a dart into his backside, latches on to a sweet through-ball from Sodje and equalises with a sublime shot in the corner of the net. The geography teacher hurls his daughter into the air and laughs in my face, spittle shooting in all directions. 'Put that in your pipe and eat it ...' he sneers, somewhat confusingly. I make my excuses and leave – his roar of 'Bring on the Oldham' ringing in my ears – and despite the fleeting euphoria of a late equaliser, I fear for Brentford's future.

Just a hop, skip and a jump from here you're in another universe entirely at Stamford Bridge where, of course, you won't see Bovril or Wagon Wheels in a month of Sundays. Just Russian billionaires, celebrity fans a-go-go, and smug bastards with bulging wallets.

It is a Sunday, though, as you'd expect for an audience with The Special Ones. Par for the course, I don't have a ticket. I did try to sort something out online but, like most Premiership clubs, the Chelsea website is completely unfathomable. It's impossible even to access the message boards without signing away your life and providing intimate details of your inside-leg measurement, great-grandmother's maiden name and every credit card known to mankind. And even then you have to think up a dozen different passwords.

And you want to buy a ticket for a match? A *Chelsea* match? Phew, you've got a nerve, matey. Who do you think you are? How many gold points have you got, eh? How many platinum stars on your supporters card? What's your membership number? What's Peter Cech's favourite food? How many Russian billionaires does it take to change a light bulb? One – and hundreds to scrabble over the loose millions that fall out of his pocket while he's doing it. How many Portuguese Special Ones does it take to change a light bulb? One – and 50,000 to adore him and bathe in the blaze of light that shines out of his arse, and tell everyone they've been loyally following this light bulb since the 1980s, through the days when it barely shone at all, and now they deserve to bask in the joy of its expensive beam. Am I jealous? Probably.

I sit on the tube to Fulham Broadway listening to the supporters chuntering on about Jose this and Roman that, the names of the foreign players tripping off their tongues as if they were born to this multi-lingual multi-cultural football heaven in which they find themselves. 'I'm looking forward to seeing Maniche,' one of them says of their latest superstar signing. 'I remember him playing for Jose at Porto, the guy is class.' 'Yes,' says his mate. 'He'll be good cover for Essien. It's outrageous the way the press have vilified Essien. Outrageous.' Jesus, they're even starting to sound like football managers.

The discussion turns to Theo Walcott, the 16-year-old Southampton wonder-kid who's just been signed by Arsenal for a fee that could reach £12 million depending on appearances, apparently in the face of a much higher offer from Chelsea. 'That's all right,' says one smirking oik in a crisply washed blue-and-white scarf, 'we'll leave them to train him up for a couple of years and when he's good we'll make 'em an offer they can't refuse.' They all fall about guffawing at this, while the faint sounds of another group of fans chanting 'We are loaded, na na na' emanate from another carriage. Not so long ago it was all Chopper Harris and Eddie McCreadie round here, sending jinking wingers crashing over the advertising hoardings to lick their wounds and reassemble their limbs. Not to mention Peter Osgood and Alan Hudson clubbing up the King's Road and Peter Bonetti losing the World Cup in Mexico and obnoxious skinheads and Headhunters and the Shed and electrified fences and preposterous comments by Ken 'Batesy' Bates. A bit of humility wouldn't go amiss here, chaps.

So I don't have a ticket, but Chelsea are playing Charlton Athletic on a Sunday afternoon, for God's sake, and it's live on Sky – how hard can it be to get in? Walking to the ground, there's little of the buzz of anticipation you'd expect from a club that's the talk of English football, merely the comfortable expectation of another crushing victory over the peasants. There's precious little chanting or singing *en route* to the stadium, just the desire to be witness to the divine accumulation of another three points.

I go inside and join a queue – a curious mix of Japanese tourists and young Americans – and it's only when I reach the desk and ask for a ticket in the Shed End please that I discover I'm trying to book a room at the Chelsea Hotel (starting rate £69 per night, £250 for the luxury package – I'm tempted). The hotel was the brainchild of former chairman Ken Bates, hence the less-than-complimentary references to it by some fans as the Bates Motel.

Somebody presses a card into my hand offering to sell me a limited edition original seat from the West Stand for just £150 which is a 'most collectable antique as well as a practical piece of furniture'. Again … *tempting*, but I fear it might clash with my original piece of rotting corner flag from Hartlepool United, and I pass. I flee to join another queue and am told to wait in line for a while to see if there are any tickets available and whether I'll be allowed to spend £48 on a football match between Chelsea and Charlton.

After an inordinate wait, there's good news. 'There are a couple of tickets left, just wait here, sir,' says a shaven-headed gorilla in one of those black suit, black shirt and black tie combos that look like they're on hire from the bouncers at some particularly shadowy nightspot in a back street in Sicily. Having already sidestepped a bunch of increasingly desperate and shifty touts, I don't blink when a guy approaches. 'You looking for a ticket, mate?' he says cheerily. 'How much?' I reply glumly. 'Oh, I don't want anything for it,' he says. 'It's my mate's. He's got a season ticket but he can't make it today. I just want it to go to a good home. It's your lucky day.'

I rip it out of his hand just as the man in black beckons me forward to the ticket office, give my new best friend a quick hug, worry briefly that I may be seriously denting Mr Abramovich's down-payment on a fourth yacht, and disappear into the crowd before I'm read the riot act about non-transfer-able season tickets and end up in a darkened cell in the bowels of the stadium being horse-whipped by Mr Mourinho.

The ticket is in the Shed End, although it bears faint resem-blance to the sardine factory of yesteryear when the Shed housed one of the noisiest, most notorious and fiercest set of football fans in the land. The Shed had a culture entirely of its own. Not necessarily a *good* culture, you understand. In those dark bad old days of the 1970s the Shed was a notorious, seething mass of partisan hatred and tribal warmongering that gave birth to the infamous Headhunters who terrorised football grounds for years, forging particularly insidious and sinister right-wing tendencies into the bargain.

Ken Bates, who bought Chelsea for £1 in 1982, wanted electrified fences to solve the hooligan problem, though others thought electrification might be better served solving the Ken Bates problem. There's an old saying that if you treat people like animals then they behave like animals, and impounded behind the fences – even without electrification – the baying, howling masses squeezed into the Shed spitting bile would have put the willies up any law-abiding opposition fan. God only knows what effect they had on the unfortunate away team kicking towards their goal.

They liked to sing in the Shed, too, though oddly enough their repertoire wasn't always entirely savoury. They were one of the first crowds to mercilessly bait the opposition rather than sing up their own team – which, given a long history of disappointment and under-achievement, wasn't that surprising.

The old boy I meet in the pub after the game seems very well informed on the topic, nursing his half of stout as if his life depends on it and regaling me with variations on 'Play up you Pensioners'. He also tells me about the stirring 'From the Shores of Montezuma' – the US Marine Corps hymn adopted by Chelsea fans after the Second World War. He tries to sing it, and I wonder which war he's talking about. Spurs adopted 'Battle Hymn of the Republic' as their anthem and Chelsea went for the song of the Marines. 'From the halls of Montezuma to the shores of Tripoli', sang the Marines, hearts bursting with pride, 'we fight our country's battles in the air, on land and sea ...' The origins of this hymn are vague – some believe it started life as a Spanish folk song, others reckon it was written for the comic opera *Genevieve De Barbant* – but its lyrical references date back to the early 1800s to a conflict in Tunis between Christians and Muslims.

My mate the old drunk in the corner starts waffling on about Roy Bentley and Frank Blunstone and Peter Sillett and Jimmy Greaves and Ted Drake and sings his own version of the Marines' hymn, which he swears won them the old Division One league title in 1955. 'We will fight fight fight for Chelsea … till we win the football league …' he croaks, in a voice that's half Shane MacGowan and half, er, old drunk in the corner of a pub in west London.

Sadly, they don't sing the Marines' hymn in the Shed today. They don't sing a whole lot else, either. The original Shed wall is now a museum curiosity with a sorry little plaque outside the stadium, and the place is severely lacking in atmosphere. There is just a smattering of the Chelsea song 'Blue Is the Colour', a No. 5 hit in 1972, which established an ignominious precedent for players to be sheepishly paraded into a recording studio, stand around awkwardly in front of a mic flaunting dodgy perms and wearing some ludicrous fashion statement of the day and self-consciously mouth the words to some trite sub-Eurovision oompah trash that a couple of wide boys from the music industry had cooked up for them.

Produced by Larry Page, it was part-written by Daniel Boone, who'd had a hit in his own right the previous year with something called 'Daddy Don't You Walk So Fast', an impossibly mawkish cover of an American hit about a bloke leaving his wife only to return when he hears the plaintive cries of his little daughter. And then he goes and writes 'Blue Is the Colour' with a line imploring us to 'Come to the Shed and we'll welcome you/Wear your blue and see us through.' In 1972? Yeah, *right*. Come to the Shed and we'll welcome you … with some foul-mouthed abuse and a bucket of urine over your head. 'Blue Is the Colour' commemorated Chelsea's appearance in the 1972 League Cup Final, a season which also saw them make their mark on the European Cup Winners Cup, breaking all previous goal-scoring records with a 21-0 two-leg aggregate win over Luxembourg side Jeunesse Hautcharage, the inimitable Peter Osgood scoring eight goals in the tie.

That's always been the great paradox of Chelsea. There they are, parked in the King's Road with a flamboyant history of cocky bastards with fancy haircuts and tricky feet posing around the pitch giving it the big 'I am' like Ossie, Alan Hudson and Charlie Cooke. And cheering them on in the Shed, there'd be an angry mob of Neanderthals. It must have been like drinking champagne at the local borstal.

If nothing else, it's funny listening to a bunch of uncouth Londoners trying to get their mouths round all these wondrous foreign names. The fans often complain – with some legitimacy – that they have gone from being stereotyped as racist thugs to being seen as southern pansies who've opened the floodgates to the diving, overpaid foreign stars. Brutal nutters one minute, spineless yuppies the next: it is no wonder that Chelsea have produced so many dire songs.

The club has continued to be a haven of football culture with the sophisticated likes of Hoddle, Gullit, Zola, Vialli, Joe Cole and, er, Dennis Wise strutting daintily across the hallowed turf through the years … with a succession of dire records celebrating them. Suggs of Madness, a longstanding Chelsea fan, knocked out 'No One Can Stop Us Now' to celebrate their appearance in the 1994 FA Cup Final, though the song was hardly prophetic – Manchester United thumped them 4-0. Undeterred, Suggs tried again three years later, writing 'Blue Day' for the club to sing at the 1997 final with better results – they beat Middlesbrough 2-0, though the song was still desperate. There have also been various colour-blind mutilations of the socialist anthem 'The Red Flag', now dyed blue apparently but still flying high 'from Stamford Bridge to Wem-ber-lee'. In the loadsamoney culture that's pervaded Chelsea through the years and now reached its laughable peak with its endless supply of roubles raining down, you can't help but laugh when the fans sing their ludicrously inappropriate blue variant on 'The Red Flag'. It is, after all, a working-class anthem with a symbolic message of hope, honour and pride that's become an almost sacred motif for the international labour movement.

Inspired by the London dock strike of 1889, 'The Red Flag' is closely associated with Chicago anarchists, the Irish Land League, the Paris Commune and Russian nihilists. Striking Rand miners went to the gallows singing it in South Africa in 1922, Labour MPs entered Parliament singing it in 1945, and it's been the soundtrack to epic trade union struggles around the world for over a century. Irishman Jim Connell from County Meath, who wrote it on a London train in 1889, would doubtless be proud to learn his words have been altered so that hordes of rabid football fans can encourage the millionaire players of a football club with so much money they barely know what to do with it. The guy must be head-butting his gravestone.

Another of Chelsea's more bizarre assaults on the music world occurred when the late Laurel Aitken, Cuban-born godfather of ska and hero of the skinheads, sang 'The Zigger Zagger Song'. A cheery blast of regulation bluebeat, it evokes memories of one of football's oldest chants: 'Zigger Zagger, Zigger Zagger, oi oi oi!' I first heard it when Tommy Docherty brought his young Chelsea glamour boys – then top of Division One and including Terry Venables, Peter Osgood and George Graham – to play a friendly to open Woking's floodlights in 1964. Chelsea won the match 5-2, George Graham scored with a spectacular overhead kick and a splendid time was had by all. My dad even wrote a letter of thanks to Chelsea and received a handwritten reply along the lines of 'Nae problem, wee lad' from Tommy Doc himself. Yet my enduring memory of the night is a gaggle of youths decked out in Chelsea blue sitting on the touchline chanting 'Zigger Zagger Zigger Zagger, oi oi oi!' throughout the game. I mean, what the hell's all *that* about?

What it's about is a huge bloke with a big voice called Mickey Greenaway, the godfather of chants and football songs. Greenaway was a Shed regular from the early 1960s and is reputed to have originated most of the chants that reverberated around British football grounds through the 1960s, 1970s and 1980s. He's even credited with nicknaming the Fulham Road

Stand 'The Tramshed' when another famous longstanding Shed-ite, Cliff Webb, suggested all the Chelsea fans who fancied a sing should congregate in the same place. Inspired by the incessant singing on Liverpool's Spion Kop, Greenaway decided that the low roof, originally designed as cover for the punters at greyhound races, would provide the best acoustics to accommodate his booming voice.

It was actually a long way from the pitch, but his mates followed his lead and the songs and chants for which the Shed subsequently became famed were mostly down to him. Some knew him as 'the Zigger Zagger Man', so famous was he for the nonsense chant he loved to kick the Shed off with at matches. Nobody seems to know what was in his head when he started it, though my favourite theory is that it derives from a German drinking song *'Ein Prosit'*, which ends with everyone shouting a traditional toast of *'Zicke zacke zicke zacke, hoi hoi hoi!'* Maybe Mickey went to a German beerfest and decided to toast the rest of Stamford Bridge with his experiences?

Whatever its origins, the chant was further absorbed into British culture and other clubs had their own Zigger Zagger Men – most notably Stoke City's John Bailey. It's likely that Stoke and not Chelsea was the inspiration for Peter Terson, former resident playwright at Stoke's Victoria Theatre, to write his acclaimed play *Zigger Zagger* about a football hooligan, which was first produced in 1967. The chant's finest hour, however, came when it was amended to play a prominent role in the equally nonsensical chorus of the Spice Girls' debut hit, 'Wannabe', in 1996. Greenaway even copped a mention in Laurel Aitken's 'Zigger Zagger Song'.

Mickey Greenaway wasn't just lauded at Stamford Bridge; he was also a familiar figure to opposing fans. He hired trains to take supporters to away matches and turned up in a smart business suit with a briefcase as he set about the serious business of out-singing them all. Spurs fans once chanted 'Where's your Greenaway?' when they thought the Shed was being uncharacteristically quiet. Instantly a familiar voice roared back across the stadium: 'Zigger Zagger Zigger Zagger'. Even the Spurs fans cheered and joined in with the 'Oi Oi Oi!' bit. So celebrated was he that a group of Chelsea fans once 'kidnapped' him during a pre-season friendly at Harrow Borough and took him to their local pub just because they wanted to hear his legendary 'Zigger Zagger' in their own boozer.

Greenaway was the heart and soul of the Shed and his personality still pervades many of the songs still sung wherever football is played. It was Mickey who weaved the solemn, re-petitive epic 'Chel-sea, Chel-sea, Chel-sea, Chel-seeeaaaa' out of 'Amazing Grace', an eighteenth-century hymn written by slave trader John Newton as an act of contrition after he'd found Christ and renounced sin. It was also Mickey who introduced the utterly crazy notion of singing 'One Man Went To Mow' at Stamford Bridge – an idea so surreal that it became adopted as Chelsea's unofficial anthem.

That chant is the one thing I hear all around me today as the players trot out – an irritating children's song that takes in the full ten verses and doesn't even bother to soccer-ise the words. This is a measure of the sway of Mickey Greenaway, not to mention his rampant sense of the absurd. It seems he took a tape of music to play as he followed Chelsea on a pre-season tour of Sweden in 1981. He switched the tape on, anticipating The Specials or Adam and the Ants or Soft Cell or whatever the hell else they'd have been grooving to in 1981 … but instead, for some reason, up popped 'One Man Went To Mow'.

By the end of that Swedish tour, all the Chelsea fans were singing it, speeding it up as they went along, ridiculing anyone who stumbled while trying to cram in all the words. Simple pleasures … but it stuck. And it's all Chelsea's own: a happy medium, perhaps, between the brain-dead hoolies of yesteryear and the suave post-ironic aristocrats of today.

Mickey Greenaway introduced many other songs to the Shed in particular and football in general – 'We all follow the Chelsea, over land and sea' to the tune of 'Land of Hope and Glory' was seemingly cooked up on the train to an away game at Leicester

City. I'd dearly love to ask Mickey about his other adventures and the other songs he introduced, but sadly he's no longer around to provide the answers. He died, broke and alone, in a bedsit in Catford in 1999, at the age of 53.

The *News of the World* once fingered him in an exposé on the notorious Headhunters, who followed Chelsea, and accused him of instigating a riot in Brighton. Some said that he was at the centre of any terrace ruck going, while others swore he loved the game too much to be diverted by mindless violence. Whatever the truth, the adverse publicity seemed to crush his spirit and he simply dropped out. But he's still lovingly remembered by the old guard as a genuine Shed legend whose love of Chelsea, and talent to inspire the supporters around him, overrode the organised viciousness that afflicted so many years of his tenure at the Shed. 'He cut through the hatred by sheer force of personality – the guy was a born leader,' wrote one Priesty in an excellent tribute on the Chelsea FC Refuge fan website.

I'm not sure what Mickey Greenaway would make of the Shed today. I mean, the stadium is fantastic, and it's hard not to suck in your breath as you forage for your seat and take in the magnificent spectacle. But the pitch is a mess that makes even Brentford's modest Griffin Park turf look like a carpet. You'd think that with all that money and perfectionism, Mr Abramovich and Mr Mourinho might provide something better than a glorified cowpat on which their pampered stars can parade their skills.

But hey, it's great theatre anyway. You look down in awe at the immaculate physical specimens representing a magnificent array of nations marching out so full of pride and self-regard to play for two teams from London. Frank Lampard, John Terry, Joe Cole – English lions all. Crespo, Gudjohnsen, Makelele and Carvalho are so sleek and athletic, with Irishman Damien Duff dancing down the wings. Superbly fit, brilliant footballers. It's hard not to be impressed. But it's also hard to get excited.

The match has been going about five minutes when a fat Dutchman starts clambering into a bunch of seats two rows in front of me with his supermodel wife and a gaggle of about 15 kids. There are several minutes' faffing around dispensing bulging lunch boxes and bottles of pop, which the kids all open instantly, spraying surrounding spectators with fizzy tooth-rot. We relax to enjoy the match. That's when a couple of sweaty lads arrive waving tickets and wade straight into the row now packed with munching Dutch people.

There is more kerfuffle as an argument ensues and the Dutch crew eventually concede they're in the wrong seats. Spilling tuna filling and pop along the way, they start climbing over the spectators in the next two rows *en route* to the vacant seats immediately behind me. I sigh, cover my face and shift to one a side to allow them to pass but the guy next to me, a surly Scotsman who's been glowering at the pitch since he arrived, is having none of it. 'You're not climbing over me, laddie,' he says tersely as one of the kids tries to mount him.

The fat Dutchman is outraged. 'Please be allowing us to pass, our seats are behind you,' he pleads. I shift along to allow the gang to clamber over me but the Scotsman is determined we present a united front on this one. He pulls me back into my seat: 'Don't let the buggers pass.' 'Come on, friend, be a matey,' says the Dutchman, cheeks going red, clearly getting exasperated. 'We haf come all the way from Rotterdam to see the football game.' The Scotsman is unmoved: 'Listen, pal, I don't care if you've come from the fucking moon; you're not getting past me.' 'But we are missing the game.' 'Ye should've thought about that before you sat in the wrong seats.'

By now other spectators in the vicinity are having their say. 'Let them through!' 'No, make 'em go to the end and come back along the proper row!' 'Shut up and sit down, I can't see!' 'Who asked you?' 'Shaddup the lorra youse or I'll come down there and kick you into next week.' All the action is going on in the crowd and for a minute the spirit of the old Shed threatens to re-emerge as voices raise and tempers flare.

Then suddenly a roar draws our attention back to the pitch. Chelsea have scored. A Gudjohnsen header, apparently, but none of us saw it. Braveheart next to me doesn't know if he's more excited that Chelsea have scored, or furious that he's missed the goal. He decides on the latter and turns to give the Dutchman a new volley of abuse. 'Now you've made me miss the fucken' goal!' he spits, but the fat Dutchman and his army of kids have miraculously escaped in the confusion. Then a spray of something wet and bubbly splatters my neck and I look behind to see the Dutch family settling into the row behind us. 'Are you happy now, prick?' asks the fat man, glaring at me.

The goal has inspired some singing action from the West Stand – several men going to mow, the 'It's super Chelsea … super Chelsea FC!' you hear at every ground and 'You are my Chelsea, my only Chelsea' to the tune of 'You Are My Sunshine's but mostly it's 'Carefree, wherever we may be/We are the famous CFC/We don't give a fack whoever you may be/Cos we are the famous CFC'. A-ha. Here is yet more evidence of the disparate and often inappropriate roots of foot-ball songs …

The United Society of Believers in Christ's Second Appearing were an American sect who originated in the nineteenth-century, an offshoot of the Quakers who lived in celibate communes with a strict moral code. They gained fame for two things – the excellent furniture they made, and the passionate, infectious hymns of worship they created. They sang with such ecstasy that their whole bodies jerked and shook, resulting in the popular name Shakers. One of their most popular hymns was 'Simple Gifts', written by one Shaker Elder, Joseph Brackett Jr, in 1848 with the opening line: 'Tis the gift to be simple, 'tis the gift to be free/'Tis the gift to come down where we ought to be …'

In 1963, Londoner Sydney Carter, a pacifist, teacher, poet and songwriter who had a very minor hit comedy single, 'My Last Cigarette', with Sheila Hancock, took the gorgeous 'Simple Gifts' and wrote new words to fit his own religious aesthetic of Christ as 'the incarnation of the piper who is calling us'. Carter's new chorus was 'Dance dance wherever you may be/I am the lord of the dance, said he/And I lead you all wherever you may be/I am the lord of the dance, said he ...' His version of the song, 'Lord of the Dance', became a modern folk and theological classic, and years later Michael Flatley took the title for his post-*Riverdance* Irish dancing extravaganza.

I listen to the Chelsea fans singing 'Carefree wherever we may be/We are the famous CFC ...' to the 'Simple Gifts'/'Lord of the Dance' tune and don't know whether to laugh or cry. Few singing it will know anything about Joseph Brackett Jr or the Shakers or Sydney Carter, but hey, this is folk music, you're not meant to know where it comes from.

None of it seems to be inspiring the Chelsea millionaires on the pitch who, having gone one up, casually saunter around waiting for Charlton to fall to their knees waving white flags. This is my one gripe with Jose Mourinho. Overall, he's been great for the British game. All that arrogance and attitude and those great sardonic asides, getting up the noses of the FA and opposing managers, he's been a worthy successor to the unintelligible soliloquies of his predecessor, the comedy Italian Claudio Ranieri.

Mourinho has the best players money can buy and has turned fine players into brilliant ones, but you wish his team would show more of the strut and flair demonstrated by The Special One himself, what with the coat and everything. Jose has been on a course of righteous confrontation with the authorities since he arrived – be it slating referees, chatting up Ashley Cole about a transfer under the gaze of the press or winding up opposition managers.

We can but admire the consummate professional and the sweaty ethics of team spirit and work rate he instils, but football's about fun too. Or it should be. We *want* to see Joe Cole and Damien Duff juggling with the ball by the corner flag, we *want* to see the team showboating, we *want* to see them humiliating the opposition just because they *can* and we *want* to see them sweeping forward at extreme pace and skill to score as many goals as they can. We want to see Shaun Wright-Phillips getting a game, too.

Instead we get a team, clearly superior to the opposition, happy to wind the match down and end it as 1-0 winners. It serves them right when a long ball is punted forward over Terry's head, Peter Cech ambles off his goal line to claim it, but Charlton's Marcus Bent is too quick for him and flicks it over him for the equaliser. After that it threatens to completely bellyflop for Chelsea. Carvalho is sent off for two yellows, and Charlton all but snatch an unlikely win that might just have wiped the smirks off the fans' faces.

Where's the joy? Where's the fun? Where's the *celery*? See, Chelsea have a strange relationship with celery. For reasons not obvious to anybody in the beginning and now completely lost in the surreal mists of time, in the early 1980s someone at Stamford Bridge started singing: 'Celery, celery/If she don't come, I'll tickle her bum/With a stick of celery ...' It caught on. Of *course* it caught on. A daft song about sex with an unfashionable vegetable completely unrelated to football, why *wouldn't* it catch on? Fans started arriving at matches, hauling sticks of celery out of their back pockets and waving them around at moments of high excitement like Dame Edna in an allotment, and before long Chelsea was an orgy of celery. Naturally, it all ended in tears.

At a time when football violence was rife, the police began to get increasingly nervous about the possibility of celery-related violence. At one infamous Chelsea match at Queens Park Rangers, a full-scale battle was fought between rival fans on the pitch and, when the dust settled, the pitch reeked of rotting celery. From that point, celery was officially banned from Chelsea games, giving rise to the bizarre sight of police searching fans at the gate for secreted vegetables and an unlikely terrace chant: 'You'll never ban the celery!' One or two other clubs – Gillingham, for one – picked up on the celery craze, and it remains close to the hearts of Chelsea fans. 'The Celery Song' still gets frequent airings at Stamford Bridge and the Abramovich era was ushered in with a new T-shirt proudly depicting the emblem of a celery and sickle.

The match ends 1-1 and I join the throng in a local pub to watch the Manchester United v. Liverpool match on telly, squeezing in next to the old boy in the corner cackling his way through the old Chelsea songs and offering loud suggestions about where Sir Alex Ferguson should shove his knighthood. 'They're all jealous of us,' he moans. 'Just 'cos we've got a few bob now, everyone else thinks it ain't fair. Would any of them turn down the chance of having someone like Abraha ... Bromivitch ... Britvic ... the Russian feller come into the club and spend some notes? Course they bloody wouldn't. Hypocrites, the lot of 'em!'

Wandering back through the streets of Fulham later, I see an army of young Chelsea fans stampeding towards me, singing at the tops of their voice. And they are singing 'Lord of the Dance'. The latest version: 'Debt-free wherever you may be/We're going to buy everyone we see/And we don't give a fuck/About the transfer fee/Cos we are the wealthy CFC ...'

You've got to laugh.

Beyond the Magic Roundabout

'Go West, life is peaceful there
Go West, there in the open air
Go West, where the skies are blue
Go West, this is what we'll do'
'Go West' – Pet Shop Boys

She's 81 and seriously ill but my mum becomes vibrant and animated when I mention football songs. Normally only ever heard belting out enthusiastic if troublingly imperfect interpretations of 'Jerusalem', she is suddenly once again a little girl in Swindon, belting out the terrace anthem her elder brother Ron taught her with the promise that if she got it word-perfect she'd be allowed to accompany him to the County Ground:

Molly dear, a pint of beer
Two Woodbines and a match
A tuppenny ha'penny walking stick
And off to the football match
The ball was in the centre
The referee's whistle blew
Morris in a temper
Up the field he flew
Morris passed to Denyer
But Denyer wouldn't do
Denyer passed to Fleming
And Fleming put him through
HOORAY!

Still perplexing after all these years, the notorious 'Magic Roundabout' remains a formidable guard in front of Swindon Town's County Ground as I attempt to negotiate it, wondering if anyone else in Swindon remembers my mum's song. What do the modern fans know of Morris, Denyer and Fleming, the Town goal-scoring legends of the 1920s and 1930s mentioned in the song?

A survivor of the First World War, Harry Morris cost Swindon £110 from Swansea and scored 48 goals in the 1926–27 season, including in 11 consecutive matches. When they played Arsenal in the FA Cup the following year, Gunners manager Herbert Chapman devised a new defensive strategy involving the centre half playing a deep 'centre back' role specifically to thwart Morris. It worked so well (Arsenal won the replay 1-0 after a goalless draw at the County Ground) they permanently adopted the system, which subsequently became the norm right across football. By the time Morris left on a free transfer to Clapton Orient in 1933 he'd scored 227 goals in 279 games for the Town, still a club record.

However, it's doubtful that Harry Morris would have scored half as many goals if it weren't for the crosses from right winger Bertie Denyer. Signed from West Ham in 1914, he went on to star for Swindon for 16 years, despite the rude interruption of active war service in France and West Africa.

The third member of this holy trinity, Harold Fleming, is said to have walked 30 miles from his home in Andover in order to play when he joined Swindon in 1907. Never on a Sunday, though. A devout Christian, he wouldn't play on the Sabbath or religious holidays. A fellow player, Edgar Dawes, said of him, 'He couldn't head, he couldn't shoot, but he had the most amazing body swerve and ball control.' As such, he became a target. Barnsley's tackling on him in an FA Cup semi-final in 1912 was so savage that he was badly injured, leading the *Daily Express* to inflame the north-south divide: 'To stop a clever opponent by maiming him is not football as understood in the south …' Fleming played 12 times for England, scoring a hat trick against Ireland in 1912 and starring in Swindon's 9-4 Football League debut victory over Luton Town in the newly formed Division Three in 1920. The road outside the ground running to the County Hotel is named Fleming Way in his honour.

I ask Derek Elston if he has ever heard my mum's Swindon song, and attempt to approximate her Wiltshire burr and wayward tune and sing it to him. Oddly enough, he hasn't. 'A bit before my time,' he says, though he knows the history and he's heard most of the Swindon songs in his time.

Derek, an affable 55-year-old from Northampton in a plain red scarf who likes to collect badges, hasn't missed a single Swindon Town match in almost 25 years. Not a single one. That includes Mickey Mouse cups, Anglo-Italian trophies, meaningless friendlies and everything. I sort of assume he is a single man, but nope, he's married. 'My wife often comes with me,' he says. Oh really? Where is she? 'Oh she doesn't come to the *matches*. She's not into football whatsoever. I just drop her in the town and she goes shopping.'

He's gratifyingly vague about how someone from Northants became a Swindon obsessive. Something about a friend of the family taking him to the County Ground when he was a kid and that was it – Swindon till he dies. Poor bloke had no say in it. It's the old cliché: you can change your wife or husband, but you can't change your football team. Then again, I don't think anyone would blame you, Derek, if you maybe gave Hartlepool away on a Tuesday night or Scunthorpe in the snow a miss. 'It *is* tempting sometimes,' he laughs. 'I'll do it for as long as I enjoy it and I'm fit enough to do it, but at some point something's going to occur and I'll miss one somewhere.'

Like all proper football fans, he's at a loss to explain why he careers all over the country supporting a moderate League One side who've broken his heart more times than they've made his day. 'They're just my team, that's all,' he says limply, fully aware of how naff it sounds. 'You often go thinking, well, it can't possibly be as bad as that again.'

Yes, it's the hope that kills you, that deep-rooted nagging shred of optimism that this will be the day when your boys turn into world-beaters. And as every football fan knows, you don't really appreciate the highs unless you suffer the lows. 'Actually,' says Derek, 'we've had our fair share of good times down here. We had a season in the Premiership, which was great, and we've had some good cup runs and seen some magnificent players over the years, so I can't really complain.'

Derek got official recognition from the club when he celebrated his thousandth consecutive game a couple of years ago. Unknown to him, his long-suffering wife had got in touch with the club, and before the game he was taken into the dressing room to be applauded by the players. 'I wanted the ground to swallow me up,' he says. 'It was nice, but it was blooming embarrassing.'

The highlight of Derek's years following Swindon, however, occurred when the ex-Manchester United player Lou Macari was manager in the mid-1980s. Macari had a special relationship with the Swindon fans. He was so popular that in 1985 the supporters went completely against normal campaigning policy to get managers kicked out by staging a mass protest to get him *reinstated* when the board sacked him on Good Friday. It worked, too. By the time Easter was over, Macari was back in the saddle, and he went on to pick up the next month's Manager of the Month award. Macari, a teetotaller, donated his prize – an ocean of Bells whisky – to the fans.

At away games, Derek and a couple of other fans have a ritual of reaching the ground early so that they can welcome the players off the coach and wish them luck on their way to the dressing room. One day Macari got off the coach, dropped a couple of bags at his feet and said, 'Bring the kit in, lads.' Derek looked at him quizzically. 'Come on, bring the kit in ...' They picked up the bags and followed the team into the dressing room. 'Ace, it was, absolutely ace,' says Derek. 'For four seasons, there were four of us who never ever paid to get into an away ground.' No wonder the fans liked Macari. 'Oh,

I've got so much time for that man, even after he left. He's a brilliant PR man.'

One evening game away at York City, Derek was left outside ticketless. One of the players, midfielder Peter Coyne, came out saying, 'C'mon, Lou says it's OK,' and ushered him inside the players' entrance. As Coyne disappeared into the dressing room to prepare for the match, Derek hung around outside trying to appear official until Macari put his head round the door: 'Oi, you, in here ...' Derek spent the whole match sitting on the bench next to Macari. '*Unbelievable*,' he reflects. 'I was in at the team talk before the game and again at half-time. We were getting beat so he weren't very happy. There were a few expletives in that dressing room, I can tell you. Tell you what, though, I don't know why any manager wants to watch the match from the bench. The view is abysmal.'

Derek was choked when Lou Macari left for West Ham in 1989, and his unofficial role as kit carrier disappeared when Ossie Ardiles took over as manager. 'We played some lovely football when Ossie was here but when it started to go wrong, Ossie couldn't get it back round. Then Glenn Hoddle came in, tweaked it a bit here and there but basically had the same players, and it was magnificent to watch. What he achieved here with the players we had was superb, but Glenn stood back a bit from it all. He wasn't one to get *involved*, not like Lou.'

It was Hoddle who got Swindon promoted into the top league for the first and only time in their history, in 1993 – and promptly skedaddled to Chelsea almost before the open-top bus had left the Magic Roundabout, leaving John Gorman to get a public spanking every week from the Premiership big boys. With only five wins they survived just the one season, and suffered further humiliation with a second successive relegation the next season.

I ask Derek about the greatest player he's seen in a Swindon shirt and he mentions local legend Don Rogers, the brilliant winger who destroyed Arsenal in a famous mud bath of a League Cup Final at Wembley in 1969. Derek's mate, who is wandering past at the time, vehemently disagrees: 'Nah, best player we've had is Peter Noble, without a doubt. We went to Mansfield a month before that Wembley game and Rogers never touched the ball twice the whole of the fucking game. Playing in front of a full house at Wembley is a bit different to playing Mansfield in midweek in front of 2,000.'

Great days, Derek, great days, but what do you think of the *modern* game? 'I don't think it's as entertaining as it used to be,' he says. 'A lot of that's to do with the amount of money involved. Managers get sacked too quickly. It always amazes me that if a team performs badly it's the manager who goes. If I perform badly at work, it's not the manager who gets the sack. And there's not so much atmosphere at games. That's partly to do with sitting down at matches. You go round the grounds and the chants are all much of a muchness; there's not much originality.'

Derek is a very *loud* fan. Recently he gave Swindon player Christian Roberts an earful he won't forget in a hurry. 'Well, he wound me up,' he says by way of explanation. 'He was a sub and at half-time he was showboating and that wound me up. And then he came on and his second or third pass was dire and gave away a goal. I just lost it. It ended up with our manager, Andy King, getting the sack after that game.' Just because you shouted at Christian Roberts? 'No, not *just* because of that ...'

There's not much for Derek or anyone else to shout about at today's game, a dismal 0-0 draw with Blackpool. Swindon come out like trains, miss an embarrassment of easy chances in the first 20 minutes and then deflate and hang on for dear life as Blackpool run the show. Ex-Blackburn Rovers and England international Jason Wilcox, who must be 75 if he's a day, almost snaps the Swindon bar with a thunderous shot, and only a debatable offside decision saves them when Keigan Parker finds the net. The lads behind the goal have one or two half-hearted attempts to get some singing going but it's mostly the stuff you hear everywhere else, and apart from a burst of the Town song

'When the Red Red Robin Goes Bob-Bob-Bobbing Along' when the mascot does a bit of cheerleading before the game, it's all a bit dead. 'Pretty grim, innit?' says Derek cheerily, with the air of a man who had never expected anything else.

But what Swindon *do* have going for them is newly appointed manager Iffy Onuora, a popular former Town striker and youth coach now cutting a dashing figure standing imperiously by the dugout in his sharp black suit, open-necked white shirt and shiny shaved head. If Blackpool should be reported to the fashion police for their disturbing tangerine shorts, Iffy might be the coolest dude who ever stood on a touchline. Well, him or Mourinho. I'm so fascinated by him that after the game I pretend to be a real journalist and infiltrate the post-match press conference that he conducts on the pitch in quiet, measured tones. He says nothing of consequence but it doesn't matter – he's so charismatic, you imagine his players would run naked round the Magic Roundabout for him if he asked them. But let's hope he doesn't, eh? It's not like he's Martin Allen.

In what must be one of the worst ideas of the season, Ron Atkinson is engaged as a Swindon Town 'consultant' for the purposes of some reality TV show. This is the same Ron Atkinson whose much-loved penchant for sticking his foot into his rather large mouth finally capsized him completely when he was caught on TV making a racist comment about Chelsea's Marcel Desailly. Take one look at Iffy Onuora, the cool black man on the Swindon bench, and you know the ludicrous suggestion that he'll take counsel from waffling buffoon Big Ron while Sky cameras chase them around is nonsense. Needless to say the experiment swiftly ends in tears. Iffy decides the cameras are intrusive and the *Big Ron Manager* circus moves on to Peterborough United.

So I move up the road to take in a match at Swindon's deadly local rivals Oxford United, a club with troubles enough of its own. Tonight they are playing Bristol City, another local derby of sorts with all the ingredients of a match that could get a bit spicy. This, I reckon, is what's missing in football these days – the spat factor. Yes, we all want to see skilful players being allowed to perform their tricks without fear of being bulldozed out of the ground by the cloggers at the back, and it's always good fun to see a red card being waved in the face of a hairy-arsed defender still trying to look innocent while the crowd waves cheerio at him as he starts the long walk. But all the cards being waved at the slip of a tackle are denying the game one of its most exciting traditional elements – the punch-ups.

Oh, don't look so shocked. However much we contrive to tut and disapprove when fists are raised and mass bundles occur, let's be honest, we *love* it. I mean, it never did ice hockey any harm, did it? Ask yourself – what are the images you most remember about great football matches?

OK, it may include Gazza's genius goal against the Scots, Ricky Villa beating 19 defenders before scoring for Spurs against Manchester City in the FA Cup Final in 1981, Charlie George lying on his back after *that* strike against Liverpool at Wembley in 1971 and Ryan Giggs running the length of the pitch to score in an FA Cup semi-final against Arsenal at Villa Park in 1999. And I'll never forget Kevin Keegan's sensational scissor kick for Southampton from outside the box in 1981 – it hit the net before anybody moved, but was disallowed because Mick Channon was standing offside by the corner flag. Not that I'm still bitter, obviously.

But no, mostly what we recall with most affection are the *fights*. Keegan and Billy Bremner trading punches in an FA Charity Shield match at Wembley in 1974 and then tearing their shirts off in fury as they left the pitch. Two mighty Scottish captains and iron men, Dave Mackay and Bremner, trying to rip each other's throats out. Vinny Jones's below-the-belt assault on Gazza. Sadly, professionalism and strict refereeing have all but removed this colourful tradition from the British game, but Oxford against Bristol City in the nether regions of League Two has to be worth a bundle, surely?

Piling off the M40 and searching for directions to the ground on the outskirts of Oxford, there's a road sign with a picture of a football and 'KASSAM OUT' scrawled all over it. A couple of miles up the road and there's another one, this time even bigger, written in red with such force you wonder if it might be blood. The stadium – the *Kassam* Stadium, no less – is reassuringly easy to find, and for those of us who recall the rubbish dump that passed as their previous Manor Ground it comes as a pleasant surprise. There stands a big, open, spacey – and free – car park and a bright, modern stadium.

Except ... *except* ... it's unfinished. There are lovely stands on three sides and a dirty great gap at one end behind the goal, its embarrassment covered by a few apologetic advertising hoardings. It has all the elements of a build-your-own stadium kit, as if when Oxford unwrapped the flat pack from MFI one of the sides was missing. They clearly couldn't be arsed to take it back and complain and stuck it up anyway, presumably in the belief that no one would notice.

The clear sound of chanting reverberates from the front of the stadium and I'm thinking the Bristol boys must already be inside warming themselves up for the rigours ahead, but then I suddenly realise that it's coming from the *outside*. There is a crowd of fans, a few hundred of them, wearing the yellow of Oxford, waving banners and chanting, 'What do we want? Kassam out!' Eyed warily by a growing army of nervous police they hold firm, barring the entrance to the car park as four Bristol Rovers supporters coaches edge towards them. 'We hate Kassam more than you!' chant the Oxford fans, and after an entertaining face-off the coaches start reversing on to the main road to chants of 'Cheerio Cheerio' from the Oxford mob. The coaches back up on to the main road and head towards the car park entrance at the other end of the stadium.

'Quick,' screams one of the leading demonstrators, 'get in the road and stop them – let's really piss them off!" The others glance at the traffic speeding by and look doubtful but then the guy's out there in front of it with his 'KASSAM OUT' banner and the others flood across with him, sitting in the middle of the road, their chants suddenly more urgent and excited. With the stakes raised, traffic halted on both sides of the road and a very real danger of one of the demonstrators being mown down by an impatient motorist or careless motorcyclist, the police start to look agitated and bark into their walkie-talkies.

The fans on the Bristol Rovers coaches aren't remotely bothered by this unexpected impediment to their progress into the ground and the driver in the lead coach diffuses any potential tension by inviting one of the protesters on board to deliver a handful of 'KASSAM OUT' placards, which the Rovers fans gleefully wave from the windows. It's a strangely heart-warming cameo in a worrying scene that could easily escalate into real trouble or even tragedy. Here are football fans united against a common enemy – the evil face of business and, in their eyes at least, a major shareholder with little interest in the game, its history or the football fortunes of the club at which he's pulling all the strings.

Supporters are a sentimental breed whose emotions go into overload when it comes to their own club and they will thus readily identify with others suffering at the hands of directors perceived not to be giving it their best shot. Especially at this level of the game, where there but for the grace of God go any of us. York City fans once staged a joint pitch invasion with their rivals from Brighton in protest at the behaviour of the Brighton owner of the day. Most of those waving banners and chanting 'KASSAM OUT' on the Bristol coaches will know little of Firoz Kassam and his disagreements with the Oxford fans, who accuse him of running their club into the ground. Devilment is perhaps the prime motivator here, but solidarity on the terraces between rival supporters is nevertheless a rare but inspiring sight.

And this isn't the first time that Oxford United has fallen into the clutches of a controversial businessman. Originally named Headington United, they re-branded themselves as Oxford United in 1960 and were elected to the old Fourth Division two years later as replacements for the bankrupt Accrington Stanley. For a while they enjoyed an amazing run of success. Under Jim 'Bald Eagle' Smith they went all the way up the leagues to the First Division and in 1986 even had a trip to Wembley, coming home with the Milk Cup after a resounding 3-0 victory over Queens Park Rangers.

The man with his hand on the tiller in these glory glory years, however, was not exactly famed for his integrity – one Robert Maxwell. Despite the unprecedented success, Oxford fans were dazed and confused by Maxwell's high-profile stewardship, particularly when he talked of merging Oxford with Reading to form a 'super club', Thames Valley Royals, to play in a new stadium at Didcot. The club started tumbling down the leagues, managers (including now-BBC TV pundit Mark Lawrenson) came and went and Oxford's tiny Manor Ground started falling down around their ears.

After Maxwell's unscheduled dive off his yacht in 1991, the club was bought by Robin Herd and work started on a brand new stadium at Minchery Farm. But when the growing list of creditors complained and permission to develop the council land around the ground stalled, a stalemate ensued. The construction workers bailed out leaving the new ground half-finished, and embattled Oxford limped on at the decrepit Manor Ground.

In 1999, with debts estimated at more than £15 million, Firoz Kassam bought Oxford for £1. Born in Tanzania to Indian parents, Kassam came to Britain when he was 19 in the late 1960s and got his first job washing up in an Indian takeaway in south London. By 1970 he'd opened his own fish and chip shop in Brixton and, with the help of a bank loan, followed it up with a cheap hotel. Others followed, and while he lost a lot of his businesses during the recession of the 1980s, he recovered to build up the Firoka Group's portfolio of luxury hotels, including historic Oxfordshire mansion Heythrop Park.

Oxford fans initially hailed him as the club's saviour. He completed work on the new stadium at Minchery Farm, named it after himself, put a leisure complex next to it for good measure and flogged the Manor Ground to developers (it's now a hospital). The club moved into their new stadium in 2001 and looked forward to boom times under their hero, Firoz Kassam.

Now there are hundreds of them chanting for him to get the hell out of town. Mollified by the display of solidarity from the Bristol Rovers supporters, the sit-down protest in the road is abandoned, the fans applauding the coaches as they pass. Then the mob takes police and stewards by surprise by making a dash for the plush Christchurch Suite. They pour past the hapless stewards and rampage up to the second floor where the polite society of Oxford are quietly dining, distributing their 'KASSAM OUT' notices and attempting to infiltrate the board-room.

'What's Kassam done wrong? *What's Kassam done wrong*?' the burly red-faced man clad in Oxford yellow repeats after me, disbelievingly. 'He's driven this club into the ground, that's what he's done.' A group of supporters around us are now chanting 'One greedy bastard, there's only one greedy bastard' as Kassam's alleged crimes against local football are cata-logued. One of them is that Firoz Kassam came in at number 192 in the 2005 *Sunday Times* Rich List with assets of £250 million, yet he has still overseen a long period of decline and the departure of many of the best players without putting any investment into the club.

'Listen, mate,' says another fan, sticking his face into mine, 'I saw Oxford at Wembley in '86 and if you'd said then that 20 years later we'd be on the verge of going out of the league, I wouldn't have believed you. The man has no concept of loyalty. If one of his hotels was struggling, do you think he'd get rid of its best people and not spend a penny on making it healthy again? I don't think so.'

His mate joins in: 'I've been a season ticket holder for 25 years and if we go down, that's it, I'll never come back. The man has strangled the life out of this club. He's not interested in the club, so why doesn't he sell it to someone who is?' Mr Kassam, however, has wisely decided to give this one a miss, so we can't ask him.

A swift look at the League Two table confirms that Oxford are, indeed, perilously close to the relegation positions that would see them sliding into the Conference. The team hasn't won for two months and manager Brian Talbot has been sacked (the eighth manager to leave since Kassam's reign began) and replaced by youth coach Darren Patterson, which makes nonsense of Talbot's optimistic programme notes. Or, indeed, Kassam's notes praising the fans and announcing that he has authorised Talbot to bring in new players 'at any cost'.

Inside the ground, though, the mood is different again as we gaze out of a freezing cold night towards Video World, the bowling alley, gym, cinema and sports bar that looms behind the empty end. True supporters can be brilliant in a crisis, and these Oxford fans leave all their anger, frustration and bitterness outside the turnstiles, trying to lift their team out of the mire with rousing passion.

The mutual respect between the two sets of fans is also forgotten, Oxford mocking the Bristolian accent with chants of 'Ooo-arr ooo-arr ooo-arr' while Rovers supporters respond with 'Accies for Oxford', suggesting that Oxford will soon be swapping places in the Football League with Accrington Stanley. The match itself is understandably tense, and as the early blood and thunder gives way to a dull bout of hoofball, the Rovers fans entertain themselves with ritual jibes aimed at Bristol City. As a special treat, we even get a round of the Rovers anthem 'Goodnight Irene'. This is one of the unsolved mysteries of football anthems. Why *do* Rovers fans sing a song first recorded in Louisiana State Penitentiary in 1934 by a convicted murderer?

Born in 1885, Huddie Ledbetter was a cotton picker, railroad labourer, guitarist, womaniser, hard drinker, gambler, fighter and rabble-rouser who seemed to attract trouble as he wandered around the Southern states trying to eke out a living. Imprisoned in Texas in 1916 for assault, he escaped and spent two years evading the law, only to kill a man in a fight. He was sentenced to 30 years' hard labour, but was pardoned after writing a song for the governor pleading contrition. By 1930, he was back in jail for attempted homicide.

It was there that folk song collectors John Lomax and his son Alan discovered him on a field trip through the South. They recorded Ledbetter singing 'Goodnight Irene', among other songs. Again, Ledbetter – or Leadbelly as he became popularly known – was granted a pardon on the back of his singing talent and when Alan Lomax took him on tour he was a sensation. He still had anger issues (he fell out with Lomax after threatening him with a knife) but, friendly with Woody Guthrie, he became an icon of the early American folk song revival and was an increasingly popular figure until his death from lateral sclerosis, a disease of the nerve cells, on a European tour in 1949.

'Goodnight Irene', though, went on to even greater success. Leadbelly is thought to have based his version on a song written in 1886 by Gussie L. Davis, a former janitor and railway porter who became the first black American to achieve any real degree of commercial musical success. Apart from 'Irene' he also wrote something called 'The Fatal Wedding', a cheery little number where the groom is exposed as a bigamist when his wife and child turn up at his planned second wedding. The baby dies in its mother's arms and the double-crossing husband commits suicide, leaving the two wives to shack up together.

In 1950 The Weavers – whose career as America's most popular group was soon to be abruptly ended by blacklisting as a result of the Senator McCarthy Communist witch hunt – had a No. 1 US hit with a sanitised version of the song (singing 'I'll *see* you in my dreams' rather than Leadbelly's 'I'll *have* you in my dreams', which is something else entirely).

Quite how it got from there to the terraces at Bristol Rovers is a matter of conjecture and theory. The most popular explanation is that it began at a home match with Plymouth Argyle.

When Argyle fans started sneaking out towards the end of a heavy tonking, Rovers supporters sang, 'Argyle, goodnight Argyle, Argyle goodnight ...' They were so chuffed by their own wit that they started adapting it to suit whichever opposition faced them, and when they ran out of ideas they just reverted to Irene.

'Sometimes I live in the country, sometimes I live in the town/Sometimes I have a great notion to jump in the river and drown'. The Rovers supporters were always at their most heart-felt singing that verse, particularly during a grim defeat as they surveyed the river running outside their Eastville stadium.

So Bristol Rovers sing 'Goodnight Irene' tonight and it sounds so good I'm tempted to cross the wire and join them. But having stood in front of the Rovers bus with the Oxford mob before the game started it seems a bit fickle, and the Oxford fans are such a committed bunch it's hard not to be dragged into their corner.

I'm not so sure about the row of Germans immediately behind me, who seem to be spending the whole match guffawing loudly at the ineptitude of the two teams and shouting things that are probably extremely disgusting. I daren't look round in case they're wearing lederhosen and waving ornate beer mugs.

In front, there's an even scarier sight – a row of Aldershot Town supporters. For any self-respecting Woking fan such as myself this is a wooden crucifix job, the Shots being our despised local rivals and all. But I swallow my pride, pretend I don't recognise those horrid shirts, and ask them what they're doing here. 'Sillsy, innit?' says one of them, who I suspect may have taken a drink. 'Sillsy. You know, Tim Sills – Oxford just bought him from the Shots. We thought we'd come down and give him a bit of support. He scored for 'em on Sat'day, we're hoping he'll score for us tonight.'

Temporarily ignoring the fact that they are Aldershot supporters and therefore brain-dead, it's a touching gesture. Most fans reserve their vilest vitriol for players who've had the gall to betray them by moving on and joining a different club, but here's a dozen or so who have journeyed from the Hampshire border to pay respects to their departed hero. They even attempt a chant of 'Feed the Sills and he will score', though sadly it doesn't catch on at all.

The match has 0-0 written all over it, but midway through the second half there's a bit of rough and tumble and Oxford are awarded a penalty. Steve Basham buries it and the Oxford fans do a conga round the stand. It's not pretty, but amid an increasing din from around us, the team cling on to their slender lead and get their first win for ages. While the fans hug each other in disbelief and chant 'We are staying up, say we are staying up' to the tune of the Gap Band's 1980s hit 'Oops Upside Your Head' (known to anybody who's ever been to a wedding reception as 'The Boat Race Song'), the small gathering from Aldershot run to the front and unravel a huge banner in praise of Tim Sills. Sills shakes their hands and trots off to the dressing room. I hate to say it, but respect to you Shots fans. Mr Kassam, meanwhile, is nowhere to be seen.

So it's another day, another footie match, and I betray the code of 'Goodnight Irene' and head off to Ashton Gate to check out Rovers' bitter rivals, Bristol City. Well, it seems only fair. We all know about the religious and familial divides polarising the Glasgow, Liverpool and Manchester derbies, but ... Bristol? This one's purely geographical. If you're from north of the Avon you're Rovers, and if you're south you're City. That seems simple enough, but where does it leave all us neutrals?

At the moment I'm edging towards Rovers, a club which does seem to have an endearing eccentricity, starting with their peculiar shirts that look like blue and white building blocks. Their official nickname is the Pirates in recognition of the city's maritime history, though nobody ever calls them that – the preferred reference is 'Gasheads' because their old Eastville ground was slap next door to a gasworks, and at every match half the crowd left gasping for air after being poisoned by the fumes. The mind boggles, though, at their original nickname of

Black Arabs, awarded when they were formed in 1883 and played in black shirts with diagonal gold sashes in the image of the rugby club who played next door.

There's also a strange obsession with Weetabix, which dates from an away game at Shrewsbury Town when a supporters' coach stopped at a pub *en route* for refreshments. As the pub didn't sell food one fan was presented with the kitty and dispatched to the nearest supermarket for provisions. He returned with £75 worth of Weetabix. That is excessive by any standards of breakfast cereal consumption, and when Shrewsbury came out to face Rovers that day they found their whole penalty area covered in Weetabix and an army of birds on the pitch having a feast. In a relationship redolent of Chelsea and celery, Bristol Rovers and Weetabix have been close ever since, and the bird population of Shrewsbury is on red alert whenever the Rovers come to town.

Other less savoury moments in Rovers' history include goalie Esmond Million being banned for life in 1963 for accepting a £300 bribe to throw a match against Bradford Park Avenue. Not that he was very good at it – the match ended 2-2. Even worse, humiliation has been plunged on the club in recent years by the revelation that Jeffrey Archer is a lifelong supporter (prison appearances allowing), not to mention 'Singing Bristol Rovers All the Way', a flop single by the late Rod Hull of Emu fame. Thankfully it is largely forgotten, although you may hear it if you ever stumble unawares into a local pub called the Victoria.

City, though, have the greater footballing pedigree, having been in the Football League longer (though Rovers fans will tell you they're the older club). They also appear to be the richer relation. After all, they reached the FA Cup Final in 1909 (they lost 1-0 to Manchester Utd) and Andy Cole used to play for them. However, they lose points for musical content and not just because Scott Davidson, a keyboard player with Bros and the Pet Shop Boys, was once their chairman.

Conforming to every West Country cliché in the book, they

have fostered an unhealthy alliance with cartoon bumpkin band the Wurzels. I mean, as I take my seat behind the goal the crowd are singing 'Drink Up Thy Zider'. *Voluntarily*. It's like they *want* everyone to think they're simpletons. When the record first appeared in the charts in 1967, the City fans were apparently so drunk on the success of a demolition of Hull City they spontaneously started singing it. Remarkably, they've been singing it ever since.

Chief Wurzel Adge Cutler was killed in a car crash coming home from a gig in 1974 but his band continued his 'scrumpy and western' legacy, including their association with the City. They even adapted one of their singles, 'Morning Glory', into 'One For Bristol City', which became the club's official anthem. And here I am among a crowd of families, middle-aged men, kids, yoofs and grannies, all clad in red, all on their feet and all singing 'Drink Up Thy Zider'. Planet Pluto would probably feel more natural right now.

Sadly, there's no sign of the Wurzels' biggest hit 'Combine Harvester' – a parody of Melanie's 1972 hit 'Brand New Key' – or any of their other unforgettable greats like 'I Shot J.R.', 'Sunny Weston-super-Mare' and 'I Want To Be an Eddie Stobart Driver', but there's probably a pub round here somewhere with them all on a loop. Not to mention fan nights dedicated to their classic album of rock covers, *Never Mind the Bullocks*.

Today's opponents are Swansea City so once the game kicks off the Bristol fans sing 'Always shit on the Welsh side of the Bridge' to the tune of Monty Python's 'Always Look on the Bright Side of Life'. To which Swansea wittily respond with 'Always shit on the *English* side of the Bridge'. Can you see what they did there? And it gets worse. City fans are singing 'The Red Flag', 'Hi-ho Bristol City' and then 'In-ger-land, In-ger-land', 'Sheep-sheep-sheep-shaggers' and 'Stand up if you hate the Welsh'.

There are a few scores to be settled for Bristol City today. The last time they crossed the Severn Bridge, Swansea tonked them 7-1, a result so humiliating that manager Brian Tinnion immediately resigned and slunk off into the sunset without a word to the press or even his own players. Since then they have poached Gary Johnson – once manager of the Latvia national team – from Yeovil Town and, with fortunes on the up, are looking for revenge. It turns out to be a spicy match with endless bookings and players squaring up. In first-half injury time Bristol City get a free kick on the edge of the box and Alex Russell floats it into the area. As French keeper Willy Gueret stands rooted to the spot gawping at the ball, City centre half Carey trundles up to him in slow motion and nudges it into the net.

'Drink Up Thy Zider' sing the Bristol fans in delight and, dazed and confused, Gueret glances at us with the look of a man who feels he's been transported here from a parallel universe. He may have a point. A couple of years ago he was enjoying himself, celebrating a Swansea win over Bury which ensured promotion, when the police moved in to arrest him after the Bury stewards complained he was annoying them. There were no charges, but Willy clearly believes the British are all bonkers.

Lots of zider is metaphorically drunk in the second half as Bristol withstand the Swansea barrage with a fine display by their reassuringly eccentric Brazilian (ex Woking!) keeper Adriano Basso, who even has his own song. It goes 'Oh Basso ... whoah-woo-oh'. Damn clever, that. City win the match 1-0 and the celebrating players leave the pitch clapping the fans, who respond by standing on their seats and singing songs about cider. The middle-aged couple who have been sitting next to me shake my hand vigorously and invite me for a drink. 'Sorry,' I say, 'I don't like cider.' 'Oh,' they say, with raised eyebrows and meaningful looks at one another, shuffling off towards the pub shaking their heads. They don't look back.

I have one more destination in the South West and it's the big one. Plymouth Argyle is Britain's most southerly club and the English league's most westerly. So it takes for ever to get there ... especially if you park your car in Bristol and don't remember where you left it, and have to contend with bright sunshine all the way down the M5 even though it's freezing cold.

However, I'm anticipating lots of fun in Plymouth. The omens are excellent. After all, Plymouth are one of only two teams in the Football League who play in the traditional goal-keeping colour of green (Yeovil is the other) and while there does seem to be a peculiar fixation with that silly game of rugby in this part of the world, you'd imagine that being so remote and *maritime* they would have their own pantheon of songs and culture. Such a lot of history here, after all – Francis Drake terrifying the Spaniards with his bowls, the first female MP Nancy Astor, Scott of the Antarctic getting a taste for icebergs and exploration, and sailors on every corner.

The club was formed by a bunch of posh boys from public school who were so impressed by watching the football players of the Argyll & Sutherland Highlanders win the Army cup that they nicked their name. Club legends over the years include little Sammy Black, whose attempts at heading the ball had the crowd in fits of laughter, largely because he normally played with a cigarette stub stuck behind his ear. When rumours of an imminent transfer emerged the fans were outraged and organised 'Sammy Must Not Go' demonstrations. It worked, too. Sammy stayed and dribbled up the wing for Argyle for 14 years before his retirement in 1938.

One of Sammy's teammates was one Jack Leslie, the son of a Jamaican and the only black player in England at the time. A one-club man, he was a nifty inside forward, and after his playing days were over he worked in the boot room at West Ham and cleaned Bobby Moore's boots. I'm also fascinated to learn that Michael Foot, the great orator and former Labour Party leader, is a lifelong Argyle fan. In honour of his 90th birthday in 2003, they registered him as a player and gave him the No. 90 shirt. There may have been times recently when the manager has seriously considered giving him a game.

Perhaps the weirdest game played at Plymouth's Home Park ground, though, was during the 1926 General Strike when a crowd of over 10,000 paid to see a special challenge match between the striking trade unionists and the police. Plymouth was badly hit by the strike, creating intense bitterness between the two sides with the local paper even talking of impending civil war, so a football match between the two protagonists appeared akin to lighting a fire in a dynamite factory.

To add to the madness, volunteers even manned specially commissioned tramcars to take fans to the match that were then picketed by strikers, some of whom were also trying to get to the game. The result was a free-for-all in the centre of Plymouth, but the match went ahead with a tramway band supplying the half-time entertainment. The band then marched back into Plymouth in front of a mass of protesters, with various confrontations and flashpoints along the route as mounted police tried to restore some order. The match ended 2-0 to the strikers and the dispute was settled a week later.

It's a bit of a trek out of the city centre, but Home Park is easy to find. There is oodles of room in a surprisingly sparse car park as I arrive an hour before kick-off to encounter a desolate scene. There are no floodlights on, hardly anybody around, none of the usual buzz you get outside before a game. Alarm bells clang and I double-check the paper – yep, there it is. Championship: Plymouth Argyle v. Preston North End. Kick-off 7.45 p.m.

'It's off, mate,' says a man in a pork pie hat, with a green scarf wrapped so tightly round his face he looks like Tony Hancock in a space costume. 'Frozen pitch.' Others gather round to hear the story from someone who has a mate on the ground staff. 'They've been working since lunchtime to make it playable,' he says knowledgeably, 'but the ref got down here an hour ago, took one look at it and called it off.'

A few more arrive and we have a lively debate about the need for undersoil heating, which should be paid for by the League because clubs like Argyle are strapped for cash, but nobody cares because they all live in London and they're only interested in the Premiership, but where would they be if it weren't for us little teams at the grass roots of the game? 'It's actually the drainage that's the problem,' says a chap with a posh voice. 'Thirty years ago we never had any matches cancelled. It's all to do with the drains.' An elderly gent in whiskers and a fez arrives to join the merry throng shivering in the cold and starts talking, as all old-time fans do, about the great players in the club's history.

'I've been following the Argyle home and away for 45 years,' says the oldie in the Tommy Cooper headgear. 'The best players we ever had down here were Gordon Fincham and Johnny Williams. That were when half backs were half backs.' Someone else puts the case for Jimmy Gauld. 'What a jinker he were, used to jink through defences all day.' Fez Man remembers him too: 'Ended up in prison, didn't he?' 'Dunno,' says the other guy. 'But boy, could he *jink*.' It transpires that Jimmy Gauld was indeed sent to prison, for four years in 1965 after admitting taking a bribe while playing for Swindon when they lost 6-1 to Port Vale five years earlier. 'Swindon were comfortably in the middle of the league with nothing to win or lose, so it didn't seem such a terrible thing to do,' he said by way of attempted mitigation.

I head off in search of disgruntled Preston supporters who have, after all, had one of their longest away trips of the season to get down here all for nothing. But apparently they never even got off the coaches, just turned straight round and went home again. Then someone says that a bunch of them have gone for a drink in a pub up the road.

Preston North End are one of the oldest clubs in the country and I'm keen to discuss various playing legends like Tom Finney, Bill Shankly, Alex James and Ghanaian Arthur Wharton, the first black player (probably) in English football. Wharton, who played in goal for PNE in the 1880s, may also have been the first footballer to become a publican. He was also a top sprinter and, supremely athletic, was on one occasion said to have swung on the crossbar to catch a shot at goal between his legs while three burly forwards flinging themselves at him ended up in a heap in the back of the net. It sounds unlikely, but you don't knock a good story.

I find no Preston supporters in the pub but spend the night

drinking with two hardy Argyle fans who are staring morosely into their pints and wondering what to do with themselves now the match is off. Andy, who looks a bit like a tattooed version of Alf Garnett, has a jacket covered in football badges while his mate Ron is a dead ringer for Frank Gallagher, the lank-haired patriarch of *Shameless*. They have come on the bus from Ilfracombe for the match – a major expedition in itself – but a few pints down the road are happy to discuss Argyle and their role in it. They love coming to Plymouth for matches, partly it seems because they can drink here without hassle, having been barred from most of the pubs in Ilfracombe after one or two unfortunate heated debates and an incident with a plate glass window.

Ron even claims he once played for Argyle. 'They signed me at 16 as an apprentice,' he says. 'I came on as a sub a couple of times for the first team. What a feeling that was! The adrenalin rush you get running out on that pitch in front of all the fans, there's nothing like it. *Nothing like it.*' Andy nods his head. 'Ain't nothing like it,' he confirms, even though he never played for Plymouth Argyle or, indeed, anyone else.

So what happened, Ron? 'I fell out with the manager, didn't I?' Why? 'He was an arse. I had a row with the chairman too.' Was he an arse as well? 'Yep.' Quite a feisty 16-year-old then, weren't you? 'Yep. He accused me of turning up late for training, but I never.' Why did he think you were late if you weren't? 'That's just it, I don't know. He didn't like me. I gave up playing after that. Well, I got an injury as well.'

Despite the plethora of arses supposedly at the helm in the late 1970s, Ron has remained a staunch Argyle fan ever since, supporting them through thick and thin. I ask him for his highs and he mentions the 1983–84 cup run which eventually saw them losing 1-0 to Watford in the semis. That must have been amazing cheering them on that day, eh Ron? He shuffles a bit and shakes his head. 'No, I couldn't make the match, I was otherwise engaged.' Doing what? 'I was dining at Her Majesty's Pleasure.' And eventually, out comes the story of the burglary and the stitch-up and the 16-month prison sentence and Newton Abbot prison.

'I should have been out on remand,' he says, still clearly aggrieved by the sense of injustice. 'I thought I'd be OK to get to the match, but the buggers wouldn't give me bail. In the end I listened to the game on the radio and you know what's funny?' What's funny, Ron? 'My cellmate was a Watford fan. George Reilly scored for them from a John Barnes cross. I didn't mind too much because I'd have missed the final anyway. I'd have still been inside.'

Andy admits that he's also had the odd run-in with the law but, like Ron, is keeping his nose clean these days. 'I do like a good drink though,' he says, demolishing yet another pint and nudging the empty glass pointedly in my direction. Amid such a confessional spirit and tales of altercations in Ilfracombe, I wonder if either of them has ever been involved in, you know, football *hooliganism*.

They both looked shocked. 'Oh no,' says Ron. 'What sort of idiots want to fight at football matches? I'd *never* do that.' He looks genuinely pained at the idea. 'You do get some muppets down here sometimes but it's not right, is it? I've had a few bundles in my time, but football is like, well, *sacred* – you shouldn't fight at football matches. It's ... well, it's ... *criminal*.'

It's a long way to come for a couple of pints on a freezing night, but with solid gold philosophy like this on offer for free it's been worth it.

And then hot news comes through from Oxford. Firoz Kassam has sold Oxford United for £1 to Nick Merry, a fan and successful businessman. It's not exactly altruistic. Kassam continues to own the ground and surrounding businesses, and charges Oxford for the privilege of using it. He remains defiant about his role in it all: 'I saved the club and built a £15 million stadium – the fans have short memories.' The hero of the club's glory years, Jim Smith, even returns as manager.

But when all's said and done I'd stood – *and very nearly sat* – in the road so the Bristol Rovers coach couldn't pass, and while

I didn't shout and chant like the others I did hold one of those 'KASSAM OUT' banners for a minute or two. It feels like some sort of victory for fan power. I raise a glass to Oxford United.

—— CHAPTER 3 ——

A Bridge Too Far

'At a football club there's a holy trinity – the players, the manager and the supporters. Directors don't come into it. They are only there to sign the cheques.'

Bill Shankly

Astrange sense of foreboding overtakes me as I cross the Severn Bridge. I've always been a bit Anne Robinson about Wales, what with all the egg-chasing and male voice choirs and unfeasibly long unpronounceable place names, and have tended to treat it as an inconvenient obstacle on the way to Ireland. Football and Wales never exactly seemed easy bedfellows.

Yet Cardiff City famously won the FA Cup in 1927 beating Arsenal 1-0 (ironically as a result of a bad mistake by Arsenal's Welsh goalie Lewis) to take the trophy out of England for the only time in its history. Well, the only time until the twenty-first century, of course, when they started dragging the Cup across the border every year when the final was moved to Cardiff's shiny new Millennium Stadium while Australian builders faffed around building the new Wembley.

Admittedly, no cosy night in the pub warming your feet by the fire, playing shove ha'penny, drinking pints of mild and putting the world to rights would be complete without telling the story of the Welsh icon Billy Meredith. From the tiny village of Chirk in the Ceiriog Valley on the border in North Wales, the deeply religious Meredith was working down the mines as a pony driver at 12. Despite his obvious talents as a right winger, his family wouldn't hear of allowing him to give up the job at Black Park Colliery to concentrate on football.

Eventually Meredith agreed to sign for Manchester City and became an instant hero, scoring two goals against Newton Heath (soon to change their name to Manchester United) in the first Manchester derby. Incredibly he continued to work down the pit throughout his first two years with the club until 1896, when his slinky skills, power on the ball, cheeky moustache and eccentric personality started turning him into British football's first superstar. He'd go on the pitch chewing tobacco until the cleaners refused to wash spit off his shirts and so he compromised by chewing on a toothpick as he tore down the wing. When Manchester City won the FA Cup for the first time with a 1-0 victory over Bolton at Crystal Palace in 1904, Meredith was team captain and a national hero.

He always did it *his* way and the fans loved him for it, although it didn't endear him to the authorities. Shortly after topping a newspaper poll to find Britain's most popular footballer, Meredith and the rest of the City team were banned for a season for allegedly attempting to bribe an Aston Villa player before a vital match. Billy vociferously claimed it was a stitch up and eventually the ban was lifted, but not before he'd put the wheels in motion to form the first players' union. After the ban he left City to cross the road to join their emergent greatest rivals Manchester United, where his celebrity shone even more brightly on the back of two league titles and an FA Cup win. He also led Wales to their first Home Championship victory.

The George Best of his day, Meredith was nicknamed 'Old Skinny'. He returned to Manchester City during the First World War, still chewing on his toothpick, criticising the way the game was run and campaigning for an end to the maximum wage. He played for Wales at the age of 48 and continued to play for City until 1924, by which time he was 50. Meredith died in Manchester in 1958, aged 83, and was initially buried in an unmarked grave until, years later, the PFA, Welsh FA, Manchester United and Manchester City agreed to collaborate on the upkeep of a new headstone at the city's Southern Cemetery.

So I'm thinking of Billy Meredith as I plough into Cymru, the jolly old M4 romping past Newport, Cardiff, Llantrisant, Bridgend and Port Talbot and taking us all the way to tonight's theatre of dreams – Swansea City. After 94 years at the tawdry Vetch Field with its crooked floodlights, the Swans have just moved into a glittering new £30 million 20,000-capacity all-seater home, splendidly called the Liberty Stadium.

I'm fondly imagining it is named after some heroic freedom fighter or commemorates an ancient legend when Welsh slaves threw off the shackles of their cruel English masters and took control of their own lives. The Welsh defeated Anglo-Norman colonists in Swansea in 1136: maybe it's something to do with that? 'Oh no,' says the bloke in the ticket office who relieves me of £13 for a ticket to tonight's game. 'It's named after the sponsor, a development company called Liberty Properties.' Another romantic illusion bites the dust.

Still, the Liberty Stadium has already won design awards and, all lit up on the edge of Swansea Bay looking like a white sparkly greenhouse, it's quite a sight. As I wander round it trying to find the way in, I bump into a small statue of Ivor Allchurch. Ah yes, Ivor Allchurch, the wavy blond-haired golden boy of Welsh football, who was discovered the old-fashioned way, being spotted by Swansea player Joe Sykes in a park game at the end of the Second World War.

He went on to make 445 appearances for Swansea, scoring 164 goals, and was capped 68 times by Wales, including a starring role in a rare Welsh foray into the World Cup Finals when they actually reached the last eight in Sweden in 1958. They were knocked out in the end by Brazil, the only goal of the game scored by a then unknown 17-year-old named Pele. Not a bad showing, considering Wales only made the finals by default after finishing runners-up in their qualifying group to Czechoslovakia. Israel's opponents had all refused to play them in the qualifications, so FIFA ruled there should be a lottery among the runner-up teams to determine who would take on Israel in a two-legged play-off to determine who'd fill the last World Cup Finals place. Wales were drawn out of a hat and went on to claim their place in Sweden.

After his brilliant performances in Sweden the whole world wanted to buy Allchurch, who eventually signed for Newcastle for a then astronomical £28,000 fee. He later returned to end his professional career back home in Swansea at the age of 35 in 1965, and was top scorer in his last two seasons. He died in 1997, aged 67.

But there is no statue of another legendary son of Swansea, Allchurch's great contemporary, childhood friend and international colleague John Charles. Charles, known as the 'Gentle Giant', also started his illustrious career here as a 15-year-old amateur just after the war. He didn't hang around South Wales for long and built his reputation as a brilliant centre half/centre forward after being signed by the fearsome Leeds manager Major Buckley in 1949, scoring a club record 42 goals for them in one season. He had the looks of a matinée idol and the towering physique of a heavyweight boxer, and became Britain's first major footballing export when he was signed to Italian team Juventus for a British record fee of £65,000.

It took months of negotiations before the deal was struck, with commentator Ken 'They think it's all over, it is now' Wolstenholme acting as Charles's unofficial agent. Where Jimmy Greaves, Denis Law and Ian Rush later failed, 'Il Buono Gigante' was a massive success and was voted Player of the Year in his second season in Italy. He helped Juve to three league titles and two Italian Cups, and remains a legend in Turin and Rome (he also spent a season playing for Roma). He even developed an alternative career as a crooner, entertaining the punters in the ski resorts of northern Italy.

Asked to name the greatest centre half he'd ever played against, Nat Lofthouse said 'John Charles'. When Billy Wright was asked to name the best centre *forward* he'd ever played against, he said 'John Charles'. Charles retired in 1966 after a

glittering career in which, despite being a target for unscrupu-
lous hatchet men, he was amazingly never booked or sent off.
He died in 2004.

Tonight Swansea are playing Huddersfield Town, with both
teams striving for promotion to the Championship. I'd rather
planned to adopt 'uddersfield for the night and ingratiate
myself with the Yorkshire travelling support. I'd contacted the
club and left various messages on supporters' internet message
boards but the miserable buggers didn't get back to me. So, sod
'em, it's Swansea for me and I'm all white on the night.

Swansea have the biggest match day programme in
Christendom and I devour it hungrily as I recover from the
steep climb to Row Y, right up there in the gods. It's a lovely
stadium but a shame about the PA and I genuinely can't work
out if the sound is distorted or if the announcer is talking in
Welsh. Either way, I've no idea which players have been chosen
to do the business tonight (OK, I've got this huge programme
on which the players are all numbered but it's not much use if
you're so far from the pitch you can't see the numbers),
although I do recognise the swashbuckling figure of Swansea's
Scouse superstriker Lee Trundle, mainly because the crowd
bursts into a chorus of 'Lee Trundle, my lord, Lee Trundle' to the
tune of 'Kumbaya' every time the ball goes anywhere near him.

This is an interesting one. 'Kumbaya', sung around every
scout camp fire and performed by any winsome sixth former
with an acoustic guitar and a Joan Baez fixation, originated as a
spiritual from the Gullah, an enslaved African-American people
who lived in isolation for hundreds of years in the Sea Islands
off Georgia and South Carolina. 'Kumbaya' is a dialect corruption of 'Come by here' that took root after an American
missionary had sung it in Angola. It gained common currency
in the civil rights movement of the 1960s and, like so many
symbolic right-on songs of unity and defiance, was commer-
cially exploited by Peter, Paul & Mary in the name of protest
song. It's strange to hear it being sung, here in Swansea, to sere-
nade a bustling barrel-chested Scouser in long white shorts.

In no time at all the song booms out at full volume around the stadium as Trundle scores, smashing the ball past Town keeper Phil Senior before he's even seen the danger. The hairy bloke who'd been sitting glumly next to me without a word is suddenly on his feet yelling 'I love you Lee Trundle' and not minding at all that his 10-year-old son next to him is swearing like a trooper and throwing V-signs at the small clutch of stripy-blue-shirted Huddersfield supporters congregated miserably behind the goal. By half-time it's 2-0 with a fine goal from the speedy Leon Britton and Row Y couldn't be happier. We even start up our very own outburst of the 'Tom Hark' tune. 'Di-da-da-da … di-da-da-da-da …' Oh, how I love that 'Tom Hark' tune …

See, there was a poor little black South African kid called Kwela Jake who ran away from home and school, slept in the back of a wrecked car in a disused car lot in the back streets of Johannesburg and spent his days trying to get money and dodging the cops, who were likely to beat him up if they caught him. His only worldly possession was a battered old tin penny whistle, which he used to busk on the streets for pennies. One day he made up the tune to 'Tom Hark' and went out in Jo'burg with his mate Elias, playing it. With its infectiously mischievous tune and joyous spirit it proved a good little earner even then. It proved an even bigger one when it caught the ear of a guy from a record company.

He whisked Jake and Elias into a studio, recorded the tune and gave them six guineas each for their troubles. When they emerged, they'd been magically transformed into Elias and the Zig Zag Flutes. Even more magically, the record was played on the radio. It became a hit in South Africa and by 1958 the whole world seemed to be bopping to 'Tom Hark' as it became an international hit and sold a million. It sold over five million in the end, and in April 1958 Elias and the Zig Zag Flutes reached No. 2 in the British charts, denied the top spot only by something called Marvin Rainwater singing 'Whole Lotta Woman'. It took on another life in 1980 when it was re-recorded by the Piranhas and became adopted by football fans. So yeah, let's sing 'Tom Hark' tonight in Swansea for Lee Trundle and Leon Britton and Roberto Martinez and Rory Fallon and all our other brave boys in white, but mostly let's sing it for Kwela Jake and Elias, busking all those years ago on the streets of Johannesburg.

Swansea lose points at half-time for their failure to provide Bovril or Wagon Wheels but Row Y's in fine voice, belting out 'Can't Help Falling In Love' and 'Hey Jude' and even 'Wild Rover' in anticipation of a convincing victory over the Yorkshire boys. Then it all starts to go horribly wrong. The crowd behind the goal has been singing 'La Marseillaise' as a salute to 'Big Willy', Swansea's French keeper, but the song dies in their throats as Big Willy comes flying out of his goal and demolishes a Huddersfield forward. A penalty, and very possibly a red card too. Luckily, it's only a yellow and Chris Brandon sends the penalty crashing against the bar.

But the reprieve doesn't last long as 'uddersfield get the bit between their teeth, their fans come alive for the first time and Swansea start panicking, glaring at each other accusingly as balls fly around the box. Big Willy threatens to burst a blood vessel bellowing at them. When veteran defender Martin McIntosh scores for Huddersfield with an unchallenged header from a corner in the 70th minute, consternation spreads through the stadium with the speed that my tent went up in flames at the Cambridge Folk Festival in 1976.

The little kid next to me is coming out with a string of obscenities he must have fished up from Swansea Bay, but his dad doesn't even blink. He's too busy shouting himself: 'Get some fresh legs on your quotz!' I look at him in bewilderment. Quotz? *Quotz*? It must be a Welsh thing. Inevitably, 'uddersfield get the equaliser a few minutes from time and the home fans, previously so encouraging, supportive and joyous, turn on their team big time and Swansea shrink off to a chorus of boos. 'Bloody typical ...' spits the bloke next to me with a mouth full of bile. 'Yep,' I say, sympathetically. 'What a load of quotz!'

The next day I undertake an epic drive from South to North Wales. It's a journey that seems to have no end, as I drive right off the end of the M4 and up through loads of little towns with two Ls at the start of their names, a severe lack of signposts, encroaching bleakness, high hills, narrow roads and a growing absence of cars, people, buildings or even sheep. I'm on my way to Wrexham for a 3 p.m. kick-off but, as lunchtime comes and goes, frankly a kickabout in the park would do me. I've no idea in which direction I'm going and there's no one to ask, though that may be just as well given my last experience of communing with the natives in this neck of the woods, when they all started talking in Welsh and pointed billiard cues at me.

I'm just checking to see how the emergency rations of Twix, bananas and holy water are holding up when I suddenly arrive in a town. It's called Llangollen and, surrounded by the River Dee, it's a gorgeous little place, with a castle, a railway and lots of references to King Arthur and the international Eisteddfod. Stopping in pursuit of more emergency Twix bars, I stumble across an unexpected sight – a road sign to Wrexham. Maybe, just *maybe*, I will make it in time for kick-off.

The Racecourse Stadium, Wrexham proves relatively easy to find and I even make it in time for a swift pint at the Turf pub, the site of the winning post in the days when the stadium really was a racccourse, and where the players used to change before matches. They also used to play cricket here (in fact, the football club was formed by cricketers looking for something to do in winter). Wrexham FC have played football at the Racecourse since 1872.

They've never had much glory down this way. Their highest ever Football League position was 15th in the old Second Division in 1979. But Wrexham have been regular Welsh Cup winners through the years and had a few European adventures, notably when they became the only Third Division side to reach the quarter finals of the European Cup Winners Cup in 1976, agonisingly losing 2-1 on aggregate to Belgian side Anderlecht, who went on to beat West Ham 4-2 in the final. More recent heroics include the 1992 2-1 FA Cup victory over Arsenal from a late free kick by 37-year-old Mickey Thomas. Today the Shropshire Reds are flogging tickets for a 30th anniversary Anderlecht reunion event ('tickets £10, including hotpot').

If you know what's good for you in these parts you fall to your knees in worship whenever the name of Mickey Thomas is mentioned and, whatever you do, don't make jokes about dud fivers. I said it once, but I think I got away with it. Less than two years after scoring the winner against Arsenal, Thomas was sent down for 18 months for dealing counterfeit money to trainees at Wrexham. He shared a cell with a murderer who decapitated his victim, and gathered plenty of material for his subsequent life as a radio pundit and after-dinner speaker. 'So Roy Keane's on £50,000 a week,' he'd say in mock-horror. 'So was I until the police found my printing machine.'

The judge called him a 'flash and daring adventurer', a description that appeared to please Mickey no end (the *News of the World* once flagged a story 'that will enrage every law-abiding Briton' with a front-page picture of Thomas in prison swigging from a bottle of champagne). On a separate occasion he was stabbed in the bum by his irate ex-brother-in-law after being discovered playing away from home in a car in a country lane with the bloke's new wife. They may pull faces when you mention his name at some of the other clubs he played for, including Manchester United, Chelsea, Leeds and Everton, but in Wrexham the guy is a legend.

I buy a ticket and join the hardcore red-and-white fans in the Crispin Lane End behind the goal to applaud the brand new troupe of nubile cheerleaders waving pom-poms and dancing to 'Carwash' in the centre circle while an announcer asks for suggestions of a name for them. 'Never mind a bloody name,' says a chirpy lad in the Bovril queue, 'I reckon we should play that little blonde one on the wing today. She's got more moves than most of our lot.'

Wrexham run out to the stirring sounds of 'Men of Harlech', a chest-thumping anthem commemorating the battle for

Harlech Castle in 1408 when the forces of Owain Glyndwr, the last Welshman to be Prince of Wales, and the future King Henry V locked horns. These were tough times in the battle for Welsh independence. Harlech Castle held strategic symbolism for the self-proclaimed king of Wales, and when the English attacked, Owain tried to call in the support of old allies from France and Scotland. It didn't materialise and Harlech fell after a long siege. Owain's wife and two daughters were captured and imprisoned in the Tower of London but Owain escaped to continue the battle for several years as a guerrilla freedom fighter motivating rebel forces around Snowdonia.

Most of his closest companions were captured and executed along the way, but Owain remained at large amid various rumours about how he had managed to disappear for so long, the most persistent being that he disguised himself as a Franciscan friar. Others insisted he was the real identity of folk hero Jack O'Kent, a wizard who roamed Herefordshire during the same period. After 1415 there was peace in Wales and Owain's son Maredudd accepted a pardon on his father's behalf in 1421, although Owain himself was never seen again.

Harlech Castle later also became a central battleground in the War of the Roses and the English Civil War and was first commemorated musically in 1784 in something called *March of the Men of Harlech in Musical and Poetical Relicks of the Welsh Bards*: 'March ye men of Harlech bold/Unfurl your banners in the field/Be brave as you were sires of old/And like them never yield ...' Surely that's got to be worth a goal start for Wrexham today.

However, those are not the words echoing around the Racecourse as the teams run out today. There have been quite a few variants on the 'Harlech' lyrics since, notably when it featured in the 1964 movie *Zulu*, starring Stanley Baker and Michael Caine. The film depicted a Welsh garrison singing 'Men of Harlech' as their answer to Zulu war chants when they crossed the river to defend Rorke's Drift against seemingly impossible odds in 1879, but the lyrics they sang were written specifically for the film and historians are adamant that 'Men of Harlech' was never sung in that particular battle.

Now, in the chill of a wintry Saturday in North Wales, the Wrexham fans stand behind the goal singing their own version of 'Men of Harlech':

> Here they come our mighty champions, raise your voices to the
>   anthem
> Marching like a mighty army, Wrexham is the name
> See the Reds who fight together, speak their name with pride
>   forever
> Marching like a mighty army, Wrexham is the name.

It sounds daft, but though the Racecourse is tatty and rundown and Wrexham supporters have had little to crow about over the years, the sense of pride and defiance as they sing is genuinely galvanising. Their voices gather in volume as they hit the chorus:

> Fearless in devotion, rising to promotion
> Rising to the ranks of mighty heroes, fighting foes in every land
> History only tells the story, we are here to see your glory
> Stand aside the Reds are coming, Wrexham is the name.

A bunch of supporters recorded 'Wrexham Is the Name' in 1978 and it stuck. You may hear 'Men of Harlech' sung in different forms at Cardiff and Wales matches, but right here right now it sounds a uniquely Wrexham thing.

Today's Coca Cola League Two match is against promotion-chasing Northampton Town but, firmly converted by their rousing singing, I plonk myself right in the middle of the Wrexham supporters who are banked up behind the goal and roundly abusing strapping Northampton keeper Lee Harper. 'You fat bastard' we chant at every conceivable opportunity, as well as (an oldie but a goodie) 'Who ate all the pies?' Bovril on tap and chants of 'Who ate all the pies?' – they know their proper football traditions in Wrexham.

There's a bloke close by standing on his own who hasn't reacted at all to any of the play. He has ignored all the chanting, stood in silence during the 'Wrexham Is the Name' singing and frankly looks like he's only here for the Bovril. But suddenly it's as if Mickey Thomas's ex-brother-in-law has arrived and caught him unawares. His face goes purple and he begins to roar: 'RED ARMY RED ARMY REDARMYREDARMYREDARMY ...'

Instantly the rest of the terrace is with him, bellowing a counterpoint 'Red Army' as his voice resonates around the stadium. He keeps going, and going, and going. His 'Red Army' chant goes on for about 15 minutes, rumbling incessantly without pause or deviation, just a constant dirge-like barrage, the words long ceasing to hold any meaning as they butt into each other in one seamless, repetitive stream of consciousness.

I gaze in awe at the guy, amazed by the noise coming out of him and his ability to maintain it without a break in concentration or breath. When he finally brings it to a hoarse halt without warning I sidle up to him, desperate to know how and why he does it, but he gives me a withering look and stares sullenly back at the pitch, ignoring my attempts to engage him in conversation. He doesn't say another word or join in another song or chant for the rest of the match. This is clearly a god among football supporters.

It's a good job the supporters are so lively because the match itself is dire, the sort of game at which fans have to make their own entertainment. There are many ways of doing it. A group of you put in a couple of quid each then pass the pot along the line every time there is a throw-in or corner. The one left holding the pot at the final whistle keeps it. You can also spice things up by predicting the number of offsides, or the time of the first substitution, or the number of visits to the pitch by the physio, or … well, anything really.

The Red Army keep their spirits up by singing anti-Chester songs and passing loud comment on incidental activity in the match. 'One Harry Secombe, there's only one Harry Secombe' they chant as a chubby red-faced steward who looks a dead ringer for the late great Goon and *Songs of Praise* presenter materialises in front of them. Harry goes even redder. 'You're only jealous,' he yells back. But their good humour is severely tested as the second half grows increasingly tedious and what little activity there is threatens the Wrexham goal rather than Northampton's.

Northampton ('You're a load of old Cobblers') may be dreaming of repeating their own astonishing rise through the early 1960s, which saw them promoted from Division Four to Division One in five seasons. Unfortunately, it was purely a social call and they ended up tumbling all the way down the leagues again, ending up back in the basement division. Still, in 1970 they did reach the fifth round of the FA Cup, only to be thrashed 8-2 at home by Manchester United, with George Best scoring six of them.

Twenty minutes from time, with the temperature sinking fast, there's a terrible mix-up between Wrexham's keeper Mike Ingham and one of several players called Williams and fleet-footed Cobbler Ryan Gilligan nips between them to score. The considerable spirit of the Red Army is swiftly crushed. A lone middle-aged fan who looks disconcertingly like the short Geordie from *Auf Wiedersehen, Pet* tries in vain to rally support for an unlikely equaliser. He rounds on his own supporters. 'Can you hear the Wrexham sing? No-ooo No-ooo …' A couple of disciples join his campaign to chivvy support: 'Four of us singing, there's only four of us singing.' Then someone else joins in: 'Five of us singing …' It's not enough for our man. He rounds on the others: 'Come on, you lot! Fifteen minutes left, what we going to do?' They shuffle nervously and look at their shoes the way people do on the underground when a busker comes round trying to collect money or a street person tries to flog them the *Big Issue*. He retaliates by launching into 'Silent Night': 'Silent night, holy night, all is calm, all is shite …'

The match peters out into a limp 1-0 defeat for Wrexham, who appear more like frightened hamsters than raging dragons. The lone rabble-rouser – he says his name is Bryn, but it could be Tim or Jim or Finn or Bin or Lynn or anything really – is disconsolate. But his abuse is reserved not for the team but for his fellow supporters. 'Rubbish,' he snarls at me, 'they're rubbish. What's the point of coming here if you can't get behind your side? They should be ashamed of themselves. I'm really not happy. You can't accuse the players of not trying if the fans don't try either.' He goes off swearing to himself, and I can only conjecture the grief he'll give them in the pub later. This man is surely the Sir Alex Ferguson of football supporters and that hapless Red Army is in for an extended dose of the hairdryer treatment.

I take refuge back in the Turf to find that a 1-0 defeat against Northampton is a fairly minor setback at a club that's spent the last year or so fighting for its survival. Faced with Inland Revenue debts of £900,000, Wrexham went into administration at the end of 2004 with everybody in the Turf using property developer and major shareholder Alex Hamilton as a metaphorical dartboard. He's been at the heart of a long, messy, complicated saga of 125-year ground leases, administration, break clauses, notices to quit, unpaid wages, court appearances, winding-up orders, an attempt to sell the Racecourse for property development, deals and no-deals, an attempt at a fans takeover, a High Court Appeal and a 10-point deduction by the Football League.

The Wrexham fanzine *Dismal Jimmy* carries a verbatim account of itself ambushing Alex Hamilton that would be hilarious if it wasn't so serious:

Fanzine: 'Don't you care about Wrexham, don't you care about the kids? All you care about is profit. Why don't you just give up, Alex, and clear off?'

Hamilton: 'I've been ready to do a deal. I've taken responsibility. I've been able to clear the debts. Why don't you ask the administrators? You just fictionalise it.'

Fanzine: 'In October 2004 the supporters put together a deal that would have given you more than £1 million. Why did you turn it down?'

Hamilton: 'They put no money on the table, sir.'

Fanzine: 'You'd have had your money twelve months ago. It had the full backing of the council and all the other parties.'

Hamilton: 'There was no money – it was conditional on planning deals.'

Fanzine: 'You're a tired old man who wants to make a pay day by terrorising and bullying a community in Wales because you're anti-Welsh ...'

Hamilton: 'I'm going to have to call the police – you're blocking my progress and you're wanting a fight. I'm trying to get into my home.'

The encounter ends with Mr Hamilton on the phone to the police.

If ever there was a microcosm of the battle for the soul of football, it's to be found at the Racecourse Ground. It's old and tatty but it still sells Bovril and Wagon Wheels and is home to proud, passionate fans who boldly sing 'Wrexham Is the Name' when the players run out, and will fight tooth-and-nail to keep their club while businessmen squabble over the land with no real understanding of the history it encompasses or what it means to the long-suffering disciples who hand over their £14 every week. It has also produced one of the most emotive football songs ever.

The Declan Swans are an indie band from Wrexham who are primarily noted for satirical songs about public figures. They've done a hilarious skit on the trial (and punctured bottom) of Mickey Thomas but they're more revered for crushing diatribes about Anne Robinson, Richard Madeley, Sven Goran Eriksson, Posh and Becks and other perceived enemies of Welshness. Their most famous satire, however, was 'Meet the Kilshaws', which ridiculed Alan and Judith Kilshaw who in 2001 caused national outrage when they attempted to buy baby twins off the internet. They schlepped to Arkansas to fly the girls back to North Wales, even though the babies had already supposedly been 'sold' to an American couple, and they had to give the babies back when social services stepped in. Alan went bank-rupt paying legal fees and bizarre stories about their lifestyle were splashed over the tabloids.

Using the 'Meet the Flintstones' tune as their template, the Declan Swans savaged the Kilshaws with couplets like 'Alan is a stranger to his bath/Judith is a fawkin psychopath'. It was adopted for a while on the terraces and took an even stranger turn when the Kilshaws themselves helped promote it and Judith Kilshaw got up on stage to sing with the Swans at a charity gig in a Wrexham nightclub. 'My voice is all right after a few pints,' she said, but the concert ended suddenly with a stage invasion and a brawl.

The relationship between Declan Swans and Wrexham reached its highest point, however, with another Wrexham Supporters Trust fundraiser, 'Stan's Ashes', the football song that has everything – a war hero, a love story, a social history of the mining industry, a tragic death, a grieving widow, politics and ... Wrexham FC. Dripping in pathos, the story climaxes with the death of its titular hero, Stan, from a lung disease contracted from swallowing coal dust. As per his wishes, his ashes are scattered over the Racecourse Ground. And then they plunge the knife in ...

> His memory lives on through the beautiful game
> The owner's head should hang in shame
> For his widow is 90 and wheelchair-bound
> What does she think about selling the ground?

And just in case we're left in any further doubt about the villain of the piece ...

> She fought back the tears on this dark afternoon
> And questioned the soul of this greedy tycoon:
> 'A cold uncaring heartless man
> Who mocks the normal average fan
> With little interest for the game
> A slur upon my husband's name.'

The boys in red are getting very tanked up when I leave them at the Turf, contemplating the ifs, buts and maybes of the developers and businessmen seemingly intent on ripping the soul out of football. 'Look at the place,' says Bryn (or is it Jim, Flynn, Ming or Bing?), jerking a thumb at the old stadium next door. 'It's not much really but we love it. That's what Mr Hamilton and his business cronies don't understand. But I'll tell you one thing: whatever happens in the boardrooms and courts, everybody in this pub will be fighting to their last breath to keep this club alive. And we'll do it, too, just you wait and see.'

The next day, I delve even deeper into the soul of football. See, the real carrot for this Welsh weekend football fiesta is Total Network Solutions. Is there a soccer fan in Great Britain who doesn't stifle a giggle when James Alexander Gordon reads out the results on Five Live and reaches the murky depths of the Welsh Premier League, which magically always manages to make an appearance on the pools coupon in the form of Total Network Solutions? I mean, *Total Network Solutions*. 'Oh yes, they'll be dancing on the streets of Total Network Solutions tonight,' says Sky Sports anchorman Jeff Stelling as the tickertape records another resounding win for TNS, who have become the cult football team for anyone with a taste for the absurd.

Complete strangers stop me in the street as news of my impending pilgrimage spreads and say, 'You're going to see Total Network Solutions? *Wow!*' A trip to the Bernabeu to watch Real Madrid take on Barcelona would scarcely have elicited more intrigue. 'Total Network Solutions, eh?' they ask, grinning. 'Who are they playing?' 'Airbus UK.' I leave them rolling around the floor, laughing.

Firstly, though, I have to find the bloody place. If I can't find Wrexham, then how the hell am I going to find Total Network Solutions? Bryn (or Gwyn, Wynn, Yin or Rin Tin Tin) had given me precise directions in the Turf last night. 'Oh yeah, it's not far from here. You can't miss it. Just go to Oswestry and take a right turn to Llynclys and you'll see a sign to Llansantffraid …' *Eh*? Lyn *who*? San Fran *wot*? 'That's right, mate, can't miss it.'

Miss it, I do. Several times. It's when I reach Shrewsbury and see signs for Wolverhampton that I realise I've lost the plot big time and turn round to plough back across the Welsh border. My 1983 road map lists four different towns called Llansantffraid, all in different parts of Wales, not to mention several hundred close variants. And stopping to ask people about Total Network Solutions FC draws a blank. They may be legends at 5 p.m. on *Sports Report* and Sky's *Soccer Saturday*, but TNS don't seem to have registered too much on the Welsh borders.

Eventually I pass a sign directing me down a small road to Llansantffraid and I hope it's the right one. It's hard to say when a farmer suddenly directs a herd of cows across the road in front of me. They pause to sniff my car's dangly bits and gaze at me in wonder as if to say, 'Look at this goon – he's in the wrong bloody Llansantffraid.' I drive on to find another obstacle in my path – not one, but *two* tractors crawling along the narrow road, giving me no alternative but to crawl along behind them for six miles. I bet they don't have this problem at Old Trafford.

It's Sunday lunchtime as I arrive in the tiny village of Llansantffraid-ym-Mechain, Powys and it doesn't have the ambience you'd expect from the home of the best football team in the Welsh league. I park up and observe the stillness. According to my information the 2 p.m. kick-off is less than half-an-hour away and there's not the remotest sign of life in any form, let alone a major Vauxhall Masterfit Welsh Premier League match with Airbus UK. I am now completely convinced I am in the wrong Llansantffraid entirely. I wander into a garage and ask the lad at the counter if he has any Wagon Wheels and, oh, this couldn't by any chance be the same Llansantffraid that is home to the famous football team Total Network Solutions? He looks at me blankly, and I laugh it off as if to perish the thought that anybody could possibly imagine a football team dwelt in a dozy little hamlet like this.

It's a tiny village and in truth not a particularly attractive one, although there are a couple of likely looking pubs in the Station and the Sun, with a few people dressed up in their Sunday best going in for Sunday lunch. A man in an ill-fitting suit and tie sees me looking round. 'Here for the football, are you?' he asks. I leap on him. 'Yes! Yes, I *am*. So this is where Total Network Solutions play?' 'Oh yes,' he says, 'we're all very proud of them.' Do you never miss a match, then? 'Me? Oh no, I don't often go to see them. Well, to be honest I've *never* seen them, but I hear they're very good. Last football match I went to was at Stoke City 30 years ago. I got knocked over a barrier and was nearly crushed to death. Never been to a game since. Do TNS have a match today then?' I'm hoping so. He beams and shakes my hand warmly as his wife hollers from the doorway of the pub that she wants her Sunday dinner and if he knows what's good for him he'll get his arse inside sharpish. 'For two pence,' he winks, 'I'd come with you. The ground is just up the hill by the school. You can't miss it.'

By my reckoning they should be kicking off by the time I make it up the hill to the ground, but it's deserted. I'm about to bail out again when a couple of chirpy chaps in yellow stewards coats appear. Is there a match on today then? 'Is there?' I was asking you. 'Asking me what?' If there's a match on today? 'We've got a match on today – home to Airbus UK, 3 p.m. kick-off if you can make it. Should be a cracker.' Hallelujah!

Right on cue, the Airbus UK coach clambers up the hill and negotiates a tight bend into the surprisingly extravagant car park. Sixteen rosy-cheeked lads bound off the coach, their faces lit up with excitement as they glance at the arena awaiting them. They have to dress up in ridiculous suits and ties and schlep halfway across the country and race home from their colleges or day jobs to train a couple of times a week and mind their Ps and Qs when they're out, but *this* is what it's all about.

It doesn't matter at what level of the game or at what standard you play. It's the sight and smell of the pitch, the nets going up, the adrenalin unleashed and the sense of anticipation that today you're going to play everyone else off the park … *this* is the glory of football. And these boys representing something called Airbus UK feel it just as intensely as the players of Manchester United and Wigan Athletic, who are gathering in Cardiff at around the same time for the Carling Cup Final.

But this still feels absurdly surreal. Llansantffraid has less than 1,000 inhabitants and is notable for, well, nothing really. Even the railway station closed 50 years ago. But in a fairy story straight out of a *Roy of the Rovers* annual, the village football team rose to take on the European champions. For over 30 years they were an enthusiastic amateur team, playing kick-and-rush in front of the proverbial two men and a dog, until a restructuring of Welsh football to incorporate a Welsh national league for the first time meant that, in theory at least, they could reach the highest echelons of Welsh football.

At the time Llansantffraid FC were seriously struggling and in real danger of extinction, but a couple of bold committee members decided to throw caution to the wind and test the theory. They established the ground up the hill at Treflan and effectively rebuilt the club on a more professional footing. Three promotions in four seasons followed, and in 1993 Llansantffraid proudly arrived to take their place in the top flight, the League of Wales.

The rest of Welsh football laughed, even disputing their right to take their place in the league, claiming that such a tiny outfit couldn't possibly sustain itself at such giddy heights and the whole venture was destined to end in tears with embarrassing double-figure defeats every week. It didn't work out that way. Patronised all the way, Llansantffraid not only survived, they flourished. In 1995 they won the Welsh League Cup and the following season, in the match that irrevocably changed their destiny, they reached the Welsh Cup Final. The Welsh Cup had traditionally been the property of Cardiff, Swansea and Wrexham, but for the first time that year Welsh clubs playing in the English leagues were excluded from the competition. Llansantffraid marched proudly into the spotlight and shone.

Their opponents in that Welsh Cup Final, the last match to be played at the old National Stadium in Cardiff before its demolition, were Barry Town, and it turned out to be a thriller. In front of a crowd of 2,666 the match ended at 3-3, couldn't be resolved by extra time, and Llansantffraid eventually won 3-2 on penalties. We can only imagine the heaving scenes in the village's two pubs that night, but drinks on the house weren't their only reward. As Welsh Cup winners, they qualified for the following season's European Cup Winners Cup.

Tales of that first European adventure and vodka breakfasts when they flew to Poland to get their bottoms smacked by KS Ruch Chorzow keep me entertained for hours in the TNS clubhouse after today's match. Depending on who you listen to, though, the costs of transporting Llansantffraid to Poland nearly bankrupted them, even if they did come back with a strange-looking leather-backed clock which now takes pride of place behind the bar. In those days they had no sponsorship, TV revenues or public assistance and, despite the glamour of cup finals and European matches, they essentially remained a tiny village side struggling to cope with the expenses reaped by success and the desire to maintain it.

Enter Mike Harris. Not a knight in shining armour, exactly, more a cheery, energetic bloke in shorts from Oswestry working hard to build the 'voice and data' technology company he'd founded in 1991. Mike Harris came to see a football match at Llansantffraid and liked it so much that he bought the club. Or, at least, pumped in enough sponsorship to refloat the club with a turbo engine. Thanks, Mike, said Llansantffraid, is there anything we can do for you in return? It seems only fair. Why yes, said Mike, as a matter of fact, there is. You wouldn't by any chance like to adopt the name of my company would you and change your name to Total Network Solutions? The club bit his hand off. That was in 1997, and neither party has looked back since.

Total Network Solutions has grown into a major business employing 92 people with assets of £9.1 million. In 2005, it became BT TNS when Mike Harris sold it to BT for an undisclosed figure thought to run into several millions. And Total Network Solutions the football team – or 'The Tins' as they're affectionately known – have gone from strength to strength with many more trophies, European excursions and tales to tell.

In 2003, a UEFA Cup tie ensured they took part in the first competitive match at Manchester City's new City of Manchester Stadium in front of 34,000 fans, and they became the first non-Football League Welsh club to play at Cardiff's Millennium Stadium in the return leg. Last season they did the double of both the Welsh Cup and Welsh Premier League for the first time, thus securing a place in the qualifying round of the European Champions League. They geared up for it with a friendly against Chelsea and then took on the European champions, Liverpool. They succumbed at Anfield to a Steven Gerrard hat trick and also lost 3-0 in the home leg – played, like most of their European ties, at Wrexham because their Treflan ground doesn't conform to UEFA standards.

There has subsequently been more off-the-field activity involving a merger with cash-strapped Oswestry FC and plans for a grand new stadium to be built at Oswestry to accommodate the European extravaganza, with a sports complex, youth academy and all. It's a visionary notion, but one that's already created a fair share of headscratching at the UEFA HQ. For it may be up the road but Oswestry is technically in Shropshire, which is technically in England, which is technically not in Wales, which technically means a team playing in the Welsh League and technically representing Wales in European competitions is technically not allowed.

But Mike Harris didn't get where he is today without a bit of legal know-how and he vociferously argued his corner against UEFA. After all, Derry City are located in Northern Ireland but play league matches in the Republic, and UEFA had no objection to them playing in Europe. And what would happen if Cardiff, Swansea or Wrexham won a trophy playing in the English Football League and earned the right to an appearance in the UEFA Cup? Would *they* be barred? Frankly we doubt it, Mr UEFA, we doubt it. So UEFA eventually relented and, given that Oswestry were in any case playing in the Welsh Premier League, made special dispensation for the new joint TNS/Oswestry club to compete in Europe from a new stadium just over the English border.

So, that settled, we can take respite from the biting conditions, grab a pint in the splendidly convivial Llansantffraid clubhouse and await today's match. TNS are winning the title this year at a canter – it's almost a year since they lost a league match – and there's a touch of Chelsea about the seasoned supporters suddenly tumbling into the ground.

I meet the Breeze family, all decked out in green and white hoops, who've been coming here en bloc since 2000. 'There used to be a lot of scrapping in those days, y'know fighting … sometimes with *each other*,' says mum Christine Breeze. 'Now there's a lot more, y'know, *discipline*.' The Breezes are Welsh football converts after having initially been smitten by the Premiership. Christine says she's been a Liverpool fan since she was eight, while the kids Stuart and Robert let the side down by supporting Manchester United and Arsenal. Hubby Graham didn't really like football much until they started going on family outings to Treflan and some of the away matches. 'Oh, the best one was when we played Liverpool at Anfield,' says Christine. 'It was soooo good seeing our team up against Gerrard and all the rest and we did all right too. We gave 'em a good game. I think they were surprised how well we played.'

A lad marches meaningfully into the back of the steep stand behind the goal opened by Ian Rush in 2001, enlisting the help of a gang of smaller kids squabbling among themselves at the front as he tries to get a chant circulating. It goes something like this: 'T-N-S … T-N-S … T-N-S!' They may be sweeping all before them in Welsh football but they won't win any trophies for their chanting.

The match itself is men against boys. They won't be dancing in the streets of Airbus UK after this performance, as the TNS men in their Celtic colours swiftly demonstrate their superiority with sharp passing and snappy tackling. Clean-cut Michael Wilde turns in a master class in finishing, scoring a hat trick while Airbus chase shadows. I wander around the pitch trying to suck in some romance about the place. A massive, handsome tree sprawls across the far side of the pitch, threatening to encroach on the touchline and dominating the landscape beyond the small contraption on the halfway line that looks more like a bunker than a grandstand. Standing imperiously in front of it, arms folded, is Ken McKenna, the TNS manager, spitting venom at the referee after he's ignored a tackle so late that you feel the defender should be playing for the Australian team rebuilding Wembley rather than Airbus.

A small clutch of Airbus supporters tries to keep the faith. 'There's goals in this for us,' one of them tells me, clearly trying to convince himself as that man Wilde goes close to adding a fourth goal. 'Come on you Wingmakers,' he then yells. Still, he does prove a useful informant. He tells me Airbus are based at Broughton (I nod knowingly, but have no idea where that is) and they weren't always called Airbus UK. They used to be British Aerospace FC and before that they were Hawker Siddeley and for a time they were De Havillands and Vickers-Armstrong and before that something else, but he can't remember what. 'I just call them Wingmakers, it's easier.' Personally, I'm not sure I want to ride in a plane built by this lot – they look about 12.

The little drummer boy and his mates have vacated the stand and are by the pitch pounding out an irregular beat at random intervals, punctured by yet more discordant chants of 'T-N-S' right in the ear of the young visiting goalkeeper. As the match wears on, the temperature drops and the rain starts sleeting down, the crowd of 353 paying customers rapidly diminishes. I wonder where they've all gone until I notice the bulging walls in that nice, warm, inviting clubhouse and the cheers of the crowd gathered round the TVs watching the rugby. I mean, this is North Wales and the rugby hinterland is down south, but hey, it is lovely and toasty in there and TNS *have* got three points in the bag.

Inside, with the points won, the natives are exceedingly friendly. In complete contrast to his animated, confrontational body language on the bench, manager Ken McKenna turns out to be an amiable Scouser who played at Wembley as a free-scoring striker for Runcorn in the 1994 FA Trophy Final against Woking. No joy that day, eh, Ken? I remind him. We beat you 2-1. That confrontational look I'd seen on the bench suddenly reappears. 'The game should have been off! The pitch was waterlogged. You couldn't play on it. It was only because Wembley had this tradition of never having a game called off that they played it. Anywhere else the game would have been off.' Who'd have thought it? Sour grapes after all these years ...

McKenna joined TNS as a player in 1999 and was appointed manager a couple of seasons later, presiding over their unprecedented run of success. He still can't quite believe it himself. 'This is my sixth season in charge and we've been in Europe every season. We're full-time now and it's going great, I love it here. I was told the tickets for the match with Liverpool at Anfield sold faster than for any game in their history – that tells you what they're like on Merseyside. They love a bit of romance there.'

Just for the record, Ken still lives on the Wirral and is a life-long Evertonian: 'I still go whenever I get a day off. I'm as nervous watching them as I am managing TNS. I had a couple of spells playing for Tranmere, but I've always been an Evertonian.' The highlight of his playing career, he says, was playing for Telford in an FA Cup tie against Everton at Goodison Park. I ask him what his philosophy about football is. 'Honesty,' he says instantly. 'You're very privileged to have the ability to play football at whatever level, even if it's parks foot-ball, and you've got to use that in the correct way.'

At 45, with trophies piling up in the TNS cupboard, you wouldn't discount one of the bigger English teams giving him a crack. Ken bats away the question with a deft leg glance.

'Mike Harris is probably the only person at the time who'd have given me the chance to manage so I remain loyal to him. When we finished second three years on the bounce people were calling for my head but Mike was very supportive and he kept me here. I'll always be honest with him, and if anybody does ever come in for me I'll discuss it with him first. I trust him and he trusts me and my only ambition really is to improve this club.'

Meanwhile, back at the bar, they're queuing up with anecdotes. Doug Williams, a former Llansantffraid player who is now TNS vice president, talks me through his 40 years' service with the club and his adventures as a committee member since a compound leg fracture ended his playing career in the early 1970s. They bought the clubhouse for £300 from Shrewsbury and put it up themselves. 'I remember the brewery coming down and saying how much trade did we think we'd do and I said about 70/80 barrels a year and they took me at my word,' he says. 'We're doing 170 barrels a year now.'

Looking at the speed the pints are going down, this doesn't surprise me a bit. 'I've been here from the beginning and I've enjoyed every minute of it,' he continues. 'See, we were always ambitious and we always thought it was possible what we've achieved. We struggled a bit financially for two or three years after the Welsh Cup win but Mike came in with TNS and put his money where his mouth is at the right time because I don't think we could have afforded to move the club forward and go full-time out of our own pockets.

'When we played Manchester City, Kevin Keegan came here to watch us the match before. Sat in here he was, it was amazing. The best, though, was when Chelsea came here for a friendly. Gianfranco Zola – what a man. They took him off after 80 minutes and he signed autographs on the field for every single kid. The match finished and the rest of them had all gone off and got changed and Zola was still on the pitch signing autographs ...'

Mike Hughes is full of tales of partying in Europe. 'Honest to

God, we're paupers compared to most of these bloody European teams but we can show most of them how to have a good time. When we played those Swedes in Wrexham we brought them here and had a meal in the pub up the road and we were all drinking and singing and they said it was the best time they'd ever had. It was the same with Liverpool. We brought [Liverpool chief executive] Rick Parry and the other lads here to show them where TNS play and took them down to the Station up the road, and what a night we had.

'And when we went to Poland that first time, that was unbelievable. The *vodka*. One of our lads was absolutely *paralytic*. We had problems getting him on the plane. We said we're very sorry we've got a bit of a problem, he's a little bit, y'know, *whatchamacallit*. He never opened his eyes from the time we left Warsaw to the time we got home.'

'And what about Estonia? I changed £100 there and I changed £40 back when I came home – you couldn't *spend* money there. A litre of beer was about 70p. It was brilliant. And we had a great time in Sweden. Ten o'clock in the morning we were on the beer and by half past twelve we were in this place called Ali Baba's, singing. Expensive there, mind. About £3 a pint.' You wonder how they managed to fit any football in.

But then comes the most shattering news of the day. In the wake of Mike Harris selling his company to BT, and although he will remain at the helm of the football club, Total Network Solutions FC has to *change its name*. Suddenly, I see the romance disappearing from Welsh football. What will Jeff Stelling do without his jokes about dancing on the streets of TNS?

I order a brandy for the shock and demand to know what their new name will be. They are suddenly coy, citing discussions, possible sponsorships, meetings to decide, lots of things to consider, debate to be conducted, blah blah. But one idea, Mike Hughes tells me, is that the name should be The New Saints. 'That's our nickname, you see. That's what they call us, The Saints. So we'd be The New Saints. And if that's too much of a mouthful, you can shorten it to … TNS.'

Yay! TNS *lives*. You're a genius, Mike Hughes, that's brilliant. As I leave Wales, I'm dancing through the streets of The New Saints.

— CHAPTER 4 —

Day of Destiny for the Candlestick Makers

'The beauty of Cup football is that Jack always has a chance of beating Goliath.'

Terry Butcher

The FA Cup third round used to be the most eagerly awaited day in the football calendar. It still is, if you are a part-time team of bakers and candlestick makers who've clawed your way through 28 qualifying rounds, waded through pitched battles on glorified public parks, had punch-ups with burly blacksmiths and won penalty shoot-outs 15-14 in fading light because you didn't have a florin to feed the meter to turn the floodlights on. All cheered on by one man and his dog.

Like the American presidency, the principle is that anyone can win the FA Cup. It's part of what makes Britain great. John Motson never stops telling us about his *Match of the Day* debut commentating on one of the most sensational cup upsets of them all, when non-league Hereford United turned over Newcastle United 2-1 in extra time of a third-round cup replay in a mud bath at Edgar Road in 1972. Grainy images of Ronnie Radford's staggering 40-yard strike triggering a mass pitch invasion while Motty goes apoplectic have almost come to define the FA Cup.

If we were to get foolishly sentimental and misty-eyed about this, we might even regard FA Cup third round day as a symbol of every man's hopes and dreams, when anything seems possible. It's a reminder of a more innocent, wide-eyed time when the nobodies had a genuine tilt at glory, and on occasion had a realistic chance of attaining it. Of course, that was long before corporate hospitality and Sky and a huge industry in duplicate shirts and Russian billionaires.

It was a time when the FA Cup Final was the only football match shown live on TV, a national occasion when you'd get up at 5 a.m. to claim your place on the sofa and watch the pre-match build-up that always included silly quizzes, celebrity fans, the captain identifying the quirks of his teammates (including the obligatory mention of the 'prankster', the 'thinker', the 'trendy one' and the one with 'dodgy taste in music') and, most revered of all, the moment they leave their hotel in their smart new club suits to get on the coach to Wembley. And then it was the bloke in the white suit on the pitch fighting a losing battle to lead the community singing over a growing cacophony of fans at either end of the stadium, excitedly and loudly reeling through their own proud repertoire of songs and chants.

Of course, that was when football was the exclusive domain of the working classes and an FA Cup Final appearance was the pinnacle of a player's career. Ask a player to choose between winning the Football League title and an FA Cup winner's medal and it would be a close call. Mick Channon said that after becoming a pro he couldn't bear to watch an FA Cup Final on telly because he was so eaten up by envy watching others enjoying the drama. In the 1975–76 season when Channon finally made it to the final with Second Division Southampton – and beat the glory boys of Manchester United to a hapless pulp, ha! – a poll of fans revealed they'd rather win the FA Cup than get promotion.

It's all very different in this expensively glam new footie age. Now there's barely a match that's *not* on telly and the FA Cup has slipped alarmingly down the ladder of priorities as the big clubs covet the big bucks of the European Champions League and use their visits to the footballing outposts of the lower league to give match experience to their fringe and youth players. Kick-off times get shoved all over the shop, the foreign players stampeding into British clubs have no concept of the history of the competition and, while Cardiff Millennium Stadium is undoubtedly a remarkable feat of engineering, it carries little of the majesty or sense of drama of Wembley. In 2000, of course, Manchester United were allowed not to defend the FA Cup they'd won the previous year – indeed, they were actively encouraged not to defend it – in order to go halfway across the world to compete in the Mickey Mouse World Club Championship. The romance of the FA Cup – what's that, then?

Except this year, as third round day(s) beckons, that old familiar flutter of excitement is reappearing. The FA, who are no longer quite the time-honoured bunch of old duffers who famously used to run football with cobwebs dangling over their monocles, have taken active steps to protect and restore the sense of wonder that made the old competition so alluring. The cup draw has been restored to Monday lunchtime, which at least gives any giantkillers a day or two's grace to wallow in their sense of achievement and fantasise about drawing Manchester United in the next round. The FA are also insisting that teams actually play the match at home if drawn out of the hat first, rather than concede advantage to the big team to make a quick buck. There's also the matter of Chelsea now being guaranteed to win the Premiership title for the next couple of decades, so suddenly the poor old much-maligned FA Cup becomes much more attractive again for the bigger fish as the one realistic opportunity to win a domestic honour.

So today I head for Burton Albion. The Brewers have indeed been drawn out of the hat at home to Manchester United, and on a cold January Sunday it somehow seems the only place to be. This is cliché centre as we go for a Burton and the minnows from the Conference prepare for their Cup Final, a real David v. Goliath occasion – indeed, the biggest game in their history – against the millionaires of Manchester. So, will the Brewers droop? One of the few remaining Conference sides who aren't fully pro, Burton probably have a few bakers and candlestick makers, or at least postmen – non-league sides *always* have postmen – in their line-up if we look hard enough.

Burton are a popular side in the Conference, partly because their modest funds and manager Nigel Clough's principles of passing football tend to make them easy meat for the muscle-bound fitness freaks and wily old ex-pros who trample over ideals at this end of the football pyramid these days. And, of course, Nigel's dad Brian is regarded with enduring affection throughout football. Brian himself wasn't always at the champagne end of things. His first managerial job was in the glamorous climes of Hartlepool United, where finances were so tight that Clough himself drove the team coach to matches.

Burton Albion moved into a new ground this season, the Pirelli Stadium, which in a delicious irony was officially opened just a few weeks ago by Sir Alex Ferguson, who brought a team of Manchester United youngsters to play a friendly. When the draw was made, the directors must have rued their modest ambitions to settle on a 6,000-capacity new stadium. You might have thought they'd get the pitch right, too, but in the days leading up to the game the playing surface resembled a vat of big, fat, wobbly jelly so they dumped 50 tons of sand on it to dry it out. That's the official story anyway. Conspiracy theorists suggest the sandpit tactic is but an age-old dirty tricks ploy to stop the big guns playing. The tickets were all sold in seconds, with a couple of Burton-based United fans at the head of one of the queues, and only the desperate and foolish dream of going to the match without a ticket. Yep, sad twats like me.

I did vow never to visit Burton again on the basis that it always snows and Woking play like a bunch of squidgy bananas every time they go there. But hey, this is the Cup and as soon as I enter this otherwise unprepossessing corner of East Staffordshire (everyone thinks it's in Derbyshire, but it's not), pass the imposing Pirelli factory and see the flags and floodlights, I'm glad I'm here. I still haven't got a ticket, though. 'No mate, you've got no chance of getting in without a ticket,' says a guy with about 19 kids, all decked out in Burton yellow, a wad of tickets in his hand and a Derby County badge on his lapel. 'Only the real fans have got tickets for this one.' So you'll be following the Albion when they play Stourbridge on Tuesday, will you? 'Actually I'm away a lot and this is my first match of the season.' I meet another guy who's flown in from the States for the match. 'I was born and raised in Burton so I'm a lifelong fan,' he says. 'This is such a major event in the town that I couldn't miss it.' Further interrogation reveals that he's never actually been to an Albion game before.

Passing the street vendors flogging the souvenir scarves ('half yellow for Burton, half red for Man U, £6 each, only a few left') and flags ('fly your colours for a fiver'), I meet my first tout. He's unshaven and has a beanie hat covering most of his face and a sour expression that would frighten the goldfish. He looks like a stage villain and you wonder if he's playing Bill Sykes in a local production of *Oliver*. He couldn't look shiftier if he had a sign on his back saying 'BEWARE – DODGY CHAR-ACTER'. Obviously I ask him how much. 'Two and a half,' he whispers in my face, his breath reeking of garlic. I'm instantly in my pocket digging out two one-pound coins and a 50p, but he's not amused. I raise my eyebrows at the realisation that the going price is £250 and he slithers into the undergrowth.

A large crowd is milling around outside the impressive main entrance surrounding a kilted bagpiper awaiting the arrival of the Man U coach. There are mild attempts to inspire a chant of 'Albion Albion', but they are mostly for the benefit of the local radio reporters thrusting microphones in the faces of the fans, and the main entertainment is provided by an elderly man's hapless attempts to drive a battered old double-decker bus into the narrow confines of the stadium's official car park. Ironic cheers burst out as he attempts to negotiate a narrow path between a parked Mercedes and the flood of spectators arriving at the stadium and inevitably the Mercedes gets it, dragged back and forth as a volley of instructions are bellowed at the old chap and he reverses, twists the wheel erratically and has another go. Sod the match; let this clown drive round the car park for 90 minutes and I'll be happily entertained.

The police have their hands full trying to keep the crowd at bay when the United coach pulls in, pushing forward amid a welcoming outburst of jeers. There are chants of 'Who are ya?' to a backdrop of bagpipes as Sir Alex leads his troops off the battle bus. Mostly the players are unrecognisable but there's a collective gasp as Cristiano Ronaldo appears and a spontaneous bout of applause greets the appearance of the grim-faced Wayne Rooney. He's followed by a smiling Ole Gunnar Solskjaer, the baby-faced assassin attempting to regain his place in the United team after a plague of injuries. Solskjaer gives a quick wave (the only player to acknowledge the crowd) while the last to leave the bus is Mikael Silvestre, who scowls almost as much as my friend the ticket tout.

As they disappear into the players' entrance and the man in the kilt packs his bagpipes and leaves (don't say even *he* couldn't get a ticket?) the crowd pile through the turnstiles and I'm left to mingle with the late-comers and the saddos peering through the fence trying to catch a glimpse of their heroes warming up on the pitch. 'You pulled the short straw, then?' I ask an 11-year-old policeman peering through the fence with me. 'No, we're not allowed to go inside the ground unless we're called in,' he explains animatedly. 'It's all in the hands of the stewards, but we've got an EGU inside and they'll call us in if anything looks like kicking off.' EGU? 'Evidence gathering unit … at the moment we're just waiting but the way things are going, we'll be called in soon enough. It only takes a few idiots doesn't it? Some of them have been in the pub too long and think they'll cause a bit of trouble. Shame, there's no need for it, not on a great occasion for Burton like this.'

Minutes later his prediction comes true, and he's bounding inside the ground with his mates with things apparently threatening to turn ugly. I stand with a little old lady from three roads away and we content ourselves with peering at Rooney, who is clearly visible through a gap between the two stands doing his warm-up routine and wisecracking with Wes Brown. 'Wayne! Wayne!' shouts the old lady through the gap, waving a camera lens hopefully in his direction, but he doesn't respond. 'Shame, he didn't hear me,' she says mournfully. 'He's a lovely boy, that Rooney. Lovely girlfriend, too. Did you see that programme about her on the telly? Such a sweet couple.' Which may well be the only time you hear the words 'sweet' and 'Rooney' in the same sentence in this lifetime.

In truth, my track record for blagging my way into sold-out events isn't great. Ever since I snuck into a Bob Dylan concert through a toilet window at Earls Court in 1978, my nerve has failed me. There was the Southampton v. Sunderland match when I got into the old Dell through a back gate three hours before kick-off, hid in the toilet, waited until they started letting the punters in, and then completely bottled it when challenged about my seat number.

So what are my chances of getting inside the Pirelli Stadium, where the excitement is already on overload? Not good … but I have a cunning plan. I reckon my friend the sleazy tout will start panicking as the match kicks off and drop his prices to negligible rates and beg me to take a ticket off his hands. Meanwhile, I stick tightly to my place outside the fence as a bloke on the inside passes a ticket with its stub torn off through to his mate on the outside. 'You won't get in,' says a Man U fan conspiratorially. 'I've tried that already.' 'Worth a crack though …' says his mate, snatching the ticket and neatly side-stepping the cop in his path.

I catch sight of my friendly tout lurking in the undergrowth and approach him cautiously as he thumbs a wad of tickets. 'Don't touch 'em with a bargepole, son,' says a copper, sidling up to me. I glance at the copper, who should really be calling me grandad rather than son, and try to look wide-eyed and innocent. 'Forgeries all over the place, see. They charge you £50, you can't get in and you won't get your money back. It's not worth it.'

Matters improve dramatically as an attractive young blonde woman in a red jacket, matching hat and white trousers approaches with a broad smile and gives me a free cup of Bovril. There's a whole army of them giving the stuff away, proof if any was needed that Burton Albion, with its custard pie pitch and team of candlestick makers, understands the true meaning of football. The free Bovril lifts the spirits of all of us Cinderella fans with no ticket and helps to ward off the encroaching cold of the afternoon. 'You haven't got any Wagon Wheels to go with that, have you?' I ask my benefactor, but she looks at me strangely so I move on.

The roars from inside the ground intensify as the players come out and the Burton fans rather touchingly sing 'And now you're gonna believe us, we're gonna win the Cup'. I wander to the main entrance, declare myself a member of Her Majesty's Press and get thrown out on my ear, just in time to see a young yellow-tied Burton official marching purposefully round the back of the stand, pursued by a group of disgruntled fans creating merry hell because they have legitimate tickets and nobody will let them in. They reach a gate behind the terraces and Mr Yellow Tie checks the tickets and nods to the stewards to open the gate to let them in. Magically they're joined by 50 youths who surge forward and try to force their way through while Yellow Tie and two portly stewards try to stem the tide. Equally magically a group of police arrives to yank the unticketed ones away and snap the gate shut. No sooner do they run off than a posh woman appears and taps one of the police on the shoulder: 'Excuse me, officer, I thought I should tell you that there are a load of young lads trying to climb over the wall round the other side!' As the police sprint off again, the crowd inside roar as the match kicks off.

I clamber up a hill near to the ground and join a gaggle of families who appear to be having a Henman Hill-like party, squealing with delight at every sighting of the ball. The players are matchstick men in the distance but half the pitch – including the Manchester United goal – is clearly visible, and with the aid of a radio commentary we get a good feel of the action. Someone passes a bottle of wine around, then there's a sudden flurry of action in the United goalmouth and it looks like Burton have scored. Our celebrations die in our throats when the commentator informs us the ball has been cleared off the line, but the odd dog fight and small child tantrums aside, we have a merry old time. They seem to be enjoying it in the stadium too, with the Burton fans singing 'Are you Tamworth in disguise?' at the United team, who appear to find it hard going playing through the rice pudding of a pitch.

At half-time it's 0-0 and I decide to leave. It's getting seriously cold, the labrador next to me has taken a worrying shine to my leg and Derek, his owner, is promising to kiss everyone on the hill if the score remains at 0-0 at full-time. I don't want to be cruel but Derek's not an attractive man and, as unlikely as it is to stay goalless, I don't fancy hanging around to find out. I mean, it's not like we can run on the pitch if Burton score.

Besides, I have another plan. Leicester is but a short hop from here and Leicester City have a 6.30 p.m. kick-off in their own Cup face-off with Tottenham. It sounds bizarre, but Leicester City v. Tottenham Hotspur has a wonderland ring about it – perhaps it's a subliminal reminder of childhood and one of the first FA Cup Finals I remember. Spurs won 2-0 that day in 1961 to become the first team for 64 years to complete the League and Cup double. They were led by Irish motormouth Danny Blanchflower, with iron man Dave Mackay scaring the life out of the Leicester frontline and his impossibly graceful Scots colleague John White – later tragically killed by lightning – pulling the strings in midfield. Gordon Banks and Frank McLintock were in defence for Leicester, whose team selection caused a storm before the match when rookie Hugh McIlmoyle was chosen ahead of star striker Ken Leek.

Rooney and Ronaldo are brought off the bench with the idea of killing off Burton as I race towards Leicester. No ticket awaits there either but their Walkers Stadium is rather grander than the Pirelli and I'm banking on a box office job. I sit in the Walkers' car park, biting my nails, listening to the radio and willing my chums at Burton to hang on, resist Man U's grandstand finish and hit the £500,000 jackpot heading their way from a replay at Old Trafford. It probably means they will buy Woking's star striker, but hey, this is the Cup and the plucky minnows are doing the business against the big-shot internationals.

Burton's keeper Saul Deeney resists United, and as the final whistle goes at the Pirelli I join the parade of Spurs fans being escorted down the hill from the train station by the police. Their team have been in good form and the fans are in buoyant mood, singing 'Glory glory Tottenham Hotspur ...', 'Spurs are on their way to Wembley ...' and, clearly their favourite, 'We are Tottenham, we are Tottenham, we are Tottenham from the Lane' at full volume to the tune of 'Sailing'. The harmonies aren't too hot but full marks for passion. Every so often they sing the praises of their Dutch manager Martin Jol, a man who looks more suited to one of those shabby old 1970s Saturday afternoon wrestling bouts commentated on by Kent Walton, but his big cuddly-bear persona seems to have struck a chord with the Spurs army: 'Maa-in Yule, Maa-in Yule/Maa-in Maa-in Yule/He's got no hair but we don't care/Maa-in Maa-in Yule.'

The Leicester fans gawp as the Tottenham supporters maraud along, and scatter to avoid blocking their path to the away end. You suspect this will be the way of things when the teams get out on the pitch, but this is the FA Cup, it's 11 against 11, the ball's the little round thing in the middle with a mind of its own and anything can happen. Just look at the candlestick makers from Burton Albion.

I manage to buy a ticket and find myself right behind the goal in the heart of the Leicester fans, wedged between a couple of lads decked head to toe in blue but with a real sense of resignation about the outcome. 'We're just crap, basically,' Lee tells me cheerfully. 'I've been coming about five years and we always have been.' It doesn't stop him from leaping up in the air and bellowing. 'We love you Leicester, we do, we love you Leicester, we do' to the tune of ... ah, that's the thing about football songs. They become so much part of the psyche of the game you forget the song had another life before being mutilated and regurgitated by over-excitable mobs of fans. In this case I doubt any of those singing it with such velocity have any clue as to its origins.

In fact, the original lyric of 'We love you Leicester, we do' (which you hear echoing round every ground in the country with the name of the club inserted) was 'We love the Beatles, we do'. It was originally released as a cash-in single at the height of Beatlemania in 1964 by the Vernon's Girls, a semi-novelty act formed by staff at the Vernon's Pools company in Liverpool who had previously had a couple of minor hits; their high point was a No. 16 with 'Lover Please' in 1962. Now, the odd thing about 'We Love the Beatles' was that the single was a complete flop. It didn't disturb the chart compilers for one solitary second. Yet it did pick up a bit of airplay and its nursery rhyme chorus lodged in somebody's brain. I can't confirm who it was, but the odds are 10-1 on it being a Scouser who adapted it for Liverpool and burst into song one day with it on the Kop. The song soon became a fans' favourite throughout the country.

Leicester fans, though, are singing now more with hope than conviction as Spurs quickly take control of the match. Jermaine Jenas knocks the ball into an empty net after a Robbie Keane header slides back to him off the post, and then Canadian right back Paul Stalteri sends a screamer into the roof of the Leicester net. My new best mate Lee has his head in his hands. 'It could be a cricket score, this,' he whines as the Spurs fans go through their repertoire of hits. 'Spurs are on their way to Wembley ...' they sing again, recalling the 'Ossie's Dream' single to which they danced all the way to the FA Cup Final in 1981. Feelings of warm nostalgia tumble all over me. Who can forget the hero of the song, little maestro Osvaldo Ardiles, visibly squirming as he attempted to get to grips with his big line?

'In our ranks is Ossie Ardiles/He's had a dream for a year or two/That one day he's gonna play at Wembley/And now his dream is coming true,' bellowed the rest of the Spurs team in a scary selection of rampaging haircuts and kipper ties. 'Ossie we're gonna be behind ya/Together man for man/We know you're gonna play a blinder ...' And they all turned to look at the rather confused little man, already a World Cup winner with Argentina in 1978 and now clearly wondering why he hadn't stayed there because the English are all barking. Ossie took a deep breath and, with a pained expression on his face, recited: 'In di cup for Toddingham ...' It was a classic *Top of the Pops* moment, and forget his dazzling ball control, unquenchable appetite for the game, wonderful goals and magnificent sportsmanship, *this* is why Ardiles, who pre-dated the flood of foreign stars into the British game and even had to take a year to play in France during the Falklands conflict, is so fondly regarded by every British football fan.

Ossie's legend was underlined by an appearance in the brilliantly awful football movie *Escape to Victory*, and a memorable spell as Toddingham manager from 1993 to 1994 when he pioneered an adventurous new 0-0-10 system, which basically comprised a goalkeeper playing behind ten forwards hurtling towards the opposition goal. It was great fun, producing a succession of nine-goal thrillers, but his chairman Alan Sugar couldn't see the funny side and it didn't keep him in the job. He also had a spell in charge at Swindon Town where he managed to get them into the top division only for the club to be controversially demoted over 'irregular payments', and has since managed in Argentina, Mexico, Saudi Arabia and Japan.

'Ossie's Dream' is also memorable for a genius opening line that Dylan would have been proud of: 'Ossie's going to Wembley, his knees have gone all trembly.' Chas and Dave, the kings of the rockney pub singalong, wrote it. Spurs appeared in the Cup Final four times between 1981 and 1991 and Chas and Dave wrote their official theme song each time, their Spurs catalogue including such immortals as 'Glory Glory Tottenham Hotspur', 'Hot Shot Tottenham', 'Tottenham Tottenham', 'The Victory Song (We're Off to Wembley Cos We Beat the Arsenal)' and 'When the Year Ends in One'. However, after being adopted on tour by the Libertines recently, Chas and Dave became fully-fledged cult heroes with a roof-raising appearance at the 2005

Glastonbury Festival, during which they confessed they'd never been *huge* Spurs fans and wouldn't be doing any more footie songs.

Ossie, Chas and Dave apart, Spurs have one of the proudest singing traditions of all the clubs, right from their Bill Nicholson double-winning days of the early 1960s when the 'Glory glory hallelujah' chorus from 'Battle Hymn of the Republic' would echo around White Hart Lane in a fashion guaranteed to intimidate the opposition. Manchester United fans pilfered it for their own purposes and it's played at various sporting arenas across the States, all of which is a far cry from its original role as an uplifting American Civil War hymn. It was originally written as a poem in 1861 by Julia Ward Howe for the Union army camped on the Potomac River near Washington DC. Hearing the soldiers marching to 'John Brown's Body' (written by John Steffe as part of his campaign to abolish slavery), she was challenged by a reverend friend to write words more appropriate to such an inspirational tune. 'Battle Hymn of the Republic' was the result.

It's unclear how or why it became the Tottenham anthem. You can't imagine Julia Howe's original opening lines, 'Mine eyes have seen the glory of the coming of the Lord/He is trampling on the vintage where the grapes of wrath are stored', ringing from the terraces. But longstanding fans reckon they first sang it on the terraces at Wolverhampton in April 1960, when Spurs beat Wolves 3-1 to prevent them doing the double. They then took it with them into various European campaigns, adapting it to include players' names along the way.

So full marks to the Spurs fans, but the players should be less proud. They pioneered the naff footballers-can't-sing pop song. Even their classic double-winning side of 1961 had a song, 'Tip Top for Tottenham', and Spurs were always enthusiastic advocates of the footballer as pop star. In 1967 the players celebrated their FA Cup Final appearance against Chelsea with a whole LP of dreadful cocker-knee songs that included Pat Jennings and Joe Kinnear whining their way through 'When Irish Eyes Are

Smiling', Jimmy Greaves decimating 'Strolling', Alan Mullery and Cyril Knowles hamming it up on 'Maybe It's Because I'm a Londoner' and Terry Venables launching the first of several attempts at establishing himself as football's answer to Frank Sinatra by crooning his way through 'Bye Bye Blackbird'.

Then there was Glenn Hoddle. Apart from the Wham-a-like nonsense of the infamous 'Diamond Lights' duet with Chris Waddle (it reached No. 12 in 1987), Glenn also went on record singing 'We Are the Champions' and, God help us, 'Hey Jude'. The Spurs song we all remember, though, is 'Nice One Cyril'.

Yorkshireman Cyril Knowles was a spirited full back who was signed by Bill Nicholson from Middlesbrough for £45,000 in 1964 and went on to make over 400 appearances in 12 years, cementing his iconic status by scoring two goals in a 4-2 victory over the all-conquering Leeds in 1975 to keep them in the First Division. He was already long a terrace cult hero by then, inspiring his own 'Nice One Cyril' song that was made into a hit single by Cockerel Chorus as a prelude to the 1973 League Cup Final and was featured on a telly ad. The lyrics were simple and memorable: 'Nice one Cyril, nice one son, nice one Cyril, let's have another one.' Knowles stayed in football as a coach and manager at Darlington, Torquay and Hartlepool. It was at Hartlepool that he was first diagnosed with a brain tumour, and he died aged 47 in August 1991. A stand is named in his honour at Hartlepool.

'Nice One Cyril' is about the only Tottenham song their fans *aren't* singing as their impudent little winger Aaron Lennon continues to terrorise the shell-shocked home defence this night in Leicester. Spurs, already two up, look like getting a hatful. The glum fans around me only manage to rouse themselves for a ritual round of 'Derby reject, Derby reject' every time the ball goes anywhere near Spurs' swarthy striker Grzegorz Rasiak. He may be from Poland but local rivalries always prevail. Then my pal Lee emerges from the depths of his despond to impart some startling news: 'We're bringing Elvis on.'

Bloody hell, I know things are bad and desperate times

require desperate measures, but even if he has been working in a supermarket in Ashby-de-la-Zouch these past 28 years, he'll be in no fit state to trouble England's No. 1 Paul Robinson. Not after eating all them burgers and everything. I peer along the touch-line expecting to see a portly old chap in a silver cape and blue suede boots warming up along the touchline, but instead there's a ferociously fit Ghanaian with thighs like oak trees puffing out his chest. 'Come on Elvis, do it for us, come on Elvis!'

Elvis Hammond enters the building to hopeful applause from the City faithful and Lee is up punching the air rather erratically, trying to ignite a chant of 'Elvis! Elvis!' Is he any good then, Elvis? I ask innocently. 'Oh, he's great is Elvis,' Lee assures me. 'He's the best.' I'm about to ask why, if he's so good, he wasn't on from the start, when there's a mad scramble down the other end. A floated ball into the box, a flurry of bodies, a header and there is a barrage of noise around me as everyone leaps to their feet. Elvis has scored!

'What a game, what a game,' says Lee repeatedly as the half-time whistle blows and I head for the Bovril. He's still full of it when I get back, fully convinced that Leicester are back on the glory trail. I remind him they are still losing 2-1 and he bangs out the old cliché about the stroke of half-time psychologically being such a good time to score. Personally, I've never under-stood this line of thought. Any time is a good time to score, but the best time to score is a minute from the end of the game. Surely if you score right on half-time the other team has a chance to catch their breath, readjust their tactics and psyche themselves up for a second-half onslaught? And while we're getting rid of bees in bonnets: penalty shoot-outs. Nope, Mr Commentator, penalty shoot-outs are *not* a lottery. Lotteries are balls with numbers on and completely random. Penalty shoot-outs are a test of skill and temperament and a perfectly legitimate way to decide cupties.

However, the way Leicester City steam into Tottenham in the second half seems to throw my theory about a good time to score goals completely out of the window. Spurs are shaken as

Leicester pound their goal below us to a tumultuous volley of encouragement from Lee and his mates. The appearance of Gary Lineker, here anchoring live TV coverage going all round the world, at a window in the posh bit inspires even more excitement. 'Oh Gary Gary/Gary Gary Gary Gary Lineker' chant all the fans in recognition of his sterling service with both teams. The Leicester fans are so buoyant they even give Paul Robinson some stick. 'You're shit – aaaaah' they chorus gleefully as Robinson pumps a goal kick deep into opposing territory. The England keeper seems genuinely amused, swivelling round to give them a smile and a wave. It's all warming up nicely.

Yet even supercool Robinson begins to wilt and look flustered after a series of breathtaking saves under intense pressure from Leicester, and he is finally beaten when a shot hits his own defender Michael Dawson and rockets past him into the net. Lee has his arms round my neck and the whole place is jumping. We certainly don't hear a peep out of the cocker-knees down the other end. All we need now is a winner, and amazingly we get it in the last minute when Leicester's bustling striker Mark de Vries suddenly finds himself in acres of space in the penalty area and coolly slides the ball past Robinson.

Lee is dancing. I am dancing. Everyone is dancing. We want to spend all night dancing. And drinking. And hugging. And singing Elvis songs. Only football can do this …

— CHAPTER 5 —

Old Gold, Claret, Baggies and Blues

'Inhabitants of big cities needed a cultural expression of their urbanism which went beyond the immediate ties of kin and locality. A need for rootedness as well as excitement is – that seems most evident in the behaviour of football crowds.'

Richard Holt, sports historian

I'm heading for the Midlands for a Friday night match between Wolves and Luton Town and I am experiencing a very strange, heady surge of excitement. Wolves. Wolverhampton. *Wolverhampton Wanderers*. One of the most magical names in British football, with a truly illustrious history: Molineux. Billy Wright. A Beverly Sister. Derek Dougan. Gold-and-black shirts. John Richards. The country's first floodlights. Andy Gray. Wembley, 1960. Steve Bull. Honved, 1954 ...

Ah yes, Honved, 1954. All English eyes were looking to Wolves that night to restore some national pride. England's misguided claims to invincibility lay in tatters after the famous international the previous year when Ferenc Puskas and his mates from Hungary came to Wembley and tonked us 6-3. The English team had watched in amazement when the Hungarians came out on the pitch 20 minutes before kick-off to warm up, something that had never occurred to anyone else before. 'I came off the pitch wondering what we had been doing all those years,' confessed a bemused Tom Finney. A rematch was quickly sought, but a year later it went even worse. The 'Magic Magyars' stuffed England 7-1, still our worst ever defeat. 'It was like playing people from outer space,' said Luton and England centre half Syd Owen at the end. So when a televised friendly match was set up between Wolves and Hungarian champions Honved, including Puskas and four other Magyar internationals, at Molineux the pride of the nation was at stake. Two down in the first 15 minutes, it looked grim, but a penalty early in the second half and two late goals sealed the game and turned Wolves into national heroes. So well done, Wolves. We owe you.

The teatime rush hour takes its toll and the M6 inevitably grinds to a halt around Birmingham as per usual – road works, crashes, Martians doing the tango across the central reservation, etc. Damn you, Birmingham! The 7.45 p.m. kick-off looms with disheartening speed. I flounder among the pile of CDs scattered on the floor and eventually emerge, triumphant, clutching Billy Bragg. On it goes and, sounding unusually morose, Bill tells a story:

> God's footballer hears the voices of angels above the
>   crowd at Molineux
> God's footballer stands on the doorstep
> And brings the good news of the kingdom to come
> While the crowd sings rock of ages, the goals bring weekly
>   wages
> Yet the glory of the sports pages
> Is but the worship of false idols and tempts him not ...

For anyone who's ever remotely dreamed of scoring a goal in a football stadium while fans cheered and sang your name, Peter Knowles did the unthinkable. Knowles, the 'God's footballer' of Bragg's song of the same name, was a brilliant Wolves winger in the 1960s; fast, tricky, determined and exciting to watch, and a bit of a pin-up to boot. The brother of Cyril Knowles of 'Nice One Cyril' fame, he was capped four times by England Under-23s, scored 64 goals in 91 games and, idolised by the Wolves fans and with an international career beckoning, had the world at his feet. And in 1969, aged 24, he chucked it all in to become a Jehovah's Witness. Suddenly people who were paying good money to watch Peter Knowles playing at Molineux were giving him the bum's rush when he knocked on their door offering them salvation.

Two weeks later it got even more bizarre. Top Chelsea striker and England international Bobby Tambling announced that he, too, was quitting the game to be baptised and to tramp the streets trying to flog copies of *The Watchtower*. It sparked wild rumours of other top players about to announce to their managers that they'd signed to play for the Jehovah's Witnesses next season. The country was in panic that religious zealots had infiltrated the national sport. And Glenn Hoddle wasn't even the Wolves manager then.

Yet it's the Knowles story that still beggars belief. Plenty of young players give up the game in their twenties but only because they have to, either through injury or insufficient talent. A desperately homesick Craig Johnston did walk out on Liverpool at 27 in 1988 to go home to Australia to look after his sister and invent the Predator football boots, but Liverpool had just lost to Wimbledon in the FA Cup Final so he wasn't thinking straight. Or maybe he couldn't cope with the shame of writing 'The Anfield Rap', the Liverpool team's infamous assault on hip hop which proved conclusively that John Barnes should let his feet do the talking yet bafflingly still made No. 3 in the charts.

Oh, let's not forget young Karol Wojtyla either, who pre-dated even Peter Knowles. Karol was reputedly a brilliant Polish keeper and there was talk that he might even be good enough to play for Poland. He gave up a promising career for religion and put football completely behind him. Later, he even changed his name. To Pope John Paul II.

I make it to Molineux with minutes to spare before kick-off to snuggle into a Black Country crowd already openly anticipating the worst. What is it about Midlands crowds? I mean, all true football fans are by nature pessimistic, that's the nature of the beast, but here they gloomily discuss the likelihood of a six-goal thrashing or torrential rain from which they will either contract pneumonia or be struck by lightning, and even if they do make it home they expect to find their wife has run off with a Jehovah's Witness. I wouldn't mind, but they're only playing Luton Town, for Godsakes.

In the early stages the managers arouse more interest than the players. There's Hoddle, of course, mad as a frog, and his opposite number tonight is Mike Newell, famed at Luton for such a laid-back approach to matches that some fans are convinced he uses the dugout to catch up on some kip. Newell has just shocked the football world by going to the press and telling them football is crooked. The authorities have feigned horror as Newell lambasts agents, accuses managers and players of taking bungs and says the whole transfer system has been abused. Players are greedy, managers are not totally straight and agents are bastards? Well, who'd have thought it, eh?

So I spend most of the first half staring at the benches lest I miss Hoddle suddenly leaping up to deliver an accusatory diatribe at the disabled or Newell delving into the magic sponge bag to pull out a megaphone and name and shame the guilty imbibers of bung. Newell's fellow managers have responded to his allegations with a deafening – and possibly telling – silence, doing their impersonations of the three non-seeing non-hearing non-speaking monkeys, and you just know nothing will come of it all despite the headlines and the righteous huffing of the FA promising an exhaustive inquiry. Football agents are clearly a despicable breed, vying with estate agents, tabloid journalists, traffic wardens, reality TV show contestants, people who take caravan holidays and Jeffrey Archer to be the first up against the wall come the revolution. But corruption has been rife since long before agents were invented.

The great Bill Nicholson, the shy, humble, honourable man who served Tottenham as player and manager for 38 years, creating the greatest team in their history and guiding them to the first double of the century in 1961, resigned in 1974. He cited one reason as the corruption inherent in the game as players made illegal demands for under-the-counter payments to join Spurs and went elsewhere when he refused to pay it. 'Players have become impossible,' said Bill Nick. 'They talk all the time about security but are not prepared to work for it. I am abused by players when they come to see me. There is no longer respect.' This, let us remember, was in 1974.

And Mike Newell is far from being the first prominent football personality to go public on the bung culture. Wilf Mannion, a legendary forward most closely associated with Middlesbrough and once described as 'the Mozart of the football pitch', claimed in a newspaper article in 1954 that illegal payments in football were rife. However, he refused to substantiate his remarks and was banned for life. He went on to run a pub in Stevenage, where he once met the Queen while wearing his carpet slippers.

The way that Luton are playing tonight you wonder if they've taken a bung themselves, and even the eternally gloomy Wolves fans are beginning to think there might be a 0-0 draw in this for them. About 25 minutes into the game a smartly dressed young man bustles into the stand and sits next to me breathing alcohol fumes. 'Don't s'pose I've missed anything interesting, have I?' I contemplate telling him that Mike Newell scratched his nose after 10 minutes and Glenn Hoddle looked like he was going to burst into a chorus of 'Jerusalem' at one point, but I think better of it and shake my head instead. 'Never do here,' he smiles, happy with my response. 'Why do we come, eh? Oh look at that, what's the point of passing to Clarke, he'll only give it away – there, what did I tell you?'

There is momentary excitement as Wolves are awarded a free kick on the edge of the Luton box and Paul Ince (age 134) lines up to take it. 'Watch this,' says my mate, leaning back in his seat. 'A tenner says he'll balloon it over the bar and it'll hit some poor disabled kid at the back of the stand.' Ince races up and whacks it. The ball balloons high over the bar into the stand. 'Hope that kid's all right,' my colleague says. Just before half-time Mark

Kennedy strikes a forlorn long shot at the Luton goal which keeper Marlon Beresford collects without blinking, and ironic cheers thunder around the ground. It's the first shot on goal of the match from either side.

Things do perk up in the second half as Ince starts running the show and ignites a move that ends with the maligned Leon Clarke thundering in a shot that Beresford pushes into the path of Wolves teenager Mark Davies, who bangs it into the net. 'Give it five minutes and they'll equalise,' says Mr Doom next to me, but this time he's wrong – it's 10 minutes. 'That's it,' he says, 'I'm off for a pint,' as nine-foot-tall Steve Howard rises unattended to serenely head Luton's equaliser. 'If you've got any sense you'll join me – there'll be no more fun here tonight.'

He's wrong again. Living up to his self-appointed 'Guv'nor' nickname, Ince strikes a sensational last-minute winner from 30 yards. The crowd can't quite believe it. 'You're not singing any more,' they chant at the small Luton contingent, who in truth were never actually singing in the first place. And then it's all 'Hi Ho Wolverhampton' and 'I was born under a Wanderers scarf'. I hang around afterwards hoping for a word with Ince, but the guy is still dancing on air and the best I can manage is a swift handshake as, grinning the night away, he disappears into one of the executive boxes to present something or other to one of the rich people who's probably too pissed to notice anyway.

I do, however, get a chat with Steve Bull – a bona fide, solid gold Wolves *legend*. He joined from rivals West Bromwich Albion in 1986, stayed for 14 years and broke every club goal-scoring record in the book with 306 goals in 561 appearances. He also played 13 times for England, the first time when Wolves were still in the old Third Division. Wolves have even named a stand after him. I've never met anyone with a stand named after them. Bully retired six years ago but he's still at Molineux for every home game, meeting and greeting and being adored. Even tonight the fans have been chanting his song:

> Stevie Bull's a tatter
> He wears an England cap
> He plays for Wolverhampton
> And he's a lovely chap
> He scores with his left foot
> He scores with his right
> And when we play the Albion
> He'll score all fucking night.

'It always make me smile when I hear it,' says Bully, amiably. 'But I get a bit embarrassed when they sing it now. I've been retired for six years. But the fans are great at Wolves, they've always been very good to me, being a Black Country lad and all.'

I don't expect him to admit this to a total stranger, but when growing up Bull's big idol was Ian Rush and he was actually a Liverpool fan. Secretly, a part of him still is. He initially signed for West Brom from non-league Tipton Town and reckons he did OK for them, but the manager of the day, Ron Saunders – a cold fish who made Sir Alf Ramsey look like Coco the Clown – told him that his first touch was a disgrace and flogged him to Wolves for £65,000. It maybe wasn't the shrewdest bit of business that Ron ever did.

Now, if there's one thing the good people of Wolverhampton despise, it's anybody and anything associated with West Bromwich Albion. They have an imaginative term of abuse for them. If you ever go to Molineux and wonder why they are singing about defecating on 'Tesco carrier bags' it's their little joke about the colours of West Brom's kit. And when they sing 'I was born under a Wanderers scarf' to the old *Paint Your Wagon* showtune 'Wanderin' Star', they add on 'Do you know where hell is? Hell is at West Brom.' So the fans didn't instantly take to the new striker without a first touch. It took Bully at least, ooh, 15 minutes to win them over.

'I think they saw I always played my heart out and worked my socks off even when I wasn't scoring and they responded to that. We bonded quite early on and the more they sang and encouraged me the more I wanted to do well for them.'

But one team's terrace idol is another's target of abuse and opposition fans hammered Bully. Aston Villa had a merry little ditty that went something like 'Stevie Bull he walks on water, everybody knows shit can float.' 'Oh I got much worse than that,' he says. 'I think West Brom and Stoke were the worst. They gave me so much stick it was unbelievable. Really horrible personal stuff about my wife and my mum, but it's the only way they can get to you.' Did you ever lose it? 'No. You can do a Cantona on them but what's the point? All it did was make me play harder. The best thing to do is score, that usually shuts them up.'

The early West Brom aberration and a fleeting Indian summer at Hereford United aside, Bully was a one-club man and when that club floundered in the lower divisions the pundits couldn't begin to imagine why he stayed. It's the Matthew Le Tissier syndrome – the modern game just doesn't have any time for quaint, old-fashioned values like loyalty, commitment and belief. At the top level it's a culture built on greed and exploitation and making as much as you can for as little as possible. Football not only didn't understand why Bully stayed at Wolves, it actually gave him stick for it. 'I know of four clubs that came in for me but there were probably more,' he says. 'There was Turin in Italy, Coventry, Newcastle and Celtic.' You weren't tempted? 'I'm a homely lad. I was happy at Wolves. I got on well with everyone, the crowd loved me, so I figured why spoil it? Looking back, I guess I could have gone to Italy for a couple of years for the experience and then come back to Wolves, but I've no regrets. I stayed loyal to Wolves and they stayed loyal to me.'

Bull talks eloquently of the Wolves history and how honoured he feels to have a stand in his name – an accolade he feels he scarcely deserves, as the adjacent erection is named after Billy Wright, another Wolves stalwart with over 100 England caps, most of them as captain. Bully starts getting all misty-eyed at the very mention of Billy Wright's name. 'I was gobsmacked when [Wolves chairman and benefactor] Sir Jack Hayward said he wanted to name a stand after me. I mean, Billy Wright, fair enough, one of the true greats of the game and what a *gentleman*. He still came to matches right up to his death and he was such a great bloke. He never moaned, never had a bad word to say about anyone, and he was a great player.'

As well as doing the ambassador gig at Molineux, Steve also runs a couple of companies and plays the odd charity game, but harbours ambitions of coaching and dreams of one day managing Wolves. 'No I don't interfere with Glenn Hoddle and the team but I did a bit of coaching at Hereford and really enjoyed it. So one day, yeah, my dream job would be managing Wolves.'

In the meantime he remains one of their most passionate supporters, forgetting his corporate duties to yell along with the rest of the fans. He refutes the often-voiced theory that the atmosphere in games isn't what it used to be or that all-seater stadiums have been the ruin of terrace anthems. 'I think the atmosphere at games here is better than it's ever been. They still sing all the songs and they keep coming up with new ones. Wolves fans are the best.' But then he would say that, wouldn't he?

The Brummie triumvirate of Birmingham City, Aston Villa and West Brom is always curious to the outsider. Persistent under-achievers the lot of 'em, they are always bickering among themselves, forever either thrashing around doing doggy paddle in the top league or making a big splash doing the butterfly trying to get there. At Villa they've got 'Deadly' Doug Ellis, the grumpy old man of the Midlands, who seems to get his jollies out of humiliating managers, hiring them at regular intervals just so he can fire them a short time afterwards. Ellis v. the fans v. the players v. the manager v. Ellis: that's the routine at Villa Park, and it's served them well for years.

They've got a dreadful kit, their songs aren't much cop, and nobody can remember the last time they won anything. OK, a

Villa director, Scotsman William McGregor, was the driving force in setting up the Football League in 1888, and there was a time when Villa were a dominant force in that league. Unfortunately that time was over a century ago. They did enjoy a bit of success in the late 1970s/early 1980s under laugh-a-minute Ron Saunders and in 1982 they somehow managed to win the European Cup in Rotterdam when Saunders had been replaced by Tony Barton. Or, to give him his other name, WHO?

Aston Villa last won the FA Cup in 1957 and even that triumph is sullied by the memory of Peter McParland flattening the Manchester United keeper Ray Wood in the first six minutes. Wood suffered concussion and a broken cheekbone but this was the dark ages before substitutes and, incredibly, Wood returned to the fray half an hour later to wander up and down the wing in a complete daze, while centre half Jackie Blanchflower – the younger, lesser-known brother of Danny Blanchflower – played as an emergency goalkeeper, courageously keeping Villa at bay until the evil McParland popped up with two late goals to take the cup to Villa Park. Blanchflower didn't have many more matches to play; his career was prematurely ended by injuries received in the Munich air crash the following year.

You wonder, fearfully, how the current generation of Man Ure fans – and indeed the players – would respond to McParland clattering Wood to deny the Busby Babes their glory in 1957. Or, indeed, Nat Lofthouse's ferocious charge into the back of Harry Gregg, taking keeper and ball into the net as Bolton beat a United team decimated by Munich in the 1958 FA Cup Final.

There was no singing in those days. Well, apart from the pre-Cup Final community singing when some chap in a white suit would be winched on to a precarious rostrum in the middle of the pitch and, baton in hand, attempt to lead the assembled masses in song. On their best behaviour, dressed up in suits and ties for the big occasion and determined to enjoy themselves, the supporters did their best to participate in the spirit of the occasion, twirling their programmes, waving their rattles, clutching their *Daily Express* songsheets and responding to the exaggerated pleas of the white-suited one: 'C'mon now, here's one for all you Manchester United fans. I know you all know it, so sing along with me, please, to "She's a Lassie from Lancashire".'

Community singing in the FA Cup Final started in 1927 when underdogs Cardiff City came to Wembley and beat Arsenal 1-0, although brass bands at major matches were not uncommon. The Scottish *Evening Times* sponsored a pre-match 'singalong' in a cup tie between Brechin City and Celtic in the 1926–27 season, when the songsheet contained the likes of 'John Brown's Body' and 'Roamin' in the Gloamin''.

The Arsenal v. Sheffield United league match at Highbury in January 1927 marked the first live radio commentary of a football match, and a bout of community singing was also introduced before that to stir up a bit of atmosphere. The *Radio Times* printed a diagram of Highbury with the pitch numbered in different sections with the commentator calling the play by referring to numbers so listeners could follow the progress of the ball on their *Radio Times* maps.

The Welsh, of course, are famous for their love of singing and with a large contingent of miners in the 10,000 Cardiff supporters at the 1927 final, the pre-match singing was deemed a great success, particularly when guests of honour King George V and Winston Churchill were observed singing their hearts out for the lads. After that, pre-match singing at Wembley became an institution and the last hymn sung before that 1927 final, 'Abide With Me' retains a special place in the hearts of football fans.

In truth, the dirge-like hymn is far from the rousing anthem you'd want to put you in the mood for 90 minutes of blood and thunder. Henry Lyte wrote the words in 1847 when he was dying of tuberculosis. A Scottish pastor at All Saints Church in Brixham, Devon, he composed 'Abide With Me' as a religious poem to mark his farewell sermon:

Swift to its close ebbs out life's little day
Earth's joys grow dim; its glories pass away
Change and decay in all around I see
Oh Thou who changest not, abide with me.

Well, it's not 'Chirpy Cheep Cheep'. Lyte died in Nice three weeks after he wrote the poem, and it was 14 years later that Londoner William Monk, a music teacher and editor of *Hymns Ancient and Modern,* set it to his appropriately melancholy tune. 'Abide With Me' has been a British institution ever since, played at funerals of football fans every day and still a sacred ritual of Cup Finals of the modern era. Poor Elton John was reduced to a blubbing blob (no change there then, huh?) as he sat in the royal box mouthing 'Abide With Me' at Wembley as chairman of Watford when they lost in the FA Cup Final against Everton in 1984.

West Bromwich Albion are known and loved by all football trivia fans because their Hawthorns ground is the highest above sea level in the country. Like all Woking fans, I carry an abiding affection for West Brom since that unforgettable day in 1991 when the Cards, then not even in the top tier of non-league football, went to the Hawthorns and beat the Division Two side 4-2 in the third round of the Cup with a stunning hat trick by Sir Tim Buzaglo. The world seemed to suspend belief that day but sometimes in times of stress I sit and screw up my eyes and try to recapture the feeling, a surreal but unforgettable stab between heart-stopping ecstasy and shell-shocked disbelief as Buzaglo ran away from the lumbering Graham Roberts to bury Woking's first goal. The rest of it remains an incredulous blur.

At the end of the game the fans poured on to the pitch and lifted the heroic Woking players on their shoulders. But it wasn't the Woking supporters – it was the West Brom fans. They cheered and clapped our coaches as we left the ground and then came in force to support us when we went to Goodison Park to play Everton in the next round. In homage, Woking fans adopted the Baggies' trademark 'Boing boing West Brom West

Brom boing boing' chant. West Brom manager Brian Talbot was sacked immediately after the Woking match and then, in the non-league world himself as manager of Rushden & Diamonds, had to endure chants of '4-2 and you lost your job' every time he came to Woking. Football is about nothing if not history.

The speciality of West Brom fans, though, is the vilification of their nearest but not dearest. They had a field day when Graham Taylor returned as Villa manager after his 'turnip' years in charge of England. 'Taylor is a turnip,' they sang to the tune of Lonnie Donegan's 'My Old Man's a Dustman', 'He's got a turnip's head/He took the job at Villa/He must have been brain dead.' Then, when West Brom were facing one of their regular relegations from the Premiership a couple of years ago, the fans were resigned to their fate and sang, 'One go down we all go down we all go down together/Come back up win the Cup kick fuck out of the Villa.' However, the manager of the day, Gary Megson, was dismayed by its negative tone and asked the fans to stop singing it – a rare occasion when a manager has attempted to interfere in the organic process of terrace singing. Most managers tend to let them get on with it and pretend not to hear the really crude stuff, merely grateful that they are not the target of the songs.

Big Ron Atkinson had two spells managing West Brom, and also managed Villa and seemingly every other club that moved. His primary contribution to the game, however, is as the inventor of 'Ronglish' during years of punditry in which he introduced to the lexicon magical, meaningless phrases like 'early doors', 'lollipop' and 'hospital ball'. Naturally, he holds a special place in the hearts of West Brom fans, who invented a special song for him to the tune of the 1963 Crystals/Phil Spector classic 'Da Do Ron Ron': 'Who's the fattest bastard in Division One? It's you Ron Ron Ron, it's you Ron Ron.'

It's Wolves, though, who cop the most flak at the Hawthorns. Sometimes referred to as 'Yams', Wolves fans are most commonly referred to as 'Dingles' after the vulgar and unlovely family in soap opera *Emmerdale*. Whenever their spirits are down, Albion crowds can usually lift themselves with a vigorous outburst of 'Slap a Dingle'. Like every other team in the country they also sing a variant on '(Is This the Way to) Amarillo?', the song everyone considered complete tosh when Tony Christie first did it in 1971, but stick a Peter Kay funny walk on it and call it 'ironic' and it's No. 1 for months and a football crowd anthem in every ground in the country. West Brom, though, have put a particularly personal slant on it:

> Is this the way to slap a Dingle?
> With one of those we'll never mingle
> For the Wolves they have no taste
> Season ticket? What a waste.

And so on to St Andrews. Birmingham City are having a desperate season. The manager/messiah, Steve Bruce, is saying that he hasn't slept for weeks worrying where the next point is coming from. Karren Brady, football's first female chief executive, is ill in hospital, and club owner and former *Sunday Sport* and adult magazine magnate David Sullivan has savaged the greed of players who don't care enough. But still, they'll always have Jasper.

In his early days as a singing comedian on the folk music scene, Jasper Carrott would perform a lot of very funny songs about football. He wore his colours on his sleeve early on, with 'Aston Villa Skinhead Supporters Club Song', a brilliant routine that involving screwing his face up into a moronic brain-dead stare as he mimicked a fan attempting to spell Villa. 'Give us a 'V!' 'V!' 'Give us an I!' 'I!' 'Give us a … er … er … er …' 'VILLA! VILLA!' 'Actually,' he confesses when I talk to him about it, 'I did perform it at Villa once.' WHAT? 'Yeah, and I changed the name to Birmingham.' You did WHAT? For a lifelong and very high-profile Birmingham fan, this could be classed as sacrilege of the lowest order. 'No, it's not,' he says. 'It's called *survival*.'

Jasper has been a committed Birmingham fan since the mid-1950s when he was about nine and a mate invited him along to

St Andrews. He's never stopped going since, and talks passionately of scrabbling to get the autographs of old City heroes like Gordon Astall and Gil Merrick. He is still rendered speechless on the occasions when he attends celebrity showbiz functions in Birmingham and finds one of them in attendance. 'It's mad,' he says. 'I'm in awe of them because they were my childhood heroes and they're in awe of me because I've been on the telly.'

Carrott remembers well the Blues losing 3-1 to Manchester City in 1956 in the FA Cup Final. Their progress to Wembley resulted in Birmingham adopting the club anthem the supporters still sing today, 'Keep Right On to the End of the Road'. In the team at the time was a free-scoring Scotsman called Alex Govan who lived in Plymouth, and his party piece was to sing it at club functions. It was subsequently played before matches in his honour, its spirit of dogged defiance and shoulder-to-shoulder resilience in the face of all odds striking a chord with City fans amid post-war austerity.

In essence every bit as stirring as Liverpool's 'You'll Never Walk Alone', it was written in 1915 by Scotsman Harry Lauder, a solid gold superstar of his day. Apart from 'Keep Right On ...' he also wrote 'Roamin' in the Gloamin'', 'I Love a Lassie' and numerous other staple songs of the golden years of music hall. Lauder was said to be the highest-paid entertainer in the world, commanding fees of over £12,000 a night. On one occasion in 1929 he received £114,000 for performing just three songs for a radio show broadcast right across America.

Lauder was also a successful actor and author, but 'Keep Right On to the End of the Road' was special and it's unsurprising that the song's bullish spirit gnawed into the psyche of notoriously sentimental football fans. Lauder's only son John, a lawyer who became a captain in the Argyll & Sutherland Highlanders, was killed on a French battlefield during the First World War. A distraught Lauder was moved to write 'Keep Right On to the End of the Road' in the aftermath of the tragedy:

Keep right on to the end of the road
Keep right on to the end
Though the way be long, let your heart be strong
Keep right on round the bend
Though you're tired and weary still journey on
Till you come to your happy abode
Where all the love you've been dreaming of
Will be there at the end of the road.

Jasper Carrott even made it to the boardroom, becoming a director of Birmingham City in 1979. He didn't like it. 'I saw the inside of football and I wasn't too enamoured of it,' he tells me. 'I just couldn't believe the laissez-faire attitude to finance and organisation. I remember going to my first AGM and I asked the chairman a question about the financial position of the club and he waffled on about we were either making a little bit or losing a little bit. I was sitting next to the treasurer, who told me we were actually losing £6,000 a week. In 1979 that was a lot of money but nobody said a thing about it. And you'd be raising funds to go into players' pockets but turning down requests to help destitute families. That can't be right.'

A 'square peg in a round hole', Carrott was on the board for three years before resigning in protest at the decision to sack Jim Smith (who had succeeded Sir Alf Ramsey as manager in 1978) and replace him with grumpy old Ron Saunders. He felt intense relief. 'The thing is, 90 per cent of the supporters basically disagree with everything you do,' he reflects. 'They have two things to say to directors: "Sack the manager!" or "Open your wallet!"'

Carrott also got his self-esteem back. While he was a director he'd walk on the St Andrews pitch to a deafening silence but as soon as he reverted to simple fandom he was a hero again and they were all up singing 'One Jasper Carrott, there's only one Jasper Carrott'. His finest moment, he says, was when he appeared on the Wembley pitch before the Leyland DAF Cup Final in 1991, when City beat Tranmere 3-2, and over 40,000 Birmingham supporters chanted 'Jasper, Jasper, give us a wave!'

Jasper did more than that: he ran towards them. 'A massive roar went up behind the goal. I looked around to see if someone had appeared behind me but it was all for me. I just stood there milking it for a couple of minutes. It was one of the best experiences of my life. It almost makes up for all the times that opposing supporters sang "You can stick your Jasper Carrott up yer arse".'

Once, when his good friend and all-time Birmingham legend Trevor Francis was manager, he invited Jasper into the dressing room to talk to the players as a morale booster before a game. He thought better of it. 'I mean, what was I going to say? "Oh, when I played for Hockley we used to do it like this?"' He did sit on the bench with Francis, although these days he prefers to keep a safe distance from the players and manager. 'You're a supporter because you *like* moaning and bitching. You can't do that if you're close to the manager and players and you know the problems they're having. Mind you, we've had plenty to bitch about here. Birmingham fans are the most loyal in the country and they've been to hell and back. Eternal pessimists but loyal.'

So I leave Carrott to moan and bitch to his heart's content in whichever executive box he fancies tonight, and take my own place right at the back of the stand as Birmingham City take on Reading in an FA Cup fourth round replay. Reading, striding confidently to the Championship title and a place in the Premiership, field a weakened side to preserve the energy of their top players for the league battles ahead. For Steve 'Sleepless' Bruce and his embattled boys in blue, the FA Cup is the one chance of salvaging a desperate season.

I sit between a huge woman devouring a bacon buttie and a skimpy little man clutching a flask of coffee. They earnestly decline my offer to swap seats so they can be together: 'No, yowse stay where yowse are, we only fight if we sit together.' The little guy winks at me, which is a bit scary. 'Yowse know the real reason weem don't sit together?' Er, your wife takes up two seats? (This is thought, not said.) 'Superstition. Every time weem sat together, the City lose. Them's true. Tell 'im, Dorothy.'

Dorothy confirms the sad truth. If ever they sit together at a match, the Blues are doomed to fail. 'Weem a superstitious bunch here, always have been and always will be.' And they tell me the story of the gypsy's curse. When the club first moved to St Andrews in 1906, they forcibly cleared a group of gypsies from the local wasteland in order to build the stadium. The gypsies responded by putting a curse on the new ground, roughly along the lines of your-team-will-be-rubbish-and-always-will-be-if-we-have-owt-to-do-with-it.

They weren't wrong. Supporters were perennially ill, choking on the clouds of soot drifting across the ground from the railway next door. They lost two FA Cup Finals, the roof on one of the stands caved in, and 20 direct hits from the German Luftwaffe during the war led to the ultimate indignity of having to play subsequent home matches at Villa Park for a while. The odd lower league promotion, a 1963 League Cup Final win over Villa, the Leyland DAF Trophy and some hilarious 1970s haircuts apart, Birmingham's cupboard was so empty, there seemed to be a gaping hole in it. And it was all down to the gypsies, apparently.

Ron Saunders – dour, scowling, grey-haired, miserable Ron Saunders – decided it was time to do something about it when he became manager in the 1980s. He put crosses on the floodlights and painted the soles of the players boots red in an attempt to break the curse. They also paraded a whippet round to urinate on each of the corner flags. That, said Ron Saunders, should do the trick. A director's wife joined in, making peace with the gypsies and persuading them to send the seventh son of a seventh son of a seventh son along to St Andrews to lift the curse. Birmingham duly lost their next seven games. Barry Fry, their manager from 1994 to 1996, is said to have embraced the challenge of the gypsy's curse, allegedly adopting the whippet tactic but doing the urinating on the corner flag routine himself. But maybe that's just a Barry Fry thing.

There's no urinating on corner flags tonight, just what initially appears to be a metaphorical urinating on the City team as the Reading fringe players enthusiastically set about their supposedly grander hosts. Dorothy, my large next-door neighbour for the night, has already spread so far on to my seat I'm practically in the lap of the little guy. With City fielding a weakened team due to various injuries he's not expecting much and the crowd seem collectively to be watching through their fingers.

The crowd is very quiet. No 'Keep Right On to the End of the Road', no 'Don't Cry For Me Aston Villa', no 'Chim chiminee chim chiminee chim chim cheroot, we hate those bastards in claret and blue'. Oh, for the terrace inspiration that stirred Birmingham fans to sing 'I'd rather have a speedboat than Kanu' when the enigmatic striker Kanu got the ball in the match with West Brom. Or the acknowledgement of Emile Heskey's change in fortunes after a dodgy start to his St Andrews career: 'He used to be shite but now he's all right/Walking in a Heskey wonderland.' Where's Jonny Hurst when you need him?

A thirty-something self-employed solicitor and City fan based in London, Jonny carries the unlikely title of Barclays Premiership Chant Laureate after a 2004 competition endorsed by Poet Laureate Andrew Motion won him £10,000 and an open door to every Premiership ground in the country. But hang on a sec, there's something wrong. Here's a sample of his winning entry about Aston Villa's Colombian striker Juan Pablo Angel, set to Barry Manilow's camp cabaret classic 'Copacabana':

> His name is Angel and he's a showboy
> An Alice band keeps up his hair
> Juan Pablo from Col-om-bi-a
> He came to Villa to be a winner
> He succeeded overnight our very own Angel Delight
> Just hear the Villa roar with each Juan Pablo score ...

Spot anything odd about this? (Well, apart from it being rubbish, of course.) It's a song written by a Birmingham City fan, hailing the star striker of their bitterest rivals. Sorry, it doesn't matter how much that bursary is worth, it's just *not right*. Hurst's other entries include 'We will, we will Ree-bok you' to the tune of Queen's 'We Will Rock You', for Bolton Wanderers, and a skit on 'Chitty Chitty Bang Bang' in honour of James Beattie, then at Southampton. He even found the inspiration to knock up one for his own side based on Tammy Wynette's 'Stand By Your Man':

> Sometimes it's hard to be a Blues fan
> Giving all your love to just one man
> We've had some bad times
> But now there's only good times
> Thanks to Brady, Bruce, the Golds and Sul-li-van.

If there's one thing that all this proves, it's that terrace anthems can't be artificially inseminated. They evolve naturally from genuine fans drawing on the passion, identity, adrenalin, comradeship, excitement and atmosphere of the moment. Birmingham fans are less than pleased that one of their own has been glorifying the enemy for personal gain, while Villa are hardly likely to take to their hearts a chant written for them by a City fan, even if they have the stomach for a tune as naff and terrace-unfriendly as 'Copacabana'.

I do, though, like another effort in the same competition written by Sharon Marshall in praise of the golden-locked assassin Robbie Savage while he was still a Birmingham player, and set to the tune of Eric Clapton's 'Wonderful Tonight':

> It's late in the evening, he's wondering what boots to wear
> He pulls on his blue shirt and brushes his long blond hair
> And then he asks Steve Bruce, "Did I play all right?"
> And Steve says, "Lily, you played wonderful tonight!"

It's not much of a game tonight, what with Reading saving themselves for the promotion push and Birmingham being rubbish. The blubbery Dorothy and her emaciated husband are silent, waiting for more humiliation to be heaped on them. But then, shortly before half-time, Mikael Forssell, the blond Viking leading the Birmingham forward line, goes marauding into the Reading box. A succession of Reading defenders clatter into him and they all go tumbling over, but miraculously Forssell is always first up to go charging on. It happens when he reaches the keeper, too, and to the amazement of St Andrews, Forssell pokes the ball over the line to put City ahead. Dorothy reaches in her bag for a jam doughnut to celebrate.

I disappear into the underbelly of St Andrews at half-time in search of a cup of restorative Bovril, but I'm still near the back of the queue when I notice that my phone is ringing. Standing on the concourse looking across the St Andrews pitch as subs warm up and fans laugh about Forssell's goal, I get the news that my mother has terminal cancer.

I've no idea what happens in the second half.

— CHAPTER 6 —

There's Only One Man United?

'I spent a lot of money on booze, birds and fast cars. The rest I just squandered.'

George Best

In the summer of 1987, so the story goes, a bloke called Frank Newton went to see his mate Allen Busby. This guy collected unusual toys – don't ask – which were strewn around the house and much admired by visitors. For reasons best known to himself, Frank was particularly taken by a five-foot-long inflatable banana that happened to be floating around the house.

It was the eve of the new football season and, a few drinks down the road, Frank decided to do what any of us would have done in the circumstances – he dressed it up in Manchester City colours and took it with him to Maine Road for the first game of the season. The match resulted in a 2-1 victory over Plymouth Argyle with an injury-time winner by Imre Varadi. The banana, which by the end of the game had acquired a face, bobble hat, shirt and scarf, was an instant hit on the terraces. It became an unofficial mascot and accompanied Frank – and, indeed, Manchester City – throughout a difficult season of rehabilitation in the old Division Two.

A popular fixture at all Manchester City games that season, it gained almost mythical powers as the City fans called for Imre Varadi to be brought on in a match at West Brom and, in the chanting, the personalities of banana and substitute became intertwined. Varadi's subsequent appearances in the pale blue shirt were invariably accompanied by the strange sight of pogoing giant bananas at football matches throughout the land. Several novelty shops in the area did a roaring trade, and in certain parts of Manchester Varadi is still fondly known as Imre Banana.

But it didn't end there. The utter absurdity of inflatable bananas being waved at footballers was a welcome release from the post-Heysel tensions afflicting British football at the time and tickled fans to such a degree that, the following season, other teams ran on to the pitch to be greeted by the bizarre sight of all manner of large blow-up objects being waved at them. The man who started it all, Frank Newton, graduated from the banana – so 1987 – to a six-foot crocodile, and other fans went to City's first match of the season at Hull armed with such delights as a toucan, a seven-foot golf club, a Red Baron and, ye gods, a *Spitfire plane*. At Grimsby giant fish started appearing on the terraces, a huge black pudding danced behind the goal at Bury, a number of giant hammers fluttered in the wind at West Ham, canaries flew at Norwich, spotted dogs barked at Oldham, and there were even turtles swimming at Stockport.

Then, like skiffle, Rubik cubes, hula-hoops and Spicemania, in the blink of an eye it was gone. With the onset of the Premiership and Sky, football got serious again. It's not a place for mavericks, eccentrics or surreal humour any more, but the romantic in me still senses the ghost of a giant banana drifting across the grey Manchester sky and giggling like a guava as it watches over the tense City fans hustling round the glorious City of Manchester Stadium today for The Big One.

They say the Manchester derby isn't what it used to be, that the foreign players don't have a clue about the history or the intense rivalry that splits the city in half, and that domestic disputes play a poor second fiddle to the battles of Europe these days. But with Sir Alex Ferguson and Stuart Pearce shouting the odds all week, it clearly still means plenty to the fans as police on horses (you can always tell you're in the midst of a major event when there are police on horses) patrol the streets.

Built for the 2002 Commonwealth Games, the whole space-age City of Manchester Stadium complex includes a squash and tennis centre as well as an athletics arena. It is dominated outside by the extraordinary B of the Bang, Britain's tallest sculpture, which looks like the myriad explosions of a particularly volatile firework involuntarily trapped in mid-air in a perpetually frozen state. The odd rugby match, swanky business conference and Red Hot Chili Peppers concert aside, the £110 million football stadium has been leased to Manchester City for the next 250 years.

After a miserable 1-0 home defeat to Southampton, City left Moss Side's Maine Road (though not because of that) to move here at the start of the 2003–04 season. They negotiated the dazzling new smart card system of entry and seem quite at home in their plush new surroundings. You wish them well. City are always popular with neutrals – especially when they play United – and are even more so with a bona fide English icon Stuart 'Psycho' Pearce in charge, giving a solo re-enactment of *The Agony and the Ecstasy* on the touchline. Pearce's uncomplicated bulldog spirit encapsulates the characteristics of old-school football, when rolled-up sleeves and ferocious tackles meant everything and Roy Race ruled the comics. When Pearce slayed the demons of his famous 1990 World Cup penalty miss against Germany and nearly broke the net (and his blood vessels) pumping his fist at the crowd in another penalty shoot-out against Spain in Euro '96, his iconic status was assured.

Pearce is not the only City legend. There is also the case of Bernard Carl Trautmann from Bremen. Aged 10 in 1933, he joined the Hitler Youth 'because I liked sport and camping' and at 17 volunteered for the Luftwaffe, although he later admitted he knew nothing of politics, the Führer or the evils of the Nazis. A Luftwaffe paratrooper, he was ultimately awarded the Iron Cross for bravery, having been captured alternatively by the Russian Red Army, the French Resistance and the American Infantry and escaped each time. It was while fleeing from the

Americans now occupying Germany in 1945 that he jumped over a hedge straight into a couple of British soldiers who reputedly greeted him with the words, 'Hello Fritz, fancy a cup of tea?'

Trautmann was brought to England and held at a P.O.W. camp at Ashton, near Manchester, where he played a full role in the regular prisoners' football matches on makeshift pitches. His performance as a substitute goalie playing for a P.O.W. side against local side Haydock Park after hostilities had ceased in 1946 caused the football fraternity to sit up and take notice.

Gradually a semblance of normality returned to the nation and a full football programme resumed, attracting huge crowds desperate to escape the traumas of recent years and the ongoing austerity of the times to acclaim heroes like Matthews, Lawton, Mannion, Finney and Carter. Frank Swift was another. An England international, Swift was a giant of a man and his spectacular acrobatics and irrepressible sense of humour made him a Manchester City legend. So when he announced his retirement in 1949 it left a gaping void in the City goal. Still in England, Bert Trautmann was playing in goal for St Helens Town in the Liverpool County Combination League at the time and played out of his skin in a friendly match against Manchester City. City decided they'd found their replacement for Frank Swift.

It wasn't a popular signing. The scars of war were still raw and the club was bombarded with protests. Season ticket holders threatened to boycott the club and a protest demonstration attracted 20,000 angry Mancunians wielding anti-Trautmann banners. Trautmann himself received a barrage of hate mail but the club held its nerve, and the keeper's dignity and professionalism, not to mention a series of brilliant performances between the sticks, soon saw off the indignation.

The Trautmann story reached its apotheosis in 1956 when City reached the FA Cup Final. A quarter of an hour before time, with the team leading Birmingham 3-1, Bert flung himself at the feet of onrushing centre forward Peter Murphy and ended up unconscious near the penalty spot. They gave him smelling salts and when he came round, Bert had blurred vision, barely the faintest idea of who he was, let alone *where* he was, and an unbearable pain searing through his neck.

But this was Wembley, this was an FA Cup Final and there were no substitutes in those days, so Bert was stuck back together again and returned to goal to finish the job. Birmingham launched a furious assault on his goal but, reeling around like a helpless drunk, Bert still pulled off three incredible saves – none of which he later remembered. So City won the day and Trautmann climbed the famous steps with the rest of the team to receive his medal from the Queen. He was later diagnosed with a fractured neck.

Trautmann spent the next six months with his neck in plaster and suffered a personal tragedy when his infant son was killed by a car shortly after the Cup Final – an event so traumatic that it triggered the breakdown of his marriage, though few involved in football knew of these events at the time. When he stopped playing he had a brief spell managing Stockport County before moving abroad. In 2004 he was awarded an OBE. City fans concocted a song commemorating that great 1956 Cup Final victory that's still sung – albeit in vastly amended form according to which team it is aimed at – all over the country to this day:

> Bless 'em all, bless 'em all
> Bert Trautmann, Dave Ewing and Paul
> Bless Roy Little who blocks out the wing
> Bless Jack Dyson the penalty king
> And with Leivers and Spurdle so tall
> And Johnstone the prince of them all
> Come on the light blues
> It's always the right blue
> So cheer up me lads
> Bless 'em all.

'Bless 'Em All' has remained in common currency in football grounds ever since, albeit adapted in rather cruder fashion along the way. Here's the song Chelsea stylee:

> Fuck 'em all, fuck 'em all
> United, West Ham, Liverpool
> 'Cos we are the Chelsea and we are the best
> We are the Chelsea so fuck all the rest.

The original 'Bless 'Em All', officially written in 1940 by Jimmy Hughes, Frank Lake and Al Stillman, was popular with both US marines and British troops during the Second World War, with its conciliatory if slightly sardonic references to officers and its mood of optimism in adversity. It became a wartime standard, and part of the staple diet for Bing Crosby, Billy Cotton and Max Bygraves.

However, there is a strong argument that the song is actually much, much older. The great folk singer and communist Ewan MacColl once recorded a parody far more cynical and bitter than dear old Max Bygraves ever gave us, and there is plenty of evidence that it was sung in various divisions of the British military with filthy lyrics long before the Second World War, being adapted from an old folk song that first found popular voice with the army in India in the 1880s. The Royal Navy Air Service also sang it with gusto as a kind of unofficial alternative anthem after the First World War. All Jimmy Hughes did was to clean it up a bit to make it decent for public consumption. In this context, its re-emergence as a football terrace anthem seems entirely appropriate, supporting the argument that football songs are the one true living organic folk tradition.

So I think of the heroic Bert Trautmann as I join the City fans making their way to the stadium for the Manchester derby. Some of them are singing the City anthem 'Blue Moon'. Well, I say *City* anthem ... even they admit they nicked it from Crewe Alexandra who were singing it in the 1980s, and *they* nicked it from Southend United who were singing it in the 1960s. *Allegedly.*

Manchester City do have a proud history of corking songs, though, the best of them aimed at United. Like the epic 'Cantonian Rhapsody':

> Is this the Moss Side? Or is it fantasy?
> Taught by the lies from Matt Busby's theatre of dreams
> Open your eyes, look right through the lies and see
> He's just a French git deserving no sympathy
> Because he's hit 'em high, hit 'em low
> Karate kid or body blow
> Any way the sod goes don't really matter to me.

And so on. Sadly, the lack of an operatic lead singer and a conductor to work out the harmonies, descants, time changes and falsettos hampered its popularity on the terraces. I also like the (short-lived) celebration of Alan Ball's brief spell as City manager to the tune of Oasis's 'Wonderwall' (the Gallagher brothers famously being City fans), which also lauded their enigmatic Russian ball wizard Georgi Kinkladze and another German keeper, Eike Immel.

> Every run that Kinky makes is winding
> And every goal that City score is blinding
> I said maybe, Eike's gonna be the one to save me
> Cos after all – you're my Alan Ball ...

The song's writer Noel Gallagher was chuffed to bits to hear his classic song echoing around the old Maine Road stadium, but mortified to discover it was being manhandled to sing the praises of 'that fucking c**t Alan Ball'.

Another City hero was Irish beanpole striker Niall Quinn, as much admired for his appalling fashion sense as the awkward, gangling style that often left centre halves on the seat of their pants mouthing obscenities. Quinn's appearances were sometimes met with a brief flurry of Dylan's 'Mighty Quinn' but Niall's favoured attire became a true terrace cult anthem –

chanted to the 'Here we go, here we go, here we go' refrain –
which even followed him when he moved to Sunderland:

> Niall Quinn's disco pants are the best
> They go up from his arse to his chest
> They're better than Adam and the Ants
> Niall Quinn's disco pants!

I am really looking forward to this match, which promises to
be a spicy affair given City's resurgence under Pearce. There is
one tiny problem: yet again, I don't have a ticket. 'Press?' I
mutter wanly at the intimidating official at the gates, and apolo-
getically slide away to attach myself to my rightful place at the
bottom of the gateman's shoe. Instead, like loads of others, I do
three circuits of the stadium in full expectation of a ticket
wafting into our pockets in the breeze, but even the touts seem
to have given up on this one in the face of the massive police
presence. As the roars of the crowd clearly indicate the arrival of
the gladiators in the arena, I seek solace at the memorial garden
and read the headstones remembering various fans. Pride of
place goes to the headstone in tribute to Mark Vivien Foe, the
28-year-old midfielder who played his last club game for City
just weeks before collapsing and dying while playing an international for Cameroon against Colombia in France in the
summer of 2003.

Loads of people continue to drift around outside the stadium,
absorbing the explosions of sound inside which suggest City are
getting the better of the early skirmishes, and I decide it will be
a wheeze to watch it on Sky in one of the pubs outside the
ground with the stereo effects of crowd noise on the telly and
from the ground. I find the doors of the first pub, the
Manchester, firmly shut. And Mary D's Beamish Bar. And the
Queen Victoria. And the Crossroads. And every other pub
within pigeon-fancying distance of the ground.

City are one-up by the time I locate my car and two-up by the
time I find an open hostelry a couple of miles down the road. I

dash to grab my place in front of the TV, only to find the place empty except for a sleazy older man touching up a much younger woman wearing enough make-up to re-paint the Sicilian Chapel. The TV is showing a black-and-white movie on Channel 4 that probably stars David Niven (don't they all?). I look at the inappropriate couple going at it hammer and tongues with disgust: what the hell do they think they're doing? How *dare* they have a Channel 4 movie on the telly when the Manchester derby is on the other channel? I march out.

Back on the road, I see a sign that announces that Rochdale is 13 miles away and follow it. At traffic lights, I check the fixture list. There it is. League Two, 3 p.m. kick-off: Rochdale v. Stockport County, very possibly the least glamorous match of the day. Bring it on, I shout, as Alan Green bursts another blood vessel complaining about the ref on the radio. All roads lead to Rochdale.

To be honest, I'm not expecting much. Parking halfway up an impossibly steep hill outside a church I sit in the car listening to Ronaldo being sent off, van Nistelrooy whacking one in for United and then Robbie Fowler putting the final knife in for City, while simultaneously watching the Rochdale fans donning crampons and harnesses and hanging the brandy round the necks of their St Bernards as they prepare for their final assault on the Spotland summit.

I grab an oxygen mask and join them on the slow haul upwards, gasping for breath as we swap idle banter about the woes of our teams in the way footie fans always do before games. 'What he wants to do is get rid of the whole bloody lot of them and start again from scratch. Not one of 'em's any good.' 'Aye, we should win today though.' 'If we don't we should stick 'em all on a ruddy great bonfire.' I nod sagely, and consult the league table. Rochdale are hovering precariously above the relegation zone but Stockport are rock bottom, have no manager and look doomed. 'If we lose today, I'll light the first match,' I say to my new best mates, who look a little nonplussed at my very non-Rochdale accent.

Rochdale may very well be the dowdiest club in England. For a start, it's in an old mill town where rugby is king, and the ground is so small that when you see signs to 'Stadium' you think it is maybe a park and ride stop for Manchester. In 1919, Rochdale were one of seven teams to apply for the six places going in the Football League. Guess which one of the seven missed out.

They did get elected two years later but their trophy cabinet has remained bare and, for all but a couple of years, when they reached the heady heights of the old Division Three, they've remained resolutely nailed to the bottom rung. Their one massive highlight was an appearance in the 1962 League Cup Final, where they were duly tonked 4-0 by Norwich. 'We've had 70 years of consolidation,' says one of the fans gasping up the hill. 'Or 70 years of mediocrity!" All this, and their only celebrity fan is Tommy Cannon, the unfunny one in Cannon & Ball. *And* they play on top of a mountain.

However, I do discover that Rochdale's assistant manager is Tony Ford. *Tony Ford.* Don't look so mystified. Tony Ford is a name that should be embedded in the hearts of every football fan or, at least, every statistician, fact fiend or pub quiz enthusiast. Ford never played in the top flight of the Football League. Never appeared at Wembley. Never played for England (well, apart from a B international against Norway). Never appeared on *A Question of Sport* or *I'm a Celebrity Get Me Out of Here* or induced fan worship or major headlines.

Yet Tony Ford, one of the earliest black players to make a decent mark on the English game, merits our unconditional respect. An industrious right-sided midfielder and an impeccable professional, he played over 1,000 first-class matches for eight different league teams – a record for an outfield player. In fact his record of 931 Football League appearances has only been surpassed by Peter Shilton (1,005) so it's a claim unlikely ever to be beaten.

From the Nunsthorpe estate on the wrong side of Grimsby, Ford joined his hometown club in 1975 and in the next decade became a local legend. His subsequent adventures, mostly around the lower leagues, took him variously to the likes of Sunderland, Stoke, West Bromwich Albion, Bradford City, Mansfield, Scunthorpe and, yes, Rochdale, and he reckons he played at over 100 different grounds. Which isn't bad when you consider there are only 92 clubs in the Football League and he never played in the top division. He finally retired from playing in 2001 at the age of 42 and was awarded the MBE for his services to football, but amazingly attempted to launch a comeback three years later.

Ford says that at no time in his career was he ever racially abused, although in his later years he did become the target for some ageist chanting. The Rochdale fans, however, responded in affectionate manner: 'He's big, he's bad, he's older than my dad/Tony Ford, Tony Ford!' and later: 'He's nearly 63, he's got an MBE/Tony Ford, Tony Ford!' Now he is back as the assistant manager to Steve Parkin at Rochdale, a club he first visited as a teenager with Grimsby Town in 1979, when his abiding memory was sitting in the visitors' dressing room next to a puddle on the floor as snow fell through the roof and a cat crawled through the rafters.

So I doff my cap to the great man, buy *The Tony Ford Story* in the club shop and head off to the pub near the ground (disconcertingly called the Church) to read it before kick-off. But something strange is happening in this pub. It's packed with people in blue and white scarves and they're singing. Very loudly. It's not the usual rubbish about 'We all follow the Stockport over land and sea', or 'We've got the best team in the land' either. They are singing proper songs with verses and choruses that go on for ages, songs that I've never heard at football grounds anywhere before. And then I listen a bit more closely. They're using the tune of the old battle-hymn of Ulster Orangemen, 'The Sash My Father Wore', with their own words:

> We are everything in football
> That people say is sad and wrong
> But when we go to Edgeley Park
> We will sing our County song

We will raise our voice in chorus
As we did in times before
And at Edgeley Park our greatest pride
Is the scarf my father wore.

It's forever being beautiful
And the colours white and blue
I wore it proudly round my neck
At Chesterfield and Crewe
My father was a County fan
Like my grandfather before
And at Edgeley Park I love to wear
The scarf my father wore ...

It goes on for many verses and it seems like the whole pub is singing as it reaches an unexpectedly gruesome denouement:

As I walked up those gallows steps
I looked down at the trap door
Then he pulled the switch
He made me twitch and I knew I was no more
And as I swung from to and fro
My body's now a wreck
But there was no rope that strung me up
'Twas the scarf around my neck!

These were Stockport County fans, the same Stockport County who haven't won a game for three months, who amassed a paltry 26 points when humiliatingly relegated last season and who are rock bottom of this division and, by inference, the worst team in the Football League. They don't even have a manager and they look like they've got a one-way ticket into the Conference, yet they are raising the roof on this splendid little pub and marching off to the game with drums, bugles and a constant barrage of songs and chants.

'Don't matter what division we're in, we could be in the

Blue is the colour as Chopper Harris, Alan Hudson and the rest bring Chelsea into disrepute in 1972.

The new Wham? Hoddle and Waddle get stuck into 'Diamond Lights'.

If they only knew what they were starting... England's 1970 World Cup squad sing 'Back Home'.

The first superstar and Manchester legend Billy Meredith.

'It's only a broken neck!' Bert Trautmann (Man City and Germany) with Gil Merrick (Birmingham and England).

Would you buy a used copy of *The Watchtower* from this man? Peter Knowles of Wolves and the Jehovah's Witnesses.

Where's your funky moped now, mate? Jasper Carrott
milks the applause of the Birmingham City fans.

The man with a stand – Wolves legend Steve Bull.

Dancing on the streets of Total Network Solutions: the Breeze family.

Fan fever hots up among the barmy army at Wick Academy.

Rebel, rebel...the Not the Manchester United Show gets on the road.

Fan as superstar: United folk hero Pete Boyle.

Top and Bottom: The Kop in full cry at Anfield.

Happy Hammers celebrate winning the
Cup in 1975.

Frankie Says... 'Abide With Me.' Cup Final
community singing at Wembley led
by Frankie Vaughan.

Still forever blowing bubbles: West Ham head for the 2006 Cup Final.

Shhh...nobody mention she's a Spurs fan! Faye White, captain of Arsenal and England.

Above: The face of an angel. Yet Leeds fan Mia Brown unwittingly nearly caused a riot.

Lee Clarkson rallies the troops at Colchester.

Cheshire League and we'd all still be there singing our hearts out,' says Ian Lancashire, one of the most boisterous of the singers. A middle-aged warehouse worker who attended his first County game in 1958 and used to take Wednesdays off work so he could see Stockport Reserves play away, he helped concoct the 'Scarf My Father Wore' song – or 'The Anthem', as all County fans call it – in a pub in Southport at a Tuesday night away game in 1973.

'Somebody mentioned "The Sash", this song that is 400 years old or something, and by the end of the night we'd got the first verse,' he says. 'Over the years we've added more verses. Some Bristol Rovers fan went on at us saying it was promoting sectarianism but it's not; the bloke who came up with some of the first lyrics is a Catholic. We've always been against sectarianism and racism and anything like that.'

Inside Rochdale's cramped Spotland ground, the noise is frankly staggering. Rochdale fans gawp as the stand designated for County followers fills up and they have to open up an extra area to fit them all in. As the drummer thumps out a beat and the bugler struggles to keep up, the songs come thick and fast. Ian Lancashire has even compiled a book of them, *A Swaying Mass of Humanity*, and they seem to be going through the full repertoire, plundering everything from Lee Marvin's 'Wanderin' Star' ('I was born under the Cheadle End/Do you know where hell is, hell is Burnerleee/Do you know where heaven is? It's here at Edge-er-ley') to the 'Blue Danube' ('A scarf of all blue, a meat pie or two, a song and a cheer, and a few pints of beer').

This lot are here to enjoy themselves, irrespective of what's occurring down on the pitch, but you can't imagine any sportsman not being stirred by the unconditional commitment of this away support, and while lacking in finesse, the lowest Football League team in the land charge at Rochdale like men possessed. And just seven minutes into the game, we see one of the best goals ever seen at Spotland, or indeed anywhere else.

The ball arrives from nowhere at the feet of County striker Jermaine Easter. With his back to goal and defenders around him, Easter flicks the ball into the air like he's casually starting a bout of keepie-uppies in the playground then executes a breathtaking overhead scissors kick. There's a gushing sound all around me as the Stockport fans suck in their breath and watch the ball, almost in slow motion, loop beyond the astonished Rochdale keeper and sail serenely into the net. A pause follows as we try to assimilate this information, and then the drum beats, the bugle blasts and the County fans are dancing on their seats, crazy with joy. They're here for a beer and a singsong; they don't really expect to score goals at all, let alone one that would make Thierry Henry beam with pride.

Ten more minutes of frantic singing follow and it's all too much for the lad behind me who, without warning, throws up down my back. The poor kid only looks about 13 – a lot younger than my coat – and is as white as a sheet. His appalled mate shrugs his shoulders while trying not to laugh and says, 'I told him he shouldn't have had that second pint.' The crowd around us start chanting 'Pisshead' at him as his mate drags him off for some water, followed by 'One pint of shandy, he's only had one pint of shandy'. You've got to laugh. Well, the rest of them seem to think so.

Rochdale offer little threat to County, who can even afford the luxury of a second-half penalty miss, when the captain Matthew Hamshaw sends his spot kick several miles up the M66. 'One Mattie Hamshaw, there's only one Mattie Hamshaw' roar the crowd in a blind declaration of support, even if he is a prize wazzock who shouldn't be allowed near the penalty spot for the rest of his career. Hamshaw somewhat sheepishly applauds them back. At the end of the game the fans are in seventh heaven, hugging each other and loudly singing the praises of 'Big Jimbo', a.k.a. Jim Gannon, a swarthy Irishman and County legend after more than 400 games as a never-say-die defender who has now returned to the club as caretaker manager and would-be miracle man to stop the rot.

I'm a little heady having sat too close to the drum and I smell of sick, but I desperately hope that Big Jimbo pulls off his miracle. Stockport, whose unbroken run in the Football League dates back over a century, is in its first season of being run by its Supporters' Trust and the old unreconstituted socialist in me reckons the more clubs that are in the hands of real fans rather than plummy-voiced accountants in silk ties and big Jaguars the better. Stockport may be on its haunches, but after a couple of hours in the company of its astonishing fans, all the old romantic ideals about the spirit of football as the province of the working classes and the public expression of a community come flooding back.

Its unfortunate geographical location right on the edge of Manchester – the town centre is just three miles from Manchester City's old Maine Road stadium, and Stockport is technically a part of Greater Manchester – squeezes its fan base to a point where a bunker mentality prevails. Despite its proximity to Manchester, Stockport clings ferociously to its own identity with regular chants of 'Cheshire' leaving no doubts there is a cultural as well as geographical barrier between the town and the big bad city on its doorstep. The passionate singing evoked by the football club is indicative of a community that steadfastly believes in itself. As such, County fans despise Manchester City and hold Manchester United in such contempt that they refuse to use their name at all, referring to them simply as 'Trafford FC'.

County fans have their own code of conduct. You must never ever clap along when they sing 'The Anthem', never be seduced by the glamour boys up the road, never boo your own players, respect opposing fans (although the occasional vomit over neutrals is OK, apparently) and, well, sing your hearts out for the lads. Their fans are legendary in the lower leagues. When Stockport were relegated at the end of last season, the opposing Walsall fans ran on to the pitch and sprinted towards the County supporters. Police and stewards went into red alert as a full-scale ruck looked about to kick off, but when they arrived in front of the blue-and-white army, the Walsall fans simply stopped and gave them a massive round of applause, so impressive had been their support. County even took 500 fans to a pre-season friendly at non-league Leek Town.

The club certainly recognises that its greatest asset is its loyal, vociferous fan base. The club recently spent £1,000 having the biggest scarf in football – 80 metres long – for the fans to pin up at matches. The biggest laugh they had at a match was when Shrewsbury Town fans chanted 'You've only got one song' at them. Stockport supporters reckon they have at least one hundred different songs, few of them ever heard anywhere else, in common currency.

'What you've got to remember,' Ian Lancashire tells me, warming to his topic, 'is that we stuck together through the 1970s and 1980s, when we had a minus goal difference for 20 consecutive seasons. We'd get 2,000 fans at home matches and 1,500 of them would go to away games. Fans of other teams come into our pub and ask us to sing "The Anthem".'

Ian has done a lot of research into the history of County and found a 1930s newspaper reference to 'the famous County song', seemingly called 'All You Conquering Heroes' but sadly with no trace of any words. And for anyone who fondly imagines football violence began in the 1970s, he found newspaper stories from the 1890s referring to County fans throwing stones at a Southport goalkeeper and, on another occasion, a match abandoned when Lincoln City players were chased off the pitch and pursued for four miles across muddy fields.

The modern tradition of County singing, however, emanated from the 1960s with the erection of the Cheadle End – Stockport's equivalent of the Kop – where the singing remains at its most vociferous. Ian's Stockport songbook includes exactly one hundred songs, mainly knocked together in the pub before a game: 'It used to be the Bobby Peel but we fell out with the landlord, so now it's mostly the Armoury in Greek Street.' There's also a CD of songs including – wait for it – a dance mix version of 'The Anthem' featuring the multi-tracked voices of Ian and a few of his mates singing in the pub. They even released it as a single.

On one famous occasion in the 1970s they travelled at the dead of night for an away game with Torquay United. They arrived at 6 a.m. and, wandering down to the beach, encountered a squad of Bradford City fans who had headed west for their team's game at Exeter. Somebody found a ball and, at 6 a.m. on a beach in Devon, Stockport County and Bradford City fans had a full-scale match. That afternoon, much to the bemusement of Torquay supporters, they were singing a song commemorating the great beach match.

'Come and see us any time,' says Ian, 'you're always welcome in Stockport. We can sup up here, you know.' Yeah, I know. I've got the vomit stains to prove it.

My plan for the next day is to take in the lunchtime Wigan Athletic v. West Ham United game. Wigan are mixing it with the big boys, and making a decent fist of it and all. So I get to Wigan and glance at the *Non-League Football* paper … and all my carefully laid plans go flying out of the window.

The fixture I'm looking at is Nelson v. FC United of Manchester, kick-off 2 p.m. After standing outside the City of Manchester Stadium while the millionaire internationals slugged out the Manchester derby and then getting vomited over while Stockport fans proved there is hope for a small club in the shadow of the big city giants, an audience with FC United seems to represent the natural completion of my weekend-long Greater Manchester odyssey.

FC United of Manchester are the direct consequence of supporters trying to wrest control of football back from the businessmen. When strange-looking 75-year-old Lithuanian New Yorker Malcolm Glazer, a resident of Palm Beach, Florida and the son of a deserter from the Russian Army, launched his takeover of Manchester United, alarm bells started ringing with the fans. Having endured the rampant commercialisation of United, not to mention the spats between manager Sir Alex Ferguson and Irish shareholder John Magnier over Fergie's co-ownership claims to wonder horse Rock of Gibraltar, a bunch of fans said enough was enough.

Mr Glazer, the 244th richest man in America, made his fortune buying trailer parks and selling watches, bought an oil company off George Bush Sr and, in 1995, spent $192 million on the franchise of Tampa Bay Buccaneers, a no-hoper American football team with a much-reviled mucky orange kit. By 2003, when they won the Superbowl, the value of the Buccaneers had rocketed to $700 million and the kit was now a tasteful red and pewter. After a long and involved process, Glazer's company finally acquired the 98 per cent of Manchester United shares it needed to effectively own the club in June 2005. The various protests, campaigns, petitions and counter-bids assembled by Shareholders United, the fans' group set up to block Glazer, had failed. Some of these same fans now looked at a picture of this bloke wearing a stupid baseball cap, who called football 'soccer' and probably thought Rio Ferdinand was a small town some-where near San Diego. And apart from anything else, they couldn't stomach that hideous ginger beard.

Their response was to set up their own club – a club that espoused the old traditions and values of United and football generally. No, not the clogging centre halves, balls made of cement and fans beating each other to a pulp, but the re-creation of a club with real spirit and a proper affinity with its fans. A grass-roots football team set to battle through the leagues, shoulder-to-shoulder with supporters who cheerfully pay a few quid to see their boys come what may, who don't have to sign away their lives for a ticket and who are close enough to the action to get really involved. FC United of Manchester are in their first season of daring to give football back to the people, and I want to see how they're getting on.

I scour my map in search of Nelson to see if I can make it in time for a 2 p.m. kick off. I've just worked out the route and figured I can make it if I fly at 200 mph when I glance again at the small print in *Non-League Football*: Nelson v. FC United of Manchester, 2 p.m. kick-off, at *Accrington Stanley*. Nelson, apparently, don't have the facilities to handle the expected influx of FC United fans and have moved the game to Accrington's ground. So after another long study of the map and a swift wheel spin, the road to Accrington it is.

Accrington Stanley, of course, is a name entrenched in the minds of every football fan of a certain age and has quite a story of its own to tell. Even the road signs seem to evoke all manner of odd emotions about the first post-war club to wither and die. Its subsequent comeback and progress through the leagues to the Conference is the stuff of moist-eyed pub talk and a rather fine telly ad. Accrington FC were one of the 12 founding members of the Football League in 1888, and although their first incarnation was short-lived, they joined forces with a team based at the Stanley Arms pub to become Accrington Stanley. There were good times but there were more bad times and it all started to go sour in the 1950s.

See, in April 1958 Accrington Stanley bought a new stand. Stanley were on the glory trail in those days, handily placed near the top of the Third Division North and seemingly heading for the dizzy heights of Division Two. That stand seemed such a sexy idea at the time; a snazzy two-tier construction to seat 4,700 fans in comfort. They bought it off Aldershot FC for a bargain £1,450 and spent another £10,000 to bring it north and rebuild it at their Peel Park home. It was a symbol of their ambition and imminent arrival in the big time, and the good folk of Accrington watched it go up in awe and admiration ... apart from one person.

Stanley's manager was a no-nonsense Scotsman called Walter Galbraith who made Sir Alex Ferguson look like a cuddly puppy and strongly felt they should send their precious new stand back to Aldershot with rivets on. Why spend all that valuable cash on a fancy pants stand when he desperately needed money to improve the team? An age-old battle between a fiery manager and a bunch of directors who, according to Galbraith, couldn't tell an inside right from an outside toilet, was subsequently fought in this industrial neck of Lancashire. When the directors informed the manager that he would have to cut the running costs of the team to pay for the new stand, Galbraith threw a wobbly and walked.

In the subsequent years, Accrington's neighbours Blackburn Rovers and Burnley marched onwards and upwards and the crowds flocked to see them and deserted Stanley, who had to sell their best players to survive. Their form inevitably slumped and they never came close to filling that new stand. Meanwhile Fulham's Jimmy Hill, he of the preposterous beard and big ideas, led a successful players campaign to abolish the maximum wage, triggering an explosion in clubs' running costs, and Stanley's finances went into freefall. In March 1962, amid the hurly burly of a season reaching its climax, Accrington Stanley sank into the dust.

But it has risen from the ashes and, to the soundtrack of their fans interestingly singing the intro to Johnny Cash's 'Ring of Fire', they eventually end the 2005–06 season as Conference champions to continue the Football League career that was so rudely interrupted 44 years ago. A few odds and ends from their old ground remain but Peel Park is now a school playing field and Stanley's home is the rather more cumbersomely named Interlink Express Stadium. But they're still chasing the dream and keeping the great name alive.

So for a lot of reasons there is a considerable air of excitement as I park in one of the urban streets nearby and join the flock of United fans unfurling flags, whacking on their red scarves and trudging up to Nelson's temporary home. FC United's first season is being spent in the decidedly humble climes of the Moore & Co. Construction Solicitors North West Counties Football League Division Two which, let's face it, is a long way from the Premiership.

It's been a bit of a tumble, too, for Nelson, who were founder members of the Third Division North in 1921 when 9,000 came to see their first home game against Wigan Borough. The following season they won the title and arrived at the dizzy heights of Division Two, a campaign for which they prepared with an overseas tour of Spain, including a famous 4-2 victory at Real Madrid. Unfortunately, the likes of South Shields, Clapton Orient, Bury, dear old Stockport County and, yes, even Manchester United, proved far tougher nuts to crack. At the end of the season only Bristol City finished below them and they went straight back down to the Third Division North.

Then, with declining crowds, a familiar story of debts and financial hardship set in and even a fund-raising carnival designed to help them out of the mire only succeeded in chalking up a £20 loss. In 1931 they finished bottom and consequently had to apply for re-election to the Football League, but failed to get it. Cash-strapped in the Lancashire Combination League, they shut up shop in 1936 but rose again after the Second World War and, inspired by their brilliant young player manager Joe Fagan (who 30 years later took Liverpool to several glories), terrorised the Lancashire Combination. Today they find themselves in a league with an extraordinarily long name and a team of blokes mostly born in Burnley, playing a team of Manchester United rebels at Accrington Stanley's ground.

Inside, there are 2,011 mostly FC United fans (a couple of hundred more than Stanley tend to attract each week) having a rare old Sunday afternoon. Nelson have even produced a commemorative badge ('just £2.50p – bargain, mate') for the occasion, which they sell on a stall next to the glossy programme. 'Bloody hell, two quid for a programme?' says one of the fans, digging deep. 'What's it got inside, *War & Peace*?' Not exactly, but it does have a full-page Sudoku puzzle and a nice picture of Nelson keeper Billy 'The Fish' Carrington. The entrance is £7, which nearly makes the bloke behind me explode with indignation: 'Is that a family ticket, then?' The man at the gate shakes his head solemnly. 'Jesus, Joseph and Mary, I only want to buy a ticket, not one of the players!' Whatever else, FC United's existence is doing wonders for the other teams' finances. Nelson's last home gate, for a 3-1 win over Daisy Hill, was just 84, and the income from three United matches alone (they've drawn them in the cup, too) will see them through the rest of the season.

The FC United fans are banked tightly behind one of the goals, maintaining an impressive barrage of songs and chants which reach fever pitch when the team run out in classic plain red shirts, baggy white shorts and black socks, deliberately recalling the United of a more innocent, past era. There are no names on the shirts, no squad numbers – just a plain 1 to 11 – and no sponsors' names either. 'That shirt is precious,' says one fan, already getting animated beyond reason merely as a result of the No. 9 kicking off. 'Why would we want to tarnish it with a sponsor's name?'

FC United are running away with Division Two of the Moore & Co. Construction Solicitors North West Counties Football League showing a clean pair of heels to the likes of Holker Old Boys, Blackpool Mechanics and Castleton Gabriels (who they put 10 past), but even winning the title will still see them five promotions short of the Football League. Not that this is playing on anybody's minds here. The club, which plays its home fixtures at Bury and tends to attract more punters than its host, is run by supporters who have very simple and honourable objectives. The first is to 'strengthen the bonds between the club and the community which it serves and to represent the interests of the community in the running of the club'. There is no mention of winning the European Champions League.

Within three minutes, 28-year-old plumber Joz Mitten, a great-nephew of Charlie Mitten who won an FA Cup winner's medal with Manchester United in 1948, knocks in the first goal. He wheels away in triumph, Mick Channon style, to see the mass of supporters twirling their scarves above their heads like lassoes and whooping like children. There's endless banter between the crowd and players at corners, a constant repertoire of songs and particular affection reserved for Adie Orr, a lithe black striker with bright red hair. 'It's yer 'air, Adie, it's gone straight to yer 'ead, get a new 'aircut, son!' shouts one geezer as Adie sends a wayward shot into the stand behind him. Two cracking goals before half-time from classy ex-England schoolboy international Steve Torpey, once on the books of Liverpool and the man who scored the first ever FC United goal, seem to seal the match as a contest and we dash to spend the break in the warmth of Accrington's overworked bar.

Inside, among the decidedly limited exhibits of Accrington's footballing achievements, a full-scale party is going on. 'This is Spike,' says Tom, a fan I get chatting to in the crush for the bar. I look across to see a John Prescott-lookalike slumped in a seat in the corner with matted hair all over his face. 'He's been to every single game FC United have ever played and you know what? He hasn't seen a single one of them. Silly bugger goes to the bar before the game starts and doesn't come out. He hasn't seen us kick one ball yet! He knows all the players' names, mind, don't you Spike?' He gives him a nudge, and Spike wakes with a start and knocks a pint of Guinness over himself.

'The thing is,' says Tom, ignoring Spike as he takes off his Guinness-soaked coat, spraying us with the black stuff in the process, 'this is what *real* football is all about. A drink before the game, a laugh with your mates, have a chat with the players and you're close to the pitch so the ref can hear you calling him a wanker. It's much better than all that old shite at Old Trafford. I still follow 'em, mind – once a red, always a red. I was gutted when the other lot did us over yesterday but I'm glad I didn't bother trying to get a ticket. The Premiership's a nightmare now. They've priced the real fans out of football. Someone had to make a stand and that's what we're doing. It's great being in at the start of something, and the football's not bad either.'

As the second half starts, I leave Spike with his head in a puddle of Guinness while Tom joins his mates rammed against the window watching the match from the inside and singing, 'We're in the bar having a view, we're in the bar looking at you'. As FC United seem to run out of steam and Nelson pull a goal back with a late penalty, the crowd behind the goal amuse themselves by chanting at the crowd under the shelter at the side of the pitch: 'Bus stop, bus stop, give us a song,' they roar.

'We all follow United, and we sing louder than you,' the bus stop responds. Various players get their own song and for some unfathomable reason 'Under the Boardwalk' makes frequent appearances.

It's freezing cold, the football is chaotic, the pitch is bumpy and the ground is a tad scruffy but there's something that is, if not life-affirming then at least *football-affirming* about it all. Jules Spencer, a 32-year-old local government worker and a board member and one of the founding fathers of FC United, brims with pride at the achievements so far. He was chairman of the Independent Manchester United Supporters Association, whose objections to the increasingly corporate and rigid atmosphere prevailing at Old Trafford laid the foundations of this new club, where the supporters run it and make the decisions. See, even before Glazer, people used to complain about the way Manchester United was going.

'There's a sense of liberation here now,' he says reflectively. 'It's giving the club back to the supporters. They are the ones who run it and make the decisions. See, even before Glazer, people used to complain about the lack of atmosphere at Old Trafford as opposed to away matches, where you'd all be congregated together with your mates. At Old Trafford there was no cohesion and you couldn't do that, you would all be made to sit in different parts of the ground and you were always being told to sit down and be quiet.

'The hardcore United fans notoriously wouldn't wear colours and scarves; we'd be known as the men in black because we always wore dark coats as a reaction against the tat they'd force you to buy in the megastore. I thought that FC United might be the same and the supporters would sing rehashed old United songs but from the very first game they came up with their own songs and there was this great explosion of colour. There was a real feeling of release.'

That first game was a friendly at Leigh RMI (Royal Mechanics Institute), until recently a Conference side, whose spartan support looked almost comical rattling around in the spacious 10,000-capacity Hilton Park rugby stadium. There had been a frenetic couple of months leading up to it as Jules and his colleagues worked round the clock to make the rebel United club happen. An initial rally of supporters had debated long and hard whether to start a new club or stay in situ at Old Trafford and fight the enemy from within. They decided on the bolder route and 2,000 turned up at a second meeting to formulate strategy, armed with £100,000-worth of pledges of support. Much of it was the money that fans had earmarked for their next Old Trafford season ticket.

They took advice from AFC Wimbledon, the splinter club formed in 2002 in response to the FA's mad decision to allow Wimbledon FC to relocate 70 miles away and morph into Milton Keynes Dons. AFC Wimbledon likewise had to start again at the bottom of the pyramid but their first match, against Sutton United on a Wednesday night in July, attracted a staggering crowd of 4,500, and the club have made consistent progress through the leagues and largely maintained their success ever since. So AFC Wimbledon is an important template for FC United – well, them and, er, *Barcelona*, a rather more famous supporters-owned club. Barca's long-held refusal to entertain a sponsor's name to sully their shirts with filthy corporatism (sadly, now finally overturned) certainly inspired FC United's emotional decision to keep their own shirts sponsor-free.

'The Glazer takeover was announced about a week before the FA Cup Final so all we had was a couple of months to get the club going in time for the new season,' says Jules. 'We could have waited another year but we might have lost the momentum, so we had to move fast. Every day seemed like a week. You'd start the day with 20 things to do and end up with another 40 things to do at the end of it. It was a mad seven or eight weeks.

'People assume that when you set up a club the first thing you do is get a manager and a team together, but that's almost the *last* thing. You need a business plan, affiliation to a league, sort out a ground-share or your own ground – there is loads of stuff before you even think about players.'

FC United interviewed a succession of would-be managers who promised the earth, but settled on Karl Marginson, an ex-Rotherham, Macclesfield, Barrow and Stalybridge Celtic player who gets up at 3 a.m. each day to deliver fruit and veg. 'He *understood*,' says Jules. 'A lot of the press reports were speculating we would get an ex-United player, but we wanted someone who knew the game on our level and bought into the principles and instinctively understood what we're about. Karl was a United fan who used to stand at the Stretford End.'

For the second friendly, an emotional game against their spiritual brethren AFC Wimbledon, they took 1,000 fans with them. But it was the low-profile third game at Stalybridge when another 2,500 fans turned up which convinced them it really was going to work. 'The cynics said that once the novelty wore off we'd all be back to Old Trafford but it hasn't happened,' Jules continues. 'OK, a reporter asked one of our fans, it's all very well you turning up at the end of the summer when it's all new and exciting, but how will you feel when you're faced with a freezing cold terrace at Darwen in the middle of December? The fan just said, "I'll wear a big coat."' The next match, with Winsford United, subsequently became known as 'Big Coat Day' and attracted over 2,000.

Sir Alex Ferguson would be enduring squeaky bum time, particularly if he were listening to the supporter talking about the drinking sessions with the players – especially the ones *before* a game. FC United followers all tell you they remain fervent Manchester United supporters, but will never set foot in Old Trafford again until 'that American' is gone. 'I watched them for 25 years, you can't just switch that off,' says Jules Spencer. 'I watched the Man City game in a pub and have had a long face ever since we lost. I just refuse to give Glazer my money.'

So what if the Glazer family bailed out and the sun shone again at Old Trafford? Would that mean FC United were redundant and would shut up shop? 'That would be up to the supporters,' he says. 'It's their club. They're the ones who can look out on to the pitch and think, "this is ours". So it would be their decision. But this club isn't just an anti-Glazer statement and I think they'd want to carry on.'

I look at the laughing, chanting mass of people waving their red scarves, singing their songs and heading for the bar and I know that he's right.

— CHAPTER 7 —

Walk On, Walk On

'The self-appointed representative of the Kop came on the field to greet me. He gave me a kiss and the smell of booze on his breath nearly knocked me off my feet. He kissed me, then he kissed the grass in front of the Kop and went back to join his mates in the crowd.'

Kevin Keegan on his 1971 Liverpool debut (taken from
The Kop by Stephen F. Kelly)

I'm at Anfield, on a Saturday afternoon. They don't stand shoulder-to-shoulder on the Kop any more, but five minutes before kick-off the place is still ablaze with emotion. The sense of nervous anticipation palpably intensifies and you feel the surge of pride, hope and expectation reverberate around you as all eyes focus on the players' tunnel. Suddenly, through the blurry mist of red, you see Steven Gerrard, the sallow-faced local hero who looks like he should be working down the chippy, running out at the front of the team.

The effect is electrifying. Seating room only be damned; everyone in the Kop rises as one in a ferocious roar of approval that must intimidate the opposition every bit as much as running out under the famous 'This Is Anfield' sign that was specifically designed to put the hex on them. You glance up to encounter a sea of red and white scarves held aloft in defiant, belligerent salute and, as you gawp at the thrilling majesty of it all, the cheers fade and their voices in unison cut through the din.

'When you walk through a storm …' The whole of the Kop is up, scarves symbolically still, radiant against the sky. 'Hold your head up high …' The players are now down in front of the goal now, applauding us, a look of awe in some of their eyes too. 'And don't be afraid of the dark …' The voices boom out as one, a solemn sense of occasion, history and belonging paradoxically encapsulated in the joy of song.

'At the end of the storm, there's a golden sky …' Just a football match? Just a football match, my arse! 'And the sweet silver song of a lark.' Their voices rise in volume, emotion and intensity, thick with passion and belief. Why, when all they're singing is a hoary old show tune? 'Walk on through the wind, walk on through the rain …' This is more than a bunch of footie fans singing their hearts out for the lads; it's cultural identity, it's a living tradition, it's a massive head rush. 'Though your dreams be tossed and blown …' It's just an old Rodgers & Hammerstein show tune from 1945. And the Kop is in full cry. There's harmonies and everything.

'Walk on, walk on …' A life-affirming song at the finale of *Carousel*, for the daughter of a wastrel showman who meets a grisly end, that's what it is. But they played it here before a game when the *other* Liverpool band, Gerry and the Pacemakers, took it to No 1, in 1963, and when the record ended the crowd just kept on singing it. And they've been singing it ever since.

'With hope in your heart …' Try not to be caught up in the theatre of it all, the extraordinary charge of emotion enveloping Anfield as the chorus trundles to its shuddering climax. 'And you'll never walk alone …' Try not to sing as if your life depends on it. 'You'll never ever walk alone …' Try not to let your heart swell and your eyes fill with water. 'Walk on, walk on, with hope in your heart …' Try not to be affected by it, to imagine this is just any old team in any old city and this is just a silly old footie match. 'And you'll never walk alone …' Try, you just try. 'You'll never walk alone …' It can't be done.

The referee blows for kick-off and you sink back into your seat in the Kop, an emotional wreck. The match begins.

Scousers are, of course, famously sentimental, romanticising every aspect of football from the idols on the pitch to the folk heroes in the crowd, goading them on to make the impossible happen. The whole persona of Liverpool's football culture is shrouded in cliché and stereotype, yet from the little kids charging a tenner a time to guard your cars outside the ground to the dodgy tracksuits and dodgier haircuts, it's hard to shrug them off.

Embedded in a gloomily downbeat urban corner of Liverpool, the legend of Anfield in general and the Kop in particular surely has no match, however much their chums from the other side of Stanley Park (and those from Old Trafford) may dispute it. Even in this strange era when the manager is Spanish, the players represent a good cross-section of the United Nations and plans are in hand for a brand new stadium, the club retains a fiercely close cultural identity with the city and the supporters are more self-aware than any other in fuelling the character of their club.

The Kop fizzes with stories, myths and legends, and some of them are even true. Chelsea had Mickey Greenaway, the king of the Shed, but the Kop had a legion of its own folk heroes who could ignite the crowd in one sudden chant that would spread like wildfire around the rest of the ground. It had 25,000 people packed so tight behind the goal that voluntary movement was impossible, the surge from the back at a moment of drama likely to carry you to a different part of the terrace. You had to beware, too, the soggy copies of the *Liverpool Echo* or the dripping plastic bags sailing over your head as conventional toilet breaks became a physical impossibility.

Incredibly, Liverpool's right to ownership of 'You'll Never Walk Alone' is disputed. A Manchester grandmother, Jane Hardwick, claims the song rang round the Old Trafford terraces long before it was ever sung at Anfield. A teenage opera singer in 1958 at the time of the Munich air disaster, she claims she rounded up a group of her mates from the New Mills Operatic Society to pay their own tribute to the Busby Babes in the aftermath of the tragedy. The Society was rehearsing *Carousel* at the time and they decided to sing 'You'll Never Walk Alone' – the big song from the show – at the first home game played by the patched-together United side. 'Soon the whole ground was singing it and many people, including me, were in tears,' she told the *Manchester Evening News*. 'It annoys me that people think the song was first sung by Liverpool fans.'

New Mills Operatic Society aside, however, there is little doubt Liverpool have spearheaded modern terrace anthems and chants. Television coverage of an England tour to South America in 1959 exposed British supporters for the first time to the colourful football culture in that part of the world, particularly the celebratory chants of 'Bra-sil cha cha cha Bras-il cha cha cha' which helped make the match such a spectacle, and palpably inspired the Brazilian team to take England to the cleaners. Coverage of the 1962 World Cup Finals in Chile, when the excitable South Americans again enhanced the spectacle, further fanned the transformation of spectators into influential participants. The ever-voluble Scousers took up the challenge and the Kop became their mouthpiece.

Everton were the original tenants of Anfield and spent eight years there until 1892 when, shortly after winning the Football League title, they decamped in a row over the rent. Club president John Houlding, a local brewer known locally as 'King John of Everton' who later went on to become the mayor of Liverpool, charged them £250-a-year rent, used his pub, the Sandon, as the club HQ and insisted that only his own products were sold at the ground. The other directors rebelled, and Everton marched out en masse to build their own ground across Stanley Park. Only three players stayed loyal to Houlding, but that was all the encouragement he needed to pick up the pieces and build a new club, Liverpool. Initially the crowds flocked to Everton's Goodison Park and Anfield was virtually deserted as the new club was launched, but success on the pitch soon had them breathing down Everton's necks.

Houlding built a steep, sloping bank of terracing in the

Walton Breck Road end of Anfield as a present to the fans who had supported them as they won their second Football League title in 1906. Ernest Edwards, the sports editor of the *Liverpool Echo*, commented that it reminded him of Spionkop Hill in South Africa, where many Liverpudlians were among the 300 Lancashire Fusiliers slaughtered by the Boers in the disastrous battle of Ladysmith in 1900. The image of the hill on which so many died was still so fresh in the minds of Liverpudlians that a terrace in their name seemed like a lasting monument to the fallen. The Kop was born.

In truth, Woolwich Arsenal had already beaten them to it, having had the same idea about their own terrace at their old Manor Ground, but the name didn't stick. The Kop wasn't even football's biggest terrace – the East Bank at Charlton's Valley, Aston Villa's Holte End and the South Bank at Molineux all regularly housed over 30,000 people. But none of them had the character or made as much noise as Liverpool's Kop end.

In 1928 they built a roof on the Kop and the roar that greeted Billy Millar's goal 50 seconds into a match against Bury seemed to explode from under the new shelter and envelop the rest of Anfield. So the Spion Kop always had a reputation for its intense atmosphere and partisan support, although it didn't evolve into football's most fabled and revered choir until the early 1960s when Beatlemania landed. Liverpool was suddenly the centre of the musical universe, and Scousers became very self-aware of their own identities and their own roles in the cultural reinvention of the city.

Sometimes when it was damp the Kop looked like it was on fire with smoke billowing out of the terrace, but it was the steam coming off the tightly cramped supporters. It bulged with dockers and railwaymen and shipyard workers and bus drivers and factory hands and labourers and bus drivers and postmen and shop assistants and welders and electricians and builders, all wishing they could have played for Liverpool, standing shoulder-to-shoulder in a heart-on-the-sleeve expression of their pride in their city and their loyalty to the shirt worn by their heroes on the pitch. Big Ron Yeats, hard-as-nails Tommy Smith, World Cup hero Roger Hunt, effervescent Scots striker Ian St John, beefy keeper Tommy Lawrence, tough-tackling Gordon Milne, the dependable Ian Callaghan (who still holds the club record for the most appearances) and the biggest hero of them all – the manager, Bill Shankly.

The first season they started singing 'You'll Never Walk Alone' at Anfield, during 1963–4, Liverpool won the Football League, triggering not only two decades of unprecedented dominance in the English game but a large helping of the trophies on offer from Europe as well. Nobody has ever doubted the inspirational role in this run of success played by the Kop, which became the envy of their rivals and a benchmark for other vociferous crowds like Manchester United's Stretford End, Chelsea's Shed and Arsenal's North Bank. The Kop's biggest fan was Shankly himself, who so identified with their passion and loyalty that he once stood with them to watch a match. You had to get to the ground two hours before kick-off to claim a place on the Kop and as the hits of the day were pumped out over the crackly tannoy, a mass karaoke doubled as the pre-match entertainment. And once the matches started the fans just kept on singing, developing their own highly individual repertoire.

The Liverpool supporters are generally credited with introducing the modern staccato chant still heard at grounds throughout the country together with the rhythmic clapping based on a 1962 Christmas hit, 'Let's Go', by American band the Routers. Locked into the Pony, one of the numerous post-Twist dance fads briefly taking America by storm at the time, it was appropriated by American cheerleaders and initially adapted at Anfield in praise of their star Scottish striker Ian St John.

The Kop-ites introduced the defiant 'We Shall Not Be Moved' to British football. An old spiritual sung by black slaves in America as 'Jesus Is My Captain, I Shall Not Be Moved', it was adapted and sung in the 1930s by the inter-racial Southern Tenant Farmers Union when they were trying to raise support for the plight of struggling Arkansas sharecroppers hit by a cut in cotton production. Subsequently adopted by the civil rights movement, it was sung on picket lines and protest marches throughout the US and recorded by various folk artists including the Freedom Singers, the Weavers, Pete Seeger, Sweet Honey in the Rock and – its most commercial incarnation – the Seekers. Once the Kop got hold of its fists-clenched message of solidarity and resistance, 'We Shall Not Be Moved' infiltrated British football and was sung by the fans of every major club in the land.

Nobody else, though, ever sang 'Scouser Tommy', a strangely mawkish tale of uncertain origin that was recorded by local singer and Radio Merseyside presenter Billy Maher. Set to the tune of 'Red River Valley', it tells the story of a British soldier mortally wounded while fighting Nazis in Libya:

> As he lay on the battlefield dying, with the blood gushing out
> of his head
> As he lay on the battlefield dying, these were the last words
> that he said …

Suddenly the song adopts a different tone entirely and poor Scouser Tommy's dying words are delivered with perky exuberance. Here is the redemptive message of the 'Liverpool till I die' attitude for all to see:

> Ooh I am a Liverpudlian, I've just come from the Spion Kop
> I like to sing, I like to shout and I get thrown out quite a lot
> We support a team that's dressed in red, it's a team that you all
> know
> It's a team we call Liverpool and to glory we go …

Among the acidic wisecracks, urine bombs and emotional overload, the Kop also had an enviable reputation for footballing knowledge and fair play, always giving opposing goalkeepers a warm reception and avoiding abusing the opposition. The worst injury that anyone ever sustained on the Kop was a woman who broke her hip when she slipped on the steps at a Billy Graham sermon at Anfield in 1984. Alas, Liverpool's honourable reputation was capsized in May 1985, when a crowd of supporters charged at Juventus fans in the Heysel Stadium in Brussels and 38 Italians and one Belgian died as a wall collapsed. The tragedy resulted in English teams being banned from Europe for five years.

This disaster, and the Hillsborough tragedy four years later, added real grief to the habitual sentimentality that Liverpool attaches to its football and the floral tributes, scarves and monuments honouring the dead that you still see at Anfield remain testament to the club's iconic status at the heart of the city. There was a lot of weeping and wailing when they finally pulled the old Kop terrace down to replace it with an all-seater stand in the wake of the Taylor Report, though in the light of the tragedies few disputed its necessity.

One of the finest renditions of 'You'll Never Walk Alone' (and one of the greatest tributes to Liverpool fans) occurred at Milan's San Siro Stadium on the Wednesday evening following the Hillsborough disaster in which 96 Liverpool fans died in 1989. Six minutes into a European Cup semi-final between AC Milan and Real Madrid the referee stopped the game to hold a minute's silence, and both the Italians and the Spaniards sang a moving rendition of the Liverpool anthem.

That last league game before the old Kop was pulled down on April 30, 1994 was inevitably an orgy of nostalgia as various Liverpool legends paraded on the pitch and the widows of Bill Shankly and Bob Paisley waved to the crowds, who responded with an incessant repertoire of their finest terrace anthems: 'Scouser Tommy', 'When the Reds Go Marching In', 'We All Live in a Red and White Kop', 'Fields of Anfield Road', 'You'll Never Walk Alone' and all. Unfortunately nobody told Norwich City they were only there to make up the numbers on that last momentous day, and the old Kop resorted to chanting, 'We only sing when we're standing' and 'You're supposed to let us win' as Jeremy Goss scored to give Norwich a 1-0 victory.

However, the Kop did have the last laugh. As the final whistle blew and the players shook hands and applauded the fans, a strange-looking character in a red fez, long khaki shorts and false moustache somehow evaded the line of police, got on the pitch and ran away with the ball. He dribbled into the penalty area, shot and punched the air in delight as the ball hit the back of the net in front of the cheering Kop. Police marched him away but the name of the man in the fez, John Garner, will forever be shrouded in Liverpool folklore as the last man to score in front of the famous old terrace.

So they say it has nothing on the old days, that it's a shadow of its former self, that the spirit isn't there and the singing's rubbish now, but there is still something special about the new all-seater Kop, even if it's only a sense of history. Or maybe it's just the people who inhabit it, who are still full of sharp one-liners, a seemingly endless repertoire of songs and a belief in the sort of miracle that saw them win the European Champions League in 2005 against all the odds.

The night before Liverpool played Bayer Leverkusen in Cologne in the last 16 in March, a couple of fans bumped into manager Rafael Benitez in the team hotel and managed to persuade him to join them in a nearby Irish bar to watch Chelsea play Manchester United on television. Immediately they had a song for the occasion: 'The famous Rafa Benitez went to the pub to see the lads/And this is what he said/Who the fuck are Man United?' This is truly folk song of the finest order.

As with most major clubs, the most committed fans aren't necessarily from Liverpool. Martin Cooper was born in Norwich and he was just seven when his dad first took him to see his hometown team play. Unfortunately they were playing Liverpool, and before the 90 minutes were up, Martin had made a lifelong pact with the Reds that has endured for over 50 years. He is now a cabbie in Cambridgeshire, but his passion for Liverpool shows no signs of abating. He's been married seven times and blames the failure of all of them on his single-minded devotion to Liverpool and constant trips around the country supporting them. One after another, the marriages dissolved in the same arguments and the same intransigence as he refused to compromise his commitment to the cause. There was some hope of longevity with his sixth wife Davina with whom he had a son Ian, named after Ian Rush. And Kenny, after Kenny Dalglish. And Alan, after Alan Hansen. And Bruce, after Grobbelaar. In fact the unfortunate boy was given the names of the entire Liverpool team which won the double in 1986, including beating Everton in the first all-Merseyside FA Cup Final.

And then there is the equally strange case of Dolly Wallinger, a devoted Northampton Town fan who adored their right back Phil Neal, who had played over 200 matches for the Cobblers. She adored him so much that when Bob Paisley made him his first signing as Liverpool manager in 1974, Dolly couldn't bear the thought of watching a Northampton side without Neal in it. So, against all the principles of being a football fan, she switched allegiances and started supporting Liverpool. Over 32 years later and with Neal long retired, she hasn't missed a game at Anfield since, and always sits directly behind the dugout. At the age of 86 and still running the Northants branch of Liverpool Supporters Club, she won the Barclays Fan of the Month award, which is fair enough given her extraordinary loyalty. I mean, *Phil Neal*? He was rubbish.

Her husband, Herbert, deserves a medal too. At the age of 90 he's stayed loyal to Northampton where he still has a season ticket. At weekends, while Dolly is sorting out the coach to Anfield, he's off to the Cobblers.

I'm back in the Kop as England take on Uruguay in a pre-2006 World Cup friendly. It's a different atmosphere entirely at England matches, where fans are bound in hope rather than expectation that England will break the habit of a lifetime and turn it on when it really doesn't matter. Going to watch the cream of the nation should feel special, and it does, if only for the pomp and circumstance that comes as part of the international trappings. Everyone stands up in the Kop as Beckham leads the troops into battle in 1966 red shirts and, despite a couple of pleas on the PA, nobody sits down while the match is on. You can put seats in the Kop but you can't make people sit on them.

We have nothing against the Uruguayans or their tiny gathering of fans hiding behind a single blue and white flag, but there's much sport to be had here at the expense of the ever-baitable Gary Neville, who recently made an arse of himself doing some sort of Mancunian Maori dance in front of Liverpool fans when Man U beat them and was quoted in the papers as saying he hated all Scousers. So, let's all boo Gary Neville – why not? It's practically a national sport.

Halfway through the first half, Uruguay score a goal. It's a brilliant goal at that. Omar Pouso volleys a swerving shot from well outside the area past Paul Robinson and the Uruguayan contingent suddenly seems to have swelled and starts doing the samba, or whatever the hell it is they do in Montevideo, around their few rows in the stand. The England players look shocked – maybe even as shocked as their manager when he discovered that the nice sheikh who'd just flown him to Dubai offering untold riches and persuaded him to share his inner thoughts about the English players and his own managerial ambitions was really a *News of the World* reporter.

It's all looking a bit gloomy, and a noisy round of 'In-ger-land In-ger-land' reverberates round Anfield in an attempt to lift the spirits, but it's hardly a chant designed to reflect the more sophisticated aspects of the beautiful game as it fills the ground with horrific mental images of angry drunken skinheads with bulging eyes rampaging round Europe waving the flag of St George. Or is that just me? We also get an airing of 'Three Lions', the great anthem put together by David Baddiel, Frank Skinner and the bloke from the Lightning Seeds for the 1996 European Championship held in England. It's that rare thing – a football song full of real wit and understanding of the fans' psyche, drawing from the sense of history ('30 years of hurt never stopped me dreaming'), theatre ('Nobby dancing'), sentiment ('it's coming home, it's coming home, football's coming home') and hope ('we can do it again'). When England played Germany in the Euro '96 semi-final at Wembley, the official anthem – some unspeakable dirge by Mick Hucknall – was drowned out by the crowd spontaneously singing 'Three Lions', as Baddiel and Skinner tried not to blubber like children.

Yet England has to carry some guilt in the whole sorry history of the pop industry plundering football. Lonnie Donegan started in 1966 with the singalong 'World Cup Willy' about a very strange-looking toy lion that had been adopted as the official mascot for the 1966 finals. It may not have done much for the credibility of the king of skiffle, and it wasn't even a chart hit, but it alerted the pop industry to the potential of treating football icons as pop stars, a process accelerated with the emergence of George Best as a sexy, photogenic teen idol who also just happened to be the greatest footballer ever produced in the British Isles.

For the 1970 World Cup in Mexico the players themselves were trooped into a recording studio for the first time to bang out 'Back Home', and the minute that it hit No. 1 the floodgates were opened. From that point every FA Cup Final team booked their time in the studio to churn out some garbage, though few ever made it on to the terraces.

In 1982 England's song was 'This Time (We'll Get It Right)' – they didn't – and a string of England embarrassments included 'We Got the Whole World at Our Feet' in 1986 and Stock, Aitken & Waterman's 'All the Way' two years later. Thankfully, New Order then took a hand and completely reinvented the whole notion of dreadful oompah footie songs with 'World In Motion', which proved that John Barnes couldn't rap to save his life but at least saw England off to the World Cup in Italy in 1990 with a bit of pride.

The way the crowd sing it now, though, there's no doubt that 'Three Lions' is the best of the lot. Reissued for the 1998 World Cup, it again echoed around stadiums, decimating the official England release '(How Does It Feel To Be) On Top of the World' by members of the squad with Echo & the Bunnymen, the Lightning Seeds and the Spice Girls. Honourable mentions in dispatches should also go to Keith Allen, who had a cameo role on 'World In Motion', contributed to the 1996 Black Grape/ Joe Strummer song 'England's Irie' and has subsequently seen it as his personal duty to knock out a song per tournament under the guise of Fat Les. Certainly the opening part of his 1998 multi-cultural mantra 'Vindaloo' has been adopted with some enthusiasm around the country by fans, though the 2002 effort 'Who Invented Fish & Chips?' died an embarrassing death.

With their team facing an embarrassing defeat by Uruguay at Anfield, the England band in the corner start playing 'The Great Escape'. Now this is more like it. Drums are a serious bone of contention among football fans but a full-scale band that can really play their instruments – you can't knock it, can you? Featuring musicians aged from 16 to 78, they used to be the Sheffield Wednesday band and were famous throughout football during the 1990s when Wednesday's East Bank Republican Army reigned supreme, the band stood at the back of the crowd belting out the club songs and the large, bald, shirtless figure of Tango Man, arguably the most recognisable football fan in the land, led the singing. Nicknamed after the strange orange character in the Tango soft drink TV ads, Tango Man, a.k.a. Paul Gregory, danced his way through matches, his large belly wobbling dangerously like an unstable mountain of jelly, defying the elements and enhancing his own legend as a hard northern bastard.

Gregory first came to national attention when television cameras caught him stripped to the waist in sub-zero temperatures in a match against Derby County in 1991. He later played up to the Tango persona by adorning a large orange hand, and a subsequent orange away kit worn by the Owls is said to have been chosen in homage to Tango Man and the other fans who whipped off their shirts in the fiercest weather as a gesture of their mind-over-matter commitment. At one point it seemed compulsory for all true Wednesday fans to go topless, especially when the climate was brass monkeys, while supporters from other clubs were anxious to prove they were just as hard. Wolves had 'Ten Bellies' and Newcastle had more than their fair share of wobbly stomachs. In fact, they still do.

As we moved towards an era of executive boxes and toned-down behaviour, this unexpected development of fan culture made football's fat cats nervous. Tango Man is no longer seen at Sheffield Wednesday and the club is not keen to help with enquiries about his whereabouts. The band are long gone too after being actively discouraged by the club, but at least now they're playing on an international stage.

It had all started with one anonymous bugler on Boxing Day, 1993. John Hemmingham, who'd played the bugle at cub scouts, stuck his instrument under his jumper and smuggled it into Hillsborough. After 80 minutes, with Wednesday winning 2-0, he raised it to his lips and played the fanfare to *Aida*, Verdi's dramatic opera of love, war and betrayal set in ancient Egypt. 'I just did it for a laugh, really,' John tells me, 'I never expected it to go anywhere.' His little turn, however, stirred up enough interest to give the bugle further airings at subsequent matches, igniting the local press into a frenzy of intrigue as they sought to solve the mystery of the phantom bugler. When John was at last unveiled the Wednesday chairman of the day, Dave Richards, phoned him up and told him to find a drummer to play with him. Gradually the Sheffield band grew. At their peak there were 15 of them, including trumpets, saxophones and even £3,500 worth of euphonium, with a large repertoire of tunes.

But a cold chill was blowing through Hillsborough. Richards left in 2000 *en route* to becoming chairman of the Premier League, four local MPs stuck their noses in demanding the sacking of manager Danny Wilson, the club's debts rose, takeover rumours spread and on the field Wednesday were on the slide. Yet the band played on … for a while anyway.

The new board didn't share Dave Richards' enthusiasm for brass in pocket and suddenly conditions and restrictions were being placed on the band. Only five musicians were allowed to play at one time and if this rule was breached, the stewards were under orders to escort the illegal sixth musician from the premises to dump his instrument. Under the scrutiny of CCTV cameras and six stewards and lots of heavy-handed policing, the band were very clearly made to feel they were not wanted, and disbanded.

'There was a vote at the club,' says John Hemmingham, 'and 85 per cent of the fans said they wanted the band to continue, but they took all the fun out of it.' By then they were also barred from playing at a lot of away grounds, mainly, says John, because other teams could see the inspirational effect they were having on the Wednesday players. 'Nobody ever said "No" to us until we'd blown their team away, then they wouldn't let us back in again! One of the funniest was at Everton when we were 2-0 up at half-time. In the second half they sent the police to stand in the middle of us and stop us playing. Some of the excuses were hilarious: issues of safety, our instruments could be used as offensive weapons, or we were a danger to other spectators. Wimbledon wouldn't let us in because they said people wouldn't be able to hear any important announcements on the tannoy. I had more respect for the clubs that came clean and said they couldn't let us play because we generated too much support for our team.'

Glenn Hoddle, though, is a man who loves his music. After seeing the band turn in a particularly inspirational performance when Wednesday played Arsenal, the then-England manager invited them to Wembley in 1996 to work their magic on the national team. They have been blowing their horns at every England game ever since, surviving Hoddle, Howard Wilkinson, Kevin Keegan, Peter Taylor and now Sven. With a standard line-up of five drummers, five trumpets, sax, trombone and cornet, with comedian Bernie Clifton joining them as an occasional celebrity sax player, they make quite a racket. 'Oh, we've heard it all,' says John. '"You can shove that trumpet up your arse", and all that, but so far nobody has actually done it. I usually say something like, "Well, your mouth's big enough, I'll put it in there." It's all in good fun.'

John introduced 'The Great Escape' into the repertoire in the crucial 1990 World Cup qualifier when England needed to draw with Italy in Rome to reach the finals. 'It just seemed right for that match and it completely took off. We'd all heard that Serie A was the big league in Europe and what a tremendous atmosphere they generated at matches and we just thought, "Right, we'll show them what creating an atmosphere is all about." We drew the match 0-0 and qualified. It was a great night.'

The band buy their own tickets and ask no favours from the FA but have managed to make themselves heard wherever England play – even in Poland when, refused entry, they spent the first half of the match playing outside the stadium and defying threats to arrest them. They had a few scrapes getting entry to the 2002 World Cup in Japan, too, but when England ran out to play there they were, blowing their tops. But do they really have any real effect on the players and impact on events on the pitch? 'Oh yes!' says John, sounding appalled by the question. 'We know the effect we have because managers and players tell us it does. If you have 3,000 people singing, the effect of a band like us behind them makes it so much more powerful.'

Bands of varying volume and personnel have since turned up from time to time at Charlton, Tottenham, Preston, Blackpool, Wycombe, Lincoln and Portsmouth but sadly are unlikely to reappear at the place it all started, Sheffield Wednesday. John Hemmingham remains a Wednesday fan although his loyalties are now split because he has a day job at Leeds United. So is there any chance of that mystery bugler suddenly making a reappearance, this time at Leeds? 'It wouldn't work. You can't artificially introduce *anything* into terrace culture. It has to be natural, it has to be spontaneous and it has to come from the fans themselves.'

Back at Anfield, John Hemmingham's trumpet does the business. England huff and puff but can't break Uruguay's door down and with only a few minutes to go, supposedly loyal fans start leaving in droves anticipating a 1-0 defeat. Whenever this happens I always pray for some last-minute drama that will be talked about for years so the early leavers will hear the roar of the crowd as they exit the stadium and curse themselves for ever more for missing it.

And it happens. England's best player, Joe Cole, whips the ball into the area and Peter Crouch, beanpole striker of this parish, flicks home the equaliser. The crowd isn't on the pitch but they think it's all over and it is now as substitute Shaun Wright-Phillips, the poor bugger who can't get a game for love nor money since joining Chelsea, skips down the wing, whips in a low cross and there's Joe Cole banging in the winner. We even get an attempt at a recreation of the 'Ian Wright Wright Wright' chant which used to echo around Highbury to the tune of 'Hot Hot Hot' for Shaun's step-dad Ian, but the hyphenated Phillips bit in the middle gets in the way and it tails off. No matter; our national honour has been salvaged, and the crowds exit Anfield smiling.

While I'm still in Lancashire, I decide to take in a match dripping in personal interest and nostalgia: Burnley v. Southampton. I was born a Woking fan but adopted Southampton as my professional team at the age of seven on a whimsical gesture of independence while feeling left out as the rest of the family cheered or jeered the football results being recounted on *Sports Report*. There were cheers from my dad when Charlton Athletic won, groans from my brother when Blackpool lost and a lap of honour round the living room from my mum when Swindon forced a 0-0 draw. As the results were announced one Saturday I gave an almighty cheer as Southampton's name was read out. The rest of the family looked at me in surprise but that was it, the die was cast for life; you don't change your football team.

I have had the world's best analysts working on this illogical decision to support Southampton ever since, and they have decided it was the fault of the cigarette cards. In my early years I collected the pictures of footballers that came free with the packs, and one particular cheery, red-cheeked chap wearing a red-and-white deckchair was the one I treasured above all others. His name was John Page and he was the captain of Southampton.

A year or so later my dad took me to my first professional match when Southampton came to London to play Charlton Athletic and when the players ran out I immediately searched for my cigarette card hero. These days you'd assume the plump bloke waddling out at the front of the team was a comedy mascot, and it almost scarred me for life to discover my first boyhood idol and the captain of my chosen football team was a bit of a porker. As the match kicked off he positioned himself in the centre half position just in front of the penalty area and didn't shift until half-time.

Around the same time Burnley were one of the top teams in the country, the one club competing with the all-conquering Spurs, and I developed an abiding admiration for their star players like Jimmy McIlroy, Jimmy Adamson, Ray Pointer, Alex Elder and John Connelly, and a distant fascination with the small Lancashire mill town whence they came.

So Burnley v. Southampton holds unique allure as I head for Burnley on a filthy Tuesday night. The radio says there is a pitch inspection before the game and, stopping at a service station *en route*, I see Sir Clive Woodward, the former England rugby supremo who is now doing something or other at Southampton (the most expensive work experience stint in history, as some Saints supporters claim). I get a coffee and place myself within handy reach of him hoping to grab a bit of chit chat, but Sir Clive is deeply engrossed in the longest phone call in history, chattering intently and chuckling intermittently. Who is he talking to then? Club chairman Rupert Lowe? Manager George Burley? Bernie Clifton? The Rugby Football Union? Alas, we will never know. Sir Clive suddenly snaps his phone shut, says, 'The match is definitely on!' and marches off without a glance in my direction.

The small town of Burnley (population 89,000) looms through the evening gloom, and as I park up the claret-and-blue scarves are already making their way up to Turf Moor. Far from the pretty village I had fondly imagined in childhood, Burnley is a hard-bitten former mill town still struggling to stave off poverty and make some sense of the glitzy modern world of Starbucks, internet cafés, theme pubs, fashion emporiums and fancy shoe shops. The electoral success that has been enjoyed here in recent years by the odious BNP is evidence of the racial tensions afflicting it. Yet there is huge pride in the town's football team, for its commendable catalogue of past triumphs and the identity it still provides the community in the lower reaches of the Championship. Burnley, the fans will tell you puffing out their chests, have more support percentage-wise from their home town than any other club in the country.

One of them is Boff from Chumbawamba, the anarchist band who had a No. 1 hit all over the world in 1997 (except Britain, where it only made No. 2) with their inspirational exhortation to fight back against the odds ('I get knocked down, I get up again') called 'Tubthumping'. They later achieved national infamy when they threw a bucket of iced water over the deputy Prime Minister John Prescott at the 1998 Brit Awards, sabotaged high-profile chat shows to pursue their own political agendas and donated most of their profits to various good causes.

Chumbawamba, who once recorded a song called 'How Dare They Call It Football?' attacking the Americanisation of the game, have had a long and successful, if controversial, career with many highs. But the biggest high of them all for Boff was watching his beloved Burnley team running out for matches to the sounds of 'Tubthumping'.

The crowds also used to try and sing it at matches but it didn't really work. 'It's actually really hard to sing without accompaniment,' laughs Boff. 'Even football chants have melodies, but take away the big drums and guitars and "Tubthumping" is pretty much all on one note. There's not really a tune at all.' There was even a suggestion that Chumbawamba would record an England World Cup song for the 1998 finals in France, but they dismissed the idea as 'a bit crap' and opted instead for 'Top of the World', a football anthem with an 'Olé Olé Olé Olé' chorus and a more international theme. 'It was all right,' says Boff. 'It didn't register at all here but we still get asked for it in Germany and France.'

Still a season ticket holder, Boff was a devoted member of the Turf Moor choir who would stand on the terraces singing at games. 'There were a couple of groups of us who were rivals. We were the music puffs and the other lot were the football thickies and we were in competition with each other.' It doesn't happen too often these days but Boff loves to hear the Burnley crowd sing. 'Yes I still sing at matches, especially away games where people are just out for a good time. I've a soft spot for the whole congregational thing where no one's in charge and no one tells you what key to sing it in. Mass psychosis can be dangerous but it's beautiful. I hate it now when they play music after you score a goal. Last season it was that Proclaimers song "500 Miles" which takes ages to get to the catchy bit. I refuse to join in. I won't join in when we sing "No one likes us we don't care" – it's brainless. And sometimes they sing "Tits, fanny and claret, that's why we love Burnley!" I hate that.'

They're a friendly bunch at Burnley. Alan Beecroft has been coming here for 48 years since his dad took him when he was five, and he has had a season ticket since the 1960s. 'I remember going to see us play Tottenham when 52,000 were here,' he says. 'We got to the ground three hours before kick-off to make sure we got in.' Alan describes himself as 'a gas chap', a description vague enough to have me imagining all manner of gas-related activities. He doesn't elaborate, telling me only that it's a job that's taken him all over the world resulting in the occasional – but still rare – absenteeism. 'This is a bad season,' he says, 'I've missed three away matches. I only missed two last season.'

Alan talks of Burnley's glory years as if they were yesterday. Winning the First Division title in 1960 and throwing it away the following season when they only needed a point from the last four matches but 'made a complete arse of it', allowing Ipswich Town to snatch it from their grasp. And then he's on about the 1962 FA Cup Final, which they lost 3-1 to Tottenham. 'We didn't play well at Wembley,' he says, shaking his head. 'We slipped up badly that day. I've got the video. It's still disappointing to watch it.'

Not too long afterwards Burnley started tumbling down the leagues ('Do you want to know why? Two words – John Bond') and slithered to their lowest point in 1987 when they looked destined to fall out of the Football League completely. They had to beat Orient in the last game of the season and then pray to God that either Torquay or Lincoln lost.

'I went through every possible emotion that day,' says Alan. 'I mean, we were bottom on merit; we were an *awful* team. We had 18,000 there for that match, incredible for a team bottom of the league, and they had to delay the kick-off to get everyone in. They were all there to write Burnley's epitaph. Nobody gave us a chance. Orient needed a point to get into the play-offs so it wasn't as if they didn't have anything to play for.

'There was so much emotion that day I couldn't take it all in. We were atrocious all match but there were two flashes of brilliance and we got two goals and won the game 2-1.' Lincoln were relegated. Somebody says that Ian Britton, the little Scotsman who headed the winning goal that day to save Burnley from the trapdoor and possibly bankruptcy, is at tonight's game, but if he is, he's not sharing a Bovril with me.

'This used to be the game of the working class,' says Alan, 'but that's all changing, especially in our community, which is one of the poorest places in England. The average income is one of the lowest in the country and we have high unemployment, yet you're asking people with very little disposable income to spend it on football. If you're spending your last few quid on a match you want to enjoy yourself and not get any grief, but if you stand up and start singing they whizz you out.'

We discuss the town's racial problems. 'The thing is, there is no *racial* problem,' says Alan quickly. 'What I'd say is there is no racial problem but there may be a *Pakistani* problem, because there have been problems between the English population and the Pakistani population over the years. But we've had all sorts of players of different nationalities playing for Burnley and as long as they play their hearts out and give 100 per cent nobody cares about their nationality or the colour of their skin. We've had plenty of black players who are worshipped here.'

I have barely got settled into my seat in front of Alan Beecroft when, 30 seconds into the game, something truly extraordinary occurs. Southampton score. This doesn't happen very often these days, and it only happens because Burnley defender Phil Bardsley deflects a cross from Southampton's walking scarecrow Alexander Ostlund into his own net. Even the few hundred Saints fans huddling at the opposite end seem too amazed to cheer so the goal is greeted in near-silence and Burnley swiftly return the ball to the centre circle and start again as if to say the previous 30 seconds had just been a practice and we should expunge it from the records.

It scarcely matters. The Saints players are so dazed by this unexpected turn of events that a few minutes later they stand and watch in admiration as Burnley's Andy Gray romps away from them, shimmies around the keeper and slides the ball into the net. I put the Bovril down and lean forward to absorb every second of what's shaping up to be a classic 5-5 draw.

Sadly, it doesn't happen. Parity resumed, both teams settle into a routine of kick-and-rush that gets them nowhere, and the most enjoyment comes from the lively Burnley mascot Bertie Bee's merciless impersonation of a fat steward waddling past him, not to mention the fans around me roundly abusing Ostlund for his 'hairy cornflake' appearance: 'Book the scruffy git', 'Give it to Steptoe!', 'Watch out, he's caught his beard in his bootlace', 'Put him in a skip', 'No one will go near him, he's got lice', 'Eh up, Swampy's got it.' And when he finally gets substituted: 'That's right, get him off and give him a bath.' It's infantile but I laugh like a drain.

Burnley's fans have long memories, too. They give a warm reception to Saints midfielder Richard Chaplow in respect to his warmly remembered spell as a Claret, but give the striker Grzegorz Rasiak almighty stick in response to crimes committed when he played against them for Derby County. 'Are you Drogba in disguise?' they chant as Rasiak collapses in a heap when one of the Clarets' players blows him a kiss.

At half-time I meet the extraordinary Dave Burnley, who is surely the most committed football fan in the land. Burnley have a long line of heroes and legends from Jimmy Adamson to Jimmy McIlroy, Leighton James, Willie Morgan and all, but at a club which lays claim to the closest ties with its community of any in the country they should build a statue of this bloke. A 52-year-old man of sallow cheeks with a claret-and-blue scarf drawn tightly round his neck, claret beanie hat bearing the Burnley crest on his head and a small earring dangling from his left ear, Dave hasn't missed a Burnley match in any competition for 32 years.

Actually it should be 37 years, but on April 10, 1974 after miners' strikes, train strikes and horrendous weather, Burnley snuck in a six-times postponed Wednesday night away game at Newcastle at the last minute and he didn't make it. Clearly, it still bothers him: 'We were due to play Newcastle no less than six times in a month: twice in the Texaco Cup Final, twice in the League, once in the FA Cup semi-final and once in the League Cup. They just put it in without anybody knowing, virtually.'

That apart, from Exeter to East Fife, friendlies to FA Cup ties, Wembley to Walsall, the Sherpa Vans Trophy to the Isle of Man Steam Packet Football Festival, every time the Clarets have trotted out to strut their stuff, Dave has been there urging them on. He is so devoted, in fact, that as a symbol of his lifelong betrothal when Burnley were relegated from the top division in 1976 he changed his name by deed poll from Dave Beeston to Dave Burnley.

Dave's attendance record is astonishing, but even more amazingly he doesn't come from Burnley and every home match involves a 150-mile round trip from his home in the village of Madeley, between Stoke-on-Trent and Crewe on the Staffordshire/Shropshire border. That sounds mad enough, but it's a village poorly served by public transport and Dave doesn't even drive. Today he hitchhiked to the match via Preston and has managed to arrange a lift back as far as Wolverhampton, but this isn't always the case.

In all weathers, Dave has frequently completed his long trek home from games with a two-and-a-half-hour walk from Crewe or Stoke station, finally making it back at some ungodly hour in the morning only to have to get up a couple of hours later for work. More often than he cares to remember he's not even been able to make it that far, and has had to sleep rough in railway stations, motorway services, shopping centres or on park benches. He has twice suffered pneumonia as a result. 'It took me three months to get rid of the last one with antibiotics,' he says. 'The doctor asked me, "How did you get in this state?" and I told him I'd been dossing out. He said, "Dave, your dossing days are over because next time you'll be dossing for life." Since then I've tried to be a bit more sensible about it. I've slept out a few times in the last couple of years but I've got so many contacts now that I can normally get lifts back to the Midlands.'

When all else fails, Dave cycles. To make sure he didn't miss the Boxing Day match at home against Stoke he started out on Christmas night, arrived at 8 a.m., watched the game (a 1-0 victory) and then cycled back to Stoke, getting home at midnight. The only other alternative would have been to have left on Christmas Eve and found someone to stay with in Burnley over Christmas – and don't think he's never done that, either.

'When we played at Brighton on Boxing Day we disguised ourselves as doctors at Sutton Hospital because we knew a nurse down there,' he reminisces. 'She said, "You've got to be a doctor to get in", so we went down with white coats and stethoscopes into the hospital, played Brighton on Boxing Day, spent £300, got away with it, but still lost 3-0. Unbelievable. That's all part of following Burnley; they always seem to let you down when you go through hell to get there.'

I have a million questions – not least one expressing my total bewilderment about him spending Christmas in Brighton disguised as a doctor – but the first has to be: If you live in

Staffs, Dave, with both Stoke City and Crewe Alexandra on your doorstep, *why Burnley*?

'It was in 1964 and everyone I knew were supporting teams at the top of the league,' he explains. 'My friend Reggie Bradshaw always supported whoever was top of the league. Liverpool were playing Tottenham and whoever won went top of the league. Liverpool won and I thought I'd beat Reg and tell him I supported Liverpool. So I knocked on his door but as soon as he opened the door he said, "I support Liverpool now, who do you support?" and stood back with a self-satisfied grin on his face. And I saw a picture of Bob Lord [the famously bombastic ex-Burnley chairman] on the back page of the *Daily Express* chastising all the Leeds United players for a big bust-up when they had lost to Leeds at Elland Road, so I said, "Well, I support Burnley." It was a throwaway comment. It meant I supported Burnley *that week*. But Reg went to Liverpool and is still a season ticket-holder there, and I'm a season ticket-holder for the 36th year at Burnley.'

The decision to change his surname by deed poll to Burnley the week after the club were relegated from the top division in 1976 was, he says a trifle dramatically, akin to formally marrying the club. 'It was me saying, "Now, you don't say anything about Burnley, because if you insult Burnley you insult my name." That was it. Everyone became more respectful from there on because they then knew how serious I was about it.'

Dave has watched them play in every division in the Football League in that time, but still winces when he recalls the 1980s, when Burnley were in the basement and nearly disappeared completely. 'That was the hardest period of my life,' he says solemnly.' The team were having a tough time and the Tories were in control. It was so bad that … well, I'd never give up on Burnley, but I was jumping into grounds and couldn't really care less. I was drinking to excess to try to forget everything; still following the team but drinking so much before a game to anaesthetise myself because for the seven years in that bottom division the standard of play was *terrible*.'

Come on, Dave, admit it: you must have occasionally been tempted to give it a miss and stay at home in front of a fire. He looks hurt I should even consider it. 'I'd never do that. Once you attach yourself to a team that's it, that's *your* team. But every time we got relegated I had to leave the country because I knew I'd get into fights with people around Stoke. So I'd leave the country alone and travel around, sleeping on trains. And then I'd come back refreshed and looking forward to the new season.'

A low rumble from the stands above us indicate the teams are out for the second half and Dave is away like a shot, determined not to miss a second. Sitting a few rows back I watch him closely. He's not animated, but he's concentrating intently, leaning forward in his seat and absorbing everything happening on the pitch. Which isn't a great deal. Most of the action occurs around the Saints goalmouth but, seemingly doing everything possible to avoid paying Brentford a few extra bob for Paul Smith, Southampton are blooding yet another new goalkeeper in Kevin Miller, who pulls off a string of startling saves. The match fizzles out at 1-1.

Dave tells me that he will be mourning the anniversary of that last missed game against Newcastle as he does every year by wearing the three-piece denim suit given to him in 1969, the year he started supporting the Clarets. 'I've expanded a bit but the suit's expanded with me and the original denim jacket is covered in stains, blood, sweat and tears.' So is this man the true heartbeat of British football or a sad nutter? He shakes my hand warmly and disappears to find his lift back to the Midlands. I watch him go with a broad smile, my belief in the true spirit of football at least partly restored.

I walk back into the town and retire to the Sparrow Hawk Hotel for a pint, giving a wide berth to a loud, motley group of blokes holding court in the corner. Through the hubbub I hear someone say, 'Matt Le Tissier was the second-best player I ever saw pull on a Southampton shirt.' Time seems to stand still as I await the next bit. 'And the best was … Terry Paine.'

I'm over there like a shot and shaking his hand. That first professional match I ever saw between Charlton and Southampton disabused me of my heroic images of John 'Tubs' Page but it gave me a new idol entirely in Terry Paine. So now me and my new best mate Brian spend the next 45 minutes telling each other how wonderful Painey was – sending pinpoint 40-yard passes from one side of the pitch to the other, raining crosses on to the head of Ron Davies so he scored 30 goals a season, and scoring some cracking goals himself. He even played in the 1966 World Cup Finals in the 2-0 victory against Mexico, and made a record 713 league appearances for Southampton in 18 years at the club. We get some more drinks in and toast the great Terry Paine. 'Mind you,' says Brian, 'he was a complete arsehole.' Painey was actually a Tory councillor at one point so Brian's probably right.

We disagree over the third best player to pull on a Saints shirt. Brian says David Armstrong and I say Mick Channon, and we discuss the 1963 FA Cup semi-final when Saints lost 1-0 at Villa Park due to the Long Hand of the Law. 'People go on about Maradona and Drogba,' says Brian, 'but the worst handball goal of all time was the one that Denis Law punched in against us in 1963. It was shameful.'

Some Burnley lads join in and I discover that former Burnley player John Connelly used to have a chippy up the road and one of them knew another ex-Claret, Brian O'Neil, who gave him some good advice about football: 'If you can't get the player, get the ball.' Somebody else reckons that 60 per cent of the world's consumption of Benedictine happens in Burnley and that Kevin Whately from *Inspector Morse*, weatherman John Ketley and some bloke on *Antiques Roadshow* are all Burnley fans. So is Alistair Campbell, but everyone hates him.

Another Southampton supporter claims to have been the last person to score a penalty at Sunderland's old ground, Roker Park, after being invited to take part in a fans' half-time shoot-out even though he was so pissed he couldn't see the goal. That's when the bloke in the kilt turns up and starts abusing everyone and talking bollocks and the manager gets irritable and it seems best to leave. We hug and giggle and say, stuff your poshos and executive boxes, *this* is what football's all about. Does anyone remember what the score was tonight? Does anyone *care*? I haven't felt this euphoric since Abba won the Eurovision Song Contest.

The next morning, my head hurts.

— CHAPTER 8 —

The Cantona Effect

'I feel close to the rebelliousness and vigour of the youth here. Perhaps time will separate us, but nobody can deny that here, behind the windows of Manchester, there is an insane love of football, of celebration and of music.'

Eric Cantona

Before I talk to you – where you from, and who do you support?'

Pete Boyle isn't aggressive but he is certainly forthright. I mumble something about Southampton. *'Southampton?'* he snarls. 'Stokes, 1976, what a *fluke* that was!'

Pete, my good man, I say, suddenly flooded by memories of that momentous May Day in 1976 when the late Bobby Stokes scuffed a shot under the body of Alex Stepney to cause one of the biggest shocks in FA Cup Final history as the humble Saints dismantled high-flying Manchester United to send me tumbling into a passionate embrace with a woman I'd never met before. Pete, there was no fluke about it; we beat you fair and square. 'Yeah, *right*,' says Pete. 'So what do you want?' A chat, I say, some merry banter. About your songs, and stuff. 'OK,' he says, 'but you'll have to buy me a pizza and a pint.' It seems like a fair deal.

Pete Boyle is the king of terrace anthems and an Old Trafford icon. He is a legend in fact – not least in his own head. Pete is responsible for a vast repertoire of songs and chants embraced so wholeheartedly by Manchester United fans that he has now released six tapes and CDs of his work and has even got a backing band and started playing gigs performing them.

There are paradoxes here, of course. Everyone has an opinion on Manchester United. And, unless you're from the red side of Manchester – or one of the other hotbeds of their fan base in the Midlands, Surrey or the West Country – it tends to be negative. Roy Keane's infamous 'prawn sandwich' outburst a few years ago about the day-tripper brigade deadening the atmosphere at Old Trafford seemed in one damning phrase to encapsulate the corporate mentality threatening to slice the heart not just out of Manchester United but the modern game generally.

Before Chelsea came arrogantly strutting past them waving their bags of gold, Manchester United were the self-styled biggest club in the world, reviled by the rest of the football fraternity, partly out of jealousy, partly out of distaste for their perceived greed and self-importance and partly out of genuine concern for where they were taking us. See, United have been embroiled in (and in some cases initiated) some of the worst excesses of commercialism and merchandising now dominating the big clubs. All that bad publicity incurred over exploiting kids with the regularity with which they changed their shirt designs now seems small fry against the horrendous juggernaut of hard-headed money men wresting control of the game without a care for the history, tradition and cultural identity so central to the ethos of the football fan.

Yet whatever else, Manchester United have always had a clear sense of football history and their own not-inconsiderable role in it. But now United has been bought, on borrowed money by a weird American bloke with a dodgy haircut whose last plaything was an American football team. As Chumbawamba would say, how *dare* they call it football?

What do the Glazers know of Billy Meredith and Johnny Carey and Sir Matt Busby and Duncan Edwards and Tommy Taylor and Dennis Viollet and Roger Byrne and Bobby Charlton and Bill Foulkes and Pat Crerand and Harry Gregg and Denis Law and Nobby Stiles and George Best and Eric Cantona and the Munich air disaster and even David Beckham? I think of the fans who have rebelled to start all over again with FC United, and once again want to shake the hand of every one of them. These are my thoughts as I drive past Old Trafford, where stewards, police and burger vans are already gathering several hours before tonight's kick-off, as I make my way to Pizza Hut to meet Pete Boyle.

He arrives in a taxi, talking at 300mph, pumping my hand vigorously while telling me about the morning's gym session and the diet that's keeping him trim and waving at passers by. He's in the middle of telling me about dropping out of uni, his new job in property management and jibing me about Southampton having to rely on an own goal by a United loanee Phil Bardsley to get a point against Burnley last night when the taxi driver returns with the mobile phone he's left in the back. He shakes the driver's hand, gives him a hug and then shakes my hand again. By the time we find a seat in the Pizza Hut I'm already exhausted.

Pete is talking about Cantona now, one of his prime heroes, and I ask if he's ever met him. This leads to the first in a long series of anecdotes: 'I always used to get ideas for songs when I was in the bath, being a failed rock star. Somebody said I should record some of them. It wasn't like now when you can make CDs in your bedroom so I went through the *Yellow Pages* to find a studio and went for the cheapest one. And I went in and recorded *Songs From a Bath Tub* in a studio in Manchester called Spirit, which is famous for having 808 State doing their big "Pacific" single and that dance song "Insanity" by Oceanic. Oh, and my favourite band The Smiths used to rehearse there.

'But – and this is the weird bit – the landlord of the pub where we drink in Manchester, the Peveril of the Peak, used to get his accordion out sometimes and he'd play all the old United songs and we'd sing along. So I said to him, "Would you come down to the studio and play on this tape I'm doing?" and he agreed. So on a dead quiet Tuesday night in February 1994 we were upstairs in the Peveril on the Peak, rehearsing. It's a proper old Irish pub – the Gallaghers were always in there

when they were starting Oasis. We were in the flat above prac-
tising this song about Cantona when the landlady comes up and
says, "Boys, there's somebody downstairs you might want to
see." So we go down, and Eric's in there playing table football.

'Now, I'm not shy, but I'm just like *staring*. I couldn't speak.
I'm usually quite cool if I meet anyone famous and there's only
two who make me feel like that – Eric and Fergie. This guy
behind the bar, Danny, he couldn't believe Pete Boyle being so
quiet, so he goes over to Eric and says, "See 'im over there, he
writes songs about you."'

The encounter may not have exactly been the start of a bosom
friendship but Cantona read the lyrics about himself, nodded
approvingly and effectively gave the royal assent. Boyle's
homages to Cantona subsequently lifted the roof at Old
Trafford: 'We'll drink a drink a drink/To Eric the king, the king
the king/He's the leader of our football team' to the tune of
'Lily the Pink'; 'Ooh aah Cantona, say ooh aah Cantona'; 'On
the first day of Christmas my true love gave to me/12 Cantonas,
11 Cantonas, 10 Cantonas …' and so on and so on.

When a bunch of film-makers decided to make a documentary about Boyle as he gigged around Ireland they even
managed to grab an interview with Cantona about Pete, and the
great Frenchman spent 10 minutes acclaiming a fellow artist
and creative talent. For his part, Boyle launched a determined
campaign to give Eric moral support through his various
clashes with authority. He turned up at the court cases
following his infamous kung-fu assault on a fan after his red
card at Crystal Palace and even appeared on *The Big Breakfast* on
TV to offer moral support and argue his corner. When Cantona
returned to Old Trafford for the Munich memorial match in
1998, Pete blagged his way into the VIP section, chairman
Martin Edwards intervened to stop him being thrown out and
Cantona welcomed him like a long-lost relative. Moments like
that, he says, make it all worthwhile.

Pete was raised ten minutes from Old Trafford and was about
five when his dad first took him to a match. He was deemed too

young to face the heartbreak wreaked on United by Bobby Stokes in that wondrous 1976 FA Cup Final but his dad relented and took him, aged seven, to his first final the following year when United went back to Wembley. Jimmy Greenhoff deflected a Lou Macari shot past Ray Clemence for the winning goal in a 2-1 victory that prevented Liverpool achieving the League, Cup and European Cup treble.

Surprisingly soon after that he started going to home games on his own and in his spare time hung around Old Trafford just because it made him feel good. One time he saw tickets being advertised for a League Cup second round match at Coventry City and, with money in his pocket, bought one. He was still barely 11 and his mum and dad were horrified by the idea of little Pete going alone on a coach to a night game in the darkest Midlands, but he kicked up such a stink that they eventually relented. 'I wouldn't let *my* kids do it,' he laughs.

Come the day of the match, Pete got to the ground at 11 a.m. – four hours before the coach was due to leave. The windscreen shattered at Spaghetti Junction and they had to change coaches with the hard lads at the back swearing blind they'd been ambushed by a Coventry posse. The big fat bloke designated as Pete's minder for the night gave him a butty to cheer him up. 'It was a rubbish game,' says Pete ruefully. 'For years I remembered it being 0-0 and I've usually got a great memory for results, but I looked it up recently and we actually got beat 1-0. The highlight for us was a disallowed Jimmy Greenhoff goal.'

With the precedent set, he started going regularly to away games as well as all the homes. He was once arrested for swearing at West Bromwich Albion but otherwise kept clear of the troubles that afflicted football through the 1980s: 'There were bad incidents but I was always clued up enough to steer clear of them.' Early on he attached himself to the singers in the United Road Paddock, which in the early 1980s had overtaken the Stretford End as the focal point of United's vocal support.

From an early age Boyle had written poetry and had even won prizes, so once he had become an integral part of the United choir and shown he wasn't backward about coming forward when it came to initiating the singing, it was a natural step to start inventing his own songs. 'We'll drink a drink a drink to Eric the king the king the king' was effectively his first Old Trafford hit, though it was in essence a re-working of an old theme, a former Reds hero Denis Law having been similarly fêted 20 years earlier. 'Wolves used to sing it to Derek Dougan, and Man City will claim it was their song because they used to sing it to Colin Bell, but *I* know it was United,' he claims. 'I recycled it for Eric but I added a load of new verses to it. At most pre-match games I'd make them raise their glasses and each "Weeee'lllll" gets longer and longer. I remember singing it with about 2,000 people outside this pub at Wembley and this policeman came up to me afterwards and said "That's fantastic".'

One of his newer successes, inspired by The Clash's 'English Civil War', is a homage to United midfielder John O'Shea, and right here in Pizza Hut he starts singing it: 'When Johnny goes marching down the wing/O'Shea, O'Shea/When Johnny goes marching down the wing/O'Shea, O'Shea/When Johnny goes marching down the wing/The Stretford End will fucking sing/ Cause we all know that Johnny's gonna score.' Our waitress looks mildly shocked.

'In the 2003 title season we played Charlton in the last home game of the season and for about 20 minutes there were about 40,000 people singing it. It started off in the Stretford End and gradually built up. At one stage Nicky Butt went up to O'Shea and said, "This is YOU!" I've met John O'Shea a couple of times and he's buzzing about it.' Pete recorded the ditty with a band and sang it in his best punk voice and there was talk of releasing it as a single, but it didn't happen and rock stardom must wait a little longer.

Like all new material he tried the John O'Shea song out first in a United pub, the Bishop Blaze, for about six weeks before taking it to a couple of away matches. If the song proves itself and achieves the required response at away games, then and only then will it be deemed ready for consumption at Old

Trafford. The romantic notion of these terrace anthems being made up on the spot and sung spontaneously by an anonymous terrace genius takes a sharp dive. 'Well you try making up a song about Djemba Djemba!' Pete exclaims. Occasionally, though, the spontaneous verse does still emerge in a moment of inspiration.

'Sometimes, right,' he says, 'I've made up a song off the cuff. You know that quote about Gary Neville hating Scousers? That came from me. I interviewed him for a fanzine and it came out. It wasn't like a nasty anti-Scouser thing, it was just in the context of being a Manchester United fan and Manchester United fans hate Scousers. Most Liverpool fans would respect that. About three weeks later we played Liverpool and this scummy journalist completely plagiarised it and there was this headline in the *Mirror* saying "NEVILLE: I HATE SCOUSERS!"

'I got a mate who is a solicitor to get an apology from the *Mirror* and I sent it to Gary. I know him anyway and we had a bit of banter about it. He said, "They all hate me cos of you!" and I said, "They all hate you anyway, Gary!" Anyway, about a week later we were playing Leeds and it just came into my head and I started singing, "Gary Neville is a Red, Gary Neville is a red, he hates Scousers." A lot of people have copied it since.'

I tell Pete about Dave Burnley, who hasn't missed a Burnley match of any description for 32 years and he's impressed. 'You've got to respect that,' he says. 'Is he a single man? See, when I went to Southampton in 1986 and we were really terrible and had a load of overpaid players who really didn't care, I did question my sanity and think "I really should get a girlfriend". But it's great looking back now to know I went through that with them.'

As it happens Pete *did* get a girlfriend – he has two children, Sophie Emma Giggs McClair Boyle and Laura Jane Cantona Boyle – and is now married to an equally fanatical United fan, a schoolteacher called Helen who he met on a coach going to London for an away game against Fulham. The now retired Brian McClair is the subject of one of Boyle's finest efforts, which he's sung to the man personally to the tune of the Elvis hit '(Marie's the Name) His Latest Flame':

> A very old man, some say today
> But he's given all he's got for years
> Sweated blood and many tears
> McClair's the name of United's flame.

There's a commendable morality to Pete's attitude to terrace anthems. He's written his fair share of diatribes about Liverpool and Manchester City over the years, but unless he comes up with something completely irresistible like 'Gary Neville is a Red, he hates Scousers', he prefers to reserve the songs demeaning the opposition for when they are actually playing them. He prefers wit and humour to gratuitous insult and recoils at some of the cruder couplets his fellow creators come up with, being particularly disturbed by a newly adopted song lauding United's outstanding South Korean international Ji-Sung Park to the tune of our old friend 'Lord of the Dance':

> Park Park wherever you may be
> You eat dogs in your own country
> But it could be worse, you could be Scouse
> Eating rats in your council house.

'It's clever, but I don't think he'd like it, know what I mean?' he says, and promptly sings me his rival Park song to the tune of 'Hark The Herald Angels Sing':

> He used to show his football skills abroad for PSV
> But then he heard the shout go up U-N-I-T-E-D
> Park now hear United sing, for he has got no fear
> The greatest ever footballer to come from South Korea.

'That's better innit?' Yes, Pete, *much* better. We talk about the rival fans who try to out-sing United as a matter of honour and he is predictably scathing about most of them. 'Newcastle and

Liverpool make a lot of noise, but can't sustain it and only tend to sing for the first and last five minutes of matches. Most of the others sing the same tired old songs slagging United off. Few have any originality and none have anything like the repertoire of United.' He grudgingly compliments Tottenham for their unique, emotional, slowed-down version of their own 'Glory Glory Hallelujah' anthem, but he reserves his highest praise for an unlikely recipient.

'At Old Trafford only one team stands out, and that's Wolves. They were the only ones who came here and sang their own original songs. Not once did they come down to the level of everybody else. Some great European fans have come. Greeks and Serbians and Croatians, all mad as hatters but great fun. See, Newcastle, Liverpool, Arsenal, all these people, they all sing "Hey Baby". We don't. We sing songs to Joy Division and Inspiral Carpets tunes. And if anyone tries to do that "Easy" chant and clap near us they get a slap.'

He's good company is Pete Boyle, and I reckon he has a valuable role in talking the hind legs off a donkey and stirring up the troops at Old Trafford to sing their hearts out for the lads and retain some of the true values of football in the face of corporate assault from all sides. Pete confesses that when the whole Glazer takeover issue arose he was tempted to go with the rebels who set up FC United. But in the end, like the master who had to put the gun to the head of faithful Old Shep, he just couldn't do it.

'I had sleepless nights about it,' he reflects. 'I admire the people behind FC United who know they're going to be there for the long haul, but as far as I'm concerned it's still supporting another club. I just love United. I love walking down to the ground, everything about it. I did my bit. I cancelled my MUTV subscription, I cancelled my club credit card, I cancelled my Cup subscription, I didn't go to one Champions League or FA Cup game at Old Trafford this season, I didn't even go to the final in Cardiff. I went down there, I ran three coaches, but I didn't go inside to the match.

I've done all that, but I just can't give up my season ticket. I love United too much.'

I love United too much. It's a magnificent reason to stay.

Later, I decide to accept Pete's invite to join the pre-match warm-up at the Bishop Blaze. Not that it's easy to get in. A gorilla on the door demands to see your match ticket and scrutinises it intently before reluctantly stepping aside to reveal a swarming mass of bodies wedged nose-to-nose from one end of the pub to the other. The bar is totally inaccessible, though anyone with SAS training can make it to the Stella trolley (£2.50 a can). But this is all about the singing – a sweaty, seething mass of voices passionately belting out an endless succession of United anthems, going seamlessly from one to the next. It isn't pretty, but dear Lord, it's powerful.

They're singing 'The Red Flag' now, and unlike Chelsea's colour-blind abomination, this Bishop Blaze version is somehow worthy of Jim Connell and the London dock strikers and the condemned South African miners and Chicago anarchists and Russian nihilists who once sang it:

> United's flag is deepest red
> It shrouded all our Munich dead
> Before their limbs grew stiff and cold
> Their heart's blood dyed its every fold
> Then raise United's banner high
> Beneath its shade we'll live and die
> So keep the faith and never fear
> We'll keep the Red Flag flying here.

The whole place is singing and the emotional impact is stunning – the cocky nouveau riche Chelsea mob should be marched in here, handcuffed to the Stella trolley and told to listen and learn. They even purloin 'Blaydon Races', a song inextricably associated with Newcastle United, and make it sound like it never had another life except right here, right now, in this heaving, sweating pub:

Oh me lads you should have seen us coming
Fastest team in the league just to see us winning
All the lads and lasses with smiles upon their faces
Walking down the Warwick Road
To see Matt Busby's aces …

The pub is yelling 'You fat bastard' at Pete Boyle but he merely smiles benevolently, lifts his T-shirt to reveal his newly gym-trained stomach and launches into a very funny song about Steven Gerrard's annual personal dilemma over whether or not to leave Liverpool for Chelsea, followed by a wonderfully sarcastic 'He's Got the Whole World In His Hands' parody aimed at Man City. Then he's leading his flock into his two favourite United songs: 'Pride of All Europe' ('We're the pride of all Europe, the cock of the north/We hate the Scousers and the Cockneys of course' to the tune of 'Just One of Those Songs') and 'Whenever I See United Play' set to 'Dirty Old Town'.

Ewan MacColl originally wrote 'Dirty Old Town' as an evocative snapshot of his own hometown Salford, not too far from here and Boylie stays faithful to MacColl's air of reflective nostalgia as he catalogues the story of his life with United:

First saw the Reds in days long gone by
The team was grand and the fans, oh my
So proud back then as I am today
Whenever I see United play.

It almost makes you wish you were a Manchester United fan. *Almost*. Then the Bishop Blaze suddenly starts to empty and I remember there's a football match to be viewed. As far as I'm concerned, the £26 I've paid for the ticket is already money well spent for the cultural education I have experienced in the Bishop Blaze. So I leave the pub and battle past the Lou Macari fish and chip shop to make my way into the Theatre of Dreams.

Tonight's opponents are West Ham United, a club with a long

and proud fan tradition of its own, and their fans are already giving a good account of themselves as I finally nail the staircase to the sky for my seat in the gods through the sea of gormless stewards. It's an historic night as 69,522 people gather in the stadium – a Premier League record – with the opening of a new tier of the stand, and there is an air of celebration around the place.

Enjoying a good season that is defying all the smart money on yesterday's promotion heroes being today's cannon fodder, the Hammers waste no time in giving their own famous anthem an airing. They sang 'I'm Forever Blowing Bubbles' when Bobby Moore led them out at Wembley in 1964 and Ronnie Boyce headed in a stoppage-time winner for a 3-2 victory over Preston in the FA Cup Final. This was the era when Merseybeat boomed, teenagers were invented and youth culture was taken seriously for the first time. England swung and the sight of Hammers fans leaving their suits and ties at home and downing the old-fashioned rattles to link arms and sway as they lifted the roof with a daft old music hall song ushered in a whole new raucous era of terrace songs and organised chanting. It was one of the first times that supporters had burst into spontaneous song at a Cup Final without being hectored by a man in a white coat.

West Ham's association with 'Bubbles', however, dates back much further than 1964. The song itself was officially written in 1919 by a Tin Pan Alley songwriting team of James Brockman, Nat Vincent and James Kendis, together with John Kellette. It became one of the era's most popular waltzes and was popularised in Britain by an actress/singer from Birmingham called Dorothy Ward. The song became a music hall favourite while Dorothy and her husband, Shaun Glenville, established a niche for themselves in panto. Shaun, a hard-drinking Irishman, played the pantomime dames while the delectable Dorothy was the country's leading principal boy. Churchill was said to lust after her, and while Shaun was in the pub Dorothy indulged the fruits of her success – Rolls Royces and expensive jewellery – and lived to the ripe old age of 96.

How 'Bubbles' fell into the hands of West Ham is a matter of conjecture. Contrary to common belief, it certainly wasn't aired at the famous first Wembley FA Cup Final in 1923 when Bolton Wanderers won 2-0 and the official Hammers song, according to the song sheets distributed beforehand, was 'Till We Meet Again', a sentimental First World War song by Raymond Egan and Richard Whiting.

There are plenty of theories, though. Being a music hall favourite, 'Bubbles' was a popular number at the piano sing-alongs for which London's East End pubs were so famous, and it wouldn't have been a giant leap for the working man to transfer the spirit of hope and aspiration encompassed by the song to the terraces at the Boleyn Ground, Upton Park. It was certainly played over the tannoy in 1927 when the Hammers already saw it as 'our song'. Some claim it was first sung in honour of a West Ham player who resembled the child in the famous Millais 'Bubbles' painting.

It may also have had a nudge from Corney Beal. The head-master of the local Park School, Beal was a mate of Hammers coach and manager Charlie Paynter and also had a talent for rhymes. He'd make up verses honouring any of the school players who performed particularly well and encourage the spectators to sing them to the 'Bubbles' tune. Clearly the Pete Boyle of the 1920s, Corney Beal is almost certainly the man who introduced Hammers fans to the idea of singing 'I'm Forever Blowing Bubbles' in praise of their team.

It's not the oldest football song, though. The curator of rare books in the National Library of Scotland came across a song thought to have been published in the 1880s called 'Dooley Fitba Club', written by James Currin and sung by a J.C. McDonald: 'Noo ye a'ken my big brither Jock/His name is Johnny Shaw/Well he's lately jined a fitba' club/For he's daft about fitba',' sang old J. C. After that, the trail runs a bit thin. There was a Dooley Swifts team in Scotland but the Dooley is likely to have been a fantasy team, 'dooley' like 'doolally' being a slang word for crazy, derived from dolorous. The 'Dooley

Fitba Club' song actually got in the pop charts, albeit in radically different form, under the guise of 'Football Crazy' ('he's footba' crazy, he's footba' mad, the footba' has taken awa' the wee bit o'sense he had') by Scottish folk duo Robin Hall & Jimmie McGregor in the 1960s.

Other early commercial recordings about the beautiful game included the Wembley crowd singing 'Abide With Me' at the 1927 Arsenal v. Fulham FA Cup Final, 'Pass Shoot Goal' by Gracie Fields from 1931, and the Sydney Kyte Orchestra's 'I Do Like To See a Game of Football' from 1932.

Another early one was 'Tip Top Tottenham Hotspur', which was released by the Totnamites to celebrate Spurs' double in 1961 and sounds like a football version of the theme from 'Top Cat': 'Hooray for the double and let's heave it up/One drink for the League and another one for the Cup'. The song even turned up on a cult 1990s three-volume album *Bend It* next to oddities like a John Charles vocal and fan songs from the relative obscur-ity of Fisher Athletic, Doncaster Rovers and Plymouth Argyle. The teams, the tracks and the whole style were assembled seemingly at random to demonstrate a social phenomenon rather than any artistic merit.

El Records' Mike Alway, the man who put the album together, remains insistent that 'Tip Top Tottenham' is a classic of the genre: 'It was extraordinary – Victor Sylvester with jazz guitar and very, very classy. I like the idea of putting it next to John Charles, who had a big bass voice and sang stuff like "16 Tons" and made four singles after he went to Juventus. I found some good foreign stuff too. When you hear a football song from Seville or Madrid you want it to sound like Seville or Madrid, and you want a Millwall record to sound like Millwall – you know, a bit threatening. But from the 1980s that stopped happening and they started using rock groups and they all sounded like Trevor Horn and crap like that. That's when the "Here We Go Here We Go Here We Go" mentality crept in and football songs stopped being interesting.'

Alway cites the case of Clyde: 'They were run by an old Scottish family and the club had been in the family for generations. One of them sent me this record they'd done and it was amazing. There were about 350 people in the crowd but they had this club song 'Bully Wee Clyde' and when they beat Forfar 3-0 to get promotion the whole crowd was singing this song and it was amazing.

'The really great years were 1966-1970 and then it stopped being about real supporters and became about clubs trying to cash in. 'Blue Is the Colour' for Chelsea and 'Good Old Arsenal' were the beginning of the end. Music is one of the reasons that footballers are making so much money today. We made them pop stars and we should be so ashamed.'

Norwich City always claim ownership of the oldest fans' song still in existence. The popular belief is that Albert T. Smith, became a Norwich director in 1905 and wrote 'On the Ball City' specifically for fans to sing at matches. Other historians, however, claim that Smith was merely a conduit and that the song actually pre-dates the formation of Norwich City in 1902. Various local clubs like Swifans, Catton, Caley and Norwich Teachers all laid claim to it as their club song, with the words adapted to suit whichever team was playing (the Teachers sang, 'On the ball Teachers, never mind your features'). Albert Smith sang it at various events, including a celebration to mark Norwich City's launch into professional football. A report in the *Eastern Daily Press* described the song as 'the popular war cry of the clubbers'.

'Oh yes, we still sing it,' Phil Harris of the Norwich City Supporters Trust tells me. 'It has rung around the San Siro and Munich's Olympic Stadium as well as Wembley.' Yet the words don't exactly trip off the tongue and lend themselves to mass terrace singing:

> On the days to call, which we have left behind
> Our boyhood's glorious game
> And our youthful vigour has declined
> With its mirth and its lonesome end
> You will think of the time, the happy time

Its memories fond recall
When in the bloom of your youthful prime
We've kept upon the ball.

Kick off, throw in, have a little scrimmage
Keep it low, a splendid rush, bravo, win or die
On the ball, City, never mind the danger
Steady on, now's your chance
Hurrah! We've scored a goal!

Norwich's amazing run to the FA Cup semi-finals in 1959 also, years later, produced the outstanding, understated 'Ballad of Crossan & Bly' by Paul Wyatt. This was not only a eulogy to the Third Division club's two heroic strikers who had caused the downfall of giants like Manchester United, Spurs and Sheffield United, it also captured a schoolboy's pain as a dream dies, along with some pertinent political points:

You can keep your 4-2-4, your lying deep, your sponsored gear
Your million-pound prima donnas in fancy shorts and puffed up
    hair
They get £1,000 a week, no wonder the game's gone wrong
Who'll take their kid to stand in a cage where a load of thugs
    belong?

You can keep your coloured playbacks, your electric scores in
    digital time
I'll just have my memories of 1959
And the yellow and green army reaching for the sky
Which'll always be the year of Crossan and Bly.

Back in the Theatre of Dreams, the row of empty seats next to me are suddenly filled by a jolly bunch of sweaty, puffed-out late-comers from Yeovil. The largest of the lot plops himself next to me and announces that he's the chairman of the Yeovil branch of the United Supporters Club or something and they've all come up in the coach. 'It's £50 for the coach and a ticket for the match. Not bad, eh?' he says. 'Ronaldo was our player of the year last season and we got to meet him. Good, eh?' Very good. What did he say? 'Oh, he didn't say much – he just stood there smiling, really. But we had our pictures taken with him and he signed loads of autographs.'

I hear Yeovil aren't bad these days, I mumble, have you ever thought of going there? You know, support your local team? Or even ... *Southampton*? 'Oh no. I've always been a Manchester United fan since I was a nipper. It's great here, innit? Good value for the money. I mean, they're putting up the prices next season but only by a couple of quid.'

On the pitch, things are looking lively. Darren Fletcher hits the post for United, Ronaldo threatens to cause mayhem, Park is sensational and there's a visible quivering among the West Ham players every time the ball goes near Rooney. Yet the Hammers captain and midfield dynamo Nigel Reo-Coker looks the best player on the pitch, Matthew Etherington panics the red backline with a series of surging runs and Marlon Harewood looks mean enough to blast anything that comes near him into the back of the net and ask questions later.

The most exciting battle, though, is between the fans. Up the M6 in their thousands, the West Ham faithful praise Pardew, conga for Reo-Coker, blow their bubbles for the lads and go on about how West Ham won the World Cup for England in 1966 through Moore, Peters and Hurst. I can see Pete Boyle some way below me on his feet, waving his arms around and shaking like a testifying southern preacher, exhorting his people to greater heights of noise. They instantly respond, drowning the Hammers with a full repertoire of their greatest hits.

On the stroke of half-time Park launches a spectacular run down the right wing, whips the ball into the box and there's van Nistelrooy clipping it past West Ham keeper Shaka Hislop, thereby igniting a short, sharp burst of 'Ruudi Ruudi Ruudi Ruudi Ruudi van Nistelrooy' to Culture Club's 'Karma Chameleon'.

United are in complete control in the second half and the

West Ham fans wilt along with their team, waving the white flag long before the end as a triumphant Boyle goes into over-drive to remember the good, the bad and the ugly. Out come the Cantona songs, the salutes to the Busby Babes and George Best and Denis Law along with a vigorous gesture of faith in current stars who have been wounded in battle. The injured Alan Smith's name echoes around the old stadium, and then they launch into 'You are my Solskjaer, my Ole Solskjaer/You make me happy when skies are grey/Oh Alan Shearer was fuckin' dearer, please don't take my Solskjaer away' to the tune of 'You Are My Sunshine'.

Gary Neville isn't playing tonight, but he isn't left out, the crowd joining in with such relish to the 'He hates Scousers' song that you know it's one of their favourites. They even make it to the verses about his sister, who is an international in her own sport: 'Tracey Neville's off her head, off her head, off her head/Tracey Neville's off her head, she plays netball.' And then their dad: 'Neville Neville is their dad, is their dad, is their dad, Neville Neville is their dad …' These are all rendered to the tune of 'London Bridge Is Falling Down'.

I begin to lose all interest in the match itself and instead resort to studying Pete and his mates in full flow. They've got the American Tim Howard in goal today and I'm rather keen to hear the song about him that pays particular attention to his medical condition of Tourette's Syndrome with its F-word overload. Alas, if they're thinking about giving it an airing, all attention is drawn away by the emergence of Ryan Giggs off the substitutes bench. Rooney may have overtaken him now, but for class, consistency and flair, Giggs has surely been the finest British player since George Best. The very sight of him running on to the pitch ignites the crowd into 'Giggs Will Tear You Apart Again' to the tune of Joy Division's 'Love Will Tear Us Apart'. The beautiful, disquieting song gathers momentum with haunting precision around the stadium, upping a gear and almost mirroring the play on the pitch as Giggs gets the ball and takes off on one of his trademark dribbles. My heart's leaping when I hear the tune, so heaven knows what it does to Giggs.

Then the ancient Sheringham comes on for West Ham and the United fans are up again, cheering one of their departed heroes: 'Oh Teddy Teddy, Teddy Teddy Teddy Teddy Sheringham'. By contrast, the West Ham supporters barely raise a smattering of hopeful applause in forlorn encouragement of the old master to pull something out of the hat and win them a point. He doesn't, and United win 1-0.

I sit in my car stuck in traffic in the Chester Road immediately outside Old Trafford for an hour or so after the game, keeping a wary eye on the coach just ahead and wondering if it's heading for Yeovil. I imagine the occupants are all sitting around gazing at Cristiano Ronaldo's signed photos. I watch the gleeful United supporters dancing down the street chattering about the game as I listen to the West Ham fans moaning on the radio phone-in about the Manchester United fans who want the club to sign Nigel Reo-Coker. And in my head a tune is playing: 'Gary Neville is a Red/HE HATES SCOUSERS!'

I mean, I loathe Gary Neville and I can't stand Manchester United. Tell me this isn't happening …

— CHAPTER 9 —

You're Only Here for the Whisky

'We hate Coca Cola, we hate Fanta too
For we're the Tartan Army and we drink Irn Bru'
Scotland fans

It seemed like a good idea at the time.

If you *really* want to know about the extremes of following football then go north, my friend. And keep going. Don't stop until you've dropped off the end. Then climb back up the cliff and find a football match. There and *only* there will you find the true meaning of football for football's sake and devoted fans displaying unconditional love. Well, that's what the voices in my head were saying, anyway.

So I head for John O'Groats. There has got to be a football team in John O'Groats. There *is*, but apparently it doesn't count: something about a summer league and kickabouts in the park and jumpers for goal posts and not being affiliated to the Scottish FA. If you want the most northerly *senior* club, then the solution lies in Wick, a few miles further south.

It's a long old haul to Wick: a six-hour drive from Glasgow through mist and tempest and hazardous terrain and crazed sheep and people who look at you in a funny way. But Alberta my bold Cavalier has the scent of the Highlands in her exhaust pipe and we power on, barely pausing to reflect on the mysteries awaiting us. 'Wick? Hmm, it's all a bit sad up there – what are you going there for?" asks the landlady in Glasgow. A football match, madam! 'That's even sadder,' she says, clearly deciding that the English are to be pitied and not hated.

Roaring into Wick after a 15-hour 700-mile trip to see Wick Academy take on Keith in a mid-table tussle in the Scots-Ad Highland League, the venture does start to seem a trifle lunatic. The small but perfectly formed Academy ground sits modestly at the entrance to a town that on the surface appears to be occupied entirely by pubs. There are 45 pubs in Wick (I know, I painstakingly counted them), plus a distillery and a brewery – well, I guess they've got to do *something* since they emptied the seas of herring and one of the fishing capitals of Europe went into steep decline in the 1900s. Now there are just 30 fishing boats in the harbour and the last vessel sailed in search of herring in 1953. But hey, Wick does have an airport, and 45 pubs, and a football team. It's not bad for a town with a population of 9,000.

The rain pummels down and the wind is merciless (well, we *are* further north than Moscow) as we down a swift cup of tea at Mrs. Bremner's Clachan B&B and make the short hop to Harmsworth Park, where a local laird had originally planned to build his house but got the willies every time he looked at the cemetery next door. An unexpectedly warm welcome lurks therein. Half expecting the match to be called off due to the elements (I remembered an Arbroath match had once been abandoned at half-time due to extreme *wind*) I'd sent a carrier pigeon on ahead with news of my plans to visit. The welcoming committee pounces the minute I set foot in the ground. News of my visit has made the local newspaper. I get a mention in the official programme and am instantly furnished with a collection of old programmes, an extensive history of the club and endless anecdotes.

'Oh we've had some big games up here,' says Ken Wood, a club committee member who, disconcertingly, comes from Kent. 'In 1984 we had a friendly with Hearts in front of 2,500. We printed 900 programmes and sold out before kick-off. We also played friendlies against Hibs and Aberdeen.' They're not entirely unfamiliar with strangers in town, either. 'Oh yes, we get a few of those … what do you call them? *Ground-hoppers*, coming up here to tick us off their list.'

I am escorted to the convivial clubroom where they queue up to shake my hand ('y'the fella frae London, then?') and furnish me with more stories from the glory days of Wick Academy. They formed in 1893 and were for many years merely an occasional team who scrambled primarily to compete in the Scottish Qualifying Cup and were assembled from various local sides, including those on Orkney. The key milestone, though, was in 1994 when they were admitted to the Highland League. Their first game, at home to Cove, attracted 1,700.

The most memorable game of recent times, however, occurred in 2001 when the Academy made it through the qualifying rounds of the Scottish Cup and were drawn at home to Threave Rovers. Nothing particularly dramatic about that, except that Wick is almost as far as you can go in the north of Scotland and Threave play at Castle Douglas in the extreme south of the country over 350 miles away – the longest journey in Scottish Cup history. 'We had telly up here for that one and everything,' says Ken Wood. 'Grampian did a whole bit on it – it was very exciting.'

Then playing in the East of Scotland League, Threave took nine hours to reach Wick across unfriendly terrain, arriving on Friday night at the Mercury Hotel (Mrs Bremner's B&B presumably not being big enough). They spent Saturday night there, too, after a thrilling 3-2 victory over Wick in front of a bumper crowd of 1,400, and you fondly imagine they were dancing in the streets of Castle Douglas that night. Sadly Threave were beaten 2-0 by Forfar in the next round, but of such occasions legends are made, and they still get animated in the boardroom at Wick when you mention Threave Rovers and the day Grampian TV cameras came to make a documentary.

Inside the clubroom, I am introduced to the personable club president Clair Harper, who asks, 'Would ye like some refreshment?' Oh it's OK, I say, just had a cup of tea with Mrs Bremner.

'Oh,' he says frowning, 'I wasn't thinking about *tea*. A wee toddy, mebbe?' Oh yes, indeed. After all, the sun appears over the yardarm very early this far north. We adjourn to the small bar. Clair Harper turns to the whisky, looks back at me and says, 'No, I think we'll get the good stuff out.' He unlocks a cupboard containing 'the good stuff' – the local pride and joy, Old Pulteney, 'the genuine maritime malt'. I didn't get this sort of treatment from Roman Abramovich.

It hits the spot with scary alacrity and by the third glass I'm making lifelong friends with the Keith FC chairman, declaring undying allegiance to Wick Academy and sharing heartfelt concerns about Russian billionaires and the iniquities of the English Premiership with anyone in earshot. 'You can't find a Wagon Wheel in the Premiership now for love or money,' I say passionately. They look at me quizzically. 'Or *Bovril* ...'

Exceedingly refreshed, we're fortified enough to face the elements as the cheerleaders – *cheerleaders!* – depart and the players of Keith and Wick Academy line up. Wick are in manly black and white stripes while the Keith chaps are decked out in a slightly more effete maroon. I'm just wondering how that icy blast of wind got inside my 18 jumpers and am surreptitiously re-adjusting my undies when Keith score. I'm not sure about the whys and wherefores and a group of us are trying to piece together the mechanics of the goal when the Scorries – Wick's nickname comes from a type of seagull – immediately bite back. Martin Gunn ('Gun-ny! Gun-ny! Gun-ny!') scores with a screaming shot from the edge of the box, and with two goals in the first three minutes I'm thinking it's going to end up 7-6.

I notice a big bloke with a lethal haircut who appears to be hiding behind the stand, furtively watching the match through his fingers. I catch his eye. 'I'm not a good watcher,' he says by way of explanation. 'I'd rather be playing than watching.' The penny drops. Amid the chatter and waterfalls of Old Pulteney in the bar, several anecdotes had circulated around 'the big man', goalkeeper Don MacMillan (or 'Psycho' as one lad lovingly refers to him), who is noted not merely for his acrobatics but a fierce temper. I heard several stories of red cards, invariably accompanied by verbal assaults on the referee and, on at least one occasion, ripping his jersey off and flinging it at the ref as he leaves the pitch. 'Och, Don's a great character all right,' they all chortled admiringly.

Sadly Don's not playing today. I assume he's halfway through a nine-match ban, but he's injured apparently: 'I don't know what I've done, it's just a wee bit sore so I thought I'd better rest it. The young boy's standing in for me. I'm carrying a few knocks and the hamstrings are a bit sore. I think it's just old age, what do ye reckon?' He seems to think I'm a physio.

Still, Don seems personable enough. He tells me he's in his fourth season with Wick and talks regretfully of the previous seasons missed due to arthritis, and his time as an upcoming young goalie with Caledonian Thistle and Ross County. Now he has a day job with an undertaker. 'Y'canna beat footba' on a Sat'day, can ye?' Oh no, I say, agreeing with him vociferously, you certainly can't. I broach the subject of his fiery temper. I hear you're a bit of a bad boy, Don …

'Och, I *used* to be. But as you get older you get wiser.' What about the time you threw your jersey at the ref? 'That was my first season here, I think. I had a bit of a disagreement with that referee, y'know? You just get frustrated sometimes. But I've mellowed now. I've had no bookings this season.'

A bunch of likely lads have gathered behind the Keith goal and are loudly offering advice to the visiting keeper: 'It's a long way back to Keith, you wanna start now.' I go to join them. A group of them used to hire a minibus, leaving at the crack of dawn for away matches, and they regale me with stories of phoning up bars *en route* to matches and getting them to open up so they could have a couple of fresheners to ease their journey. The end result was that trips to places like Inverness and Fort William invariably degenerated into a glorified pub crawl, and on more than one occasion the vociferous away support that greeted Academy in the first half disappeared completely in the second when most of the fans fell fast asleep.

It doesn't happen any more. Well, not *much*. Now they tend to content themselves with barracking the opposition from behind the goal. There's Tam, an ex-boxer, known to turn up for matches wearing an elaborate 'scorrie hat' in the club colours with wings that flap at the flick of a wire. And there's Drew, who played centre forward for the Academy in the 1960s in the days when their only match of the season was in the qualifying round of the Scottish Cup: 'There were four clubs in Wick then and they'd pick a Caithness team from Wick and Thurso to play Orkney. The best players would be picked for the Academy team so we'd have a few Orcadians playing with us too.' Did Tam play in that team too? 'Tam? No, he wasn't good enough. He was so bad he made me look good, which is why I got picked.' Tam doesn't disagree.

Drew later went on to manage one of the local teams. 'See the stocky lad in the middle?' I do. He looks the classiest player on the pitch but his mobility isn't all it might be and one man's 'stocky' is another man's 'chubby'. 'Well,' continues Drew, 'he played for Wick Rovers when I was manager and he was a great player when he was 15 or 16. He went on to Dundee and St Johnstone for a few years but didn't make it – I think there was too much of the toddy.'

These days the Highland League operates a strict rule banning alcohol from being brought into matches, so there is no chance of anyone falling asleep at half-time here. Is there? 'Well, we do have the German bar,' says Drew, looking shiftily around to see if anyone's listening. He jerks a thumb at Lidls, the German supermarket across the road. 'You can get a good carryout from there, fill up the hip flask and smuggle it in. There's also a house over the road and a very nice lady would let us in there at half-time for a toddy. It warms you up for the second half.'

Keith nick a second goal midway through the second half, and in truth look by far the superior side. Despite lots of honest toil, the Scorries go down 2-1, but in the clubroom afterwards nobody is too distraught. Having been whipping boys in their first years in the Highland League, their current mid-table status is good. 'When you consider we are just a small town so far north and Keith can draw on players from all over Aberdeen, we're doing well to compete,' says somebody in the bar as the Old Pulteney flows once more.

Internal politics, they say, took its toll and on entry into the Highland League they took on a few old players at the end of their careers, offering mad inducements like £50 a goal. A new broom swept that nonsense away and with mostly young local players the Academy are on the up again. Given the extreme geographical location, the players could hardly be anything *but* local. The nearest town of any size to Wick is Thurso, and there's such a coastal rivalry between them that talented players from Thurso would rather travel 50 miles to play for Brora Rangers than come to the Academy.

While all this is going on, the Keith lads peruse the league table to determine whether their victory has made any inroads into the lead that the likes of Deveronvale, Huntly and Buckie Thistle have over them and settle into the serious business of finding out where we're going for the post-match inquest. Or, to put it another way, 'piss-up'. A local club is nominated and we pile into the Keith team coach to take us there. Half the players have already absconded to an offie and they stagger on to the coach clutching huge cases of beer just in case they get a bit of a thirst on during the long drive back to Moray. They say they love coming to Wick to play. It's so remote they see it as a bit of an adventure. That and the fact that they always fancy themselves to get three points and Wick can always be relied upon to give them a good dinner afterwards.

Inside the club someone keeps buying me drinks and I interview everyone that moves, including somebody who was apprenticed to Blackpool in the 1950s and played in tangerine shirts worn by Stanley Matthews, Jackie Mudie and Stanley Mortensen. Mortensen, he reminds me, is the only player to have scored a hat trick in a Wembley FA Cup Final (the 'Matthews final' in 1953), and while he scored 23 goals in a 25-

match England career, he also once played for Wales. 'Oh aye,' he says when I give him the look of a man who's had too many toddies. 'In 1943, it was. Mortensen was a reserve for England that day and when Wales turned up and were a man short they asked if he could play for them. And he did.' There was clearly no scurrying around family trees to unearth Welsh grandparents in those days.

He also gives me a complete rundown on ancient football. Duncan Edwards was 'a magician with a football' and Tom Finney was 'the most complete footballer I have ever seen. In those days it was a man's game. If you take the ball and the man with it, how's that a foul? See, I was a tackler. I never lost a tackle in my life, but I only ever got booked once. Mind you I had a cartilage operation and my career was over at 21. These days all you need is a handball and a silly foul and you get sent off! We used to play a goalkeeper, two full backs, a right half, left half and centre half, outside right, outside left, centre forward, inside right and inside left. Then they started introducing 4-4-2 and all the rest of it but to me these things happen automatically. You never used to have to plan it, it just happened naturally by instinct. If ever I was put in charge of a football club I would revert back to the old ways, play the old system with wingers and full backs, because you'd still play 4-4-2 or whatever naturally if you needed to.'

Wick's player of the match today is announced as Craig Shearer, a 25-year-old midfielder born and bred in the town who's been a first team regular for seven years, playing over 200 matches for the club, and still describes it as a 'dream come true'. 'I was always a fan. I'd come to every game and think, "One day I'm gonna play here", and here I am! It's all I ever thought about, playing for Wick Academy. I'd never want to play for anybody else. It's in my heart. Even if I got offered another team I could'nae leave.'

OK, I know I've had a drink but I find this sentimentality hugely touching. So what if we're miles from anywhere and Craig freely admits he'd never be good enough to be offered a barrel load of money to play for someone else? His loyalty to the cause and the sheer passion with which he talks of playing for his local club is surely something to celebrate. All those despicable hacks who used to savage Matt Le Tissier and accuse him of lacking ambition simply because he chose to play all his career with Southampton rather than join one of the supposedly more glamorous clubs promising to double his wages should be parachuted into Caithness right now and stuck in this club with me and Craig Shearer and given a lesson in those who still play football for its own sake.

'I was a supporter of Wick Academy and now I'm a player for Wick Academy so I'm living the dream to be honest,' he says, and I'm nearly crying into my glass. 'My first game was at Brora Rangers, our big local derby match. It's a real bitter rivalry. We used to go up there and sing, "We hate Brora and we hate Brora". I could'nae believe it when I was told I was in the team. I was 18. We got a 1-1 draw so it was a good result.'

Craig continues to talk me through the highlights of his career as a Wick Academic. His first goal was 'a 25-yard shot against Huntly; it went like a bullet in the top corner'. He played in the famous Scottish Cup tie against Threave: 'Great experience. I got Man of the Match that day   I was gutted to lose, mind.' I have every belief that if I go back to Harmsworth Park in 10 years' time, Craig Shearer will still be playing for the Academy. 'Oh aye,' he says. 'I love this club. It's such a great craic and this is the best squad of players we've ever had. There's no way I want to leave.'

A dozen more life stories, garbled philosophising and fierce debates about sectarianism and tomorrow's Old Firm derby later, I take directions to the nearest offie to buy a souvenir bottle of Old Pulteney and crawl back to Mrs Bremner's guest house. It's been a hard day's night.

My head still clanging, I crawl from Mrs Bremner's fine B&B the next morning and am out of Wick, chasing the sunrise, by 6.30 a.m. There's an Old Firm derby kicking off 300 miles away in Glasgow at 12.30 p.m. and a friend of a friend's mate's girlfriend's uncle's next-door neighbour drinks with a bloke who has a ticket with my name on it. Maybe.

Random snatches of conversation from last night pound around my head: 'A ticka fae the match t'mrae? Youse gotta be frickin' joking! Nae chance, pal!' My bravado of last night seems desperately optimistic in the cold light of day when a lie-in, Mrs Bremner's breakfast and a gentle constitutional around this bracing northerly tip of Scotland seems infinitely more attractive. But Alberta the brave Cavalier is primed for the challenge and while I'm barely conscious as we sweep south through the hilly terrain, terrifying sleeping sheep and the odd insomniac laird, we plough on through the small town of Brora and down through places with exciting names like Morangie, Tain and Achnagorran and various villages familiar from scurrilous nights sampling intriguing blends of malt whisky.

I make a brief pause at Inverness to test the water on the ticket front and my fading mobile gets confusing signals. The thick Scottish accent which responds to my call suggests his Saturday night may have followed a similar pattern to my own. and after several attempts I still can't quite decipher whether he's saying 'Nae problem, pal, I've got your ticket, meet me in the Grapes at midday' or 'Fuck off, you English bastard.' Ever the optimist, I drive like the wind for Glasgow.

I'm doing it because … well, because the Old Firm derby – that's the big one really, isn't it? No other match commands the same reputation for intense rivalry as Rangers and Celtic. I met a couple of Celtic fans in Wick last night who had a minibus booked for 5 a.m. to take them to today's match. They introduced me to their mate, due to travel with them, who was a rabid Rangers fan. 'Shouldn't you two be killing each other?' I'd asked in all innocence. 'Oh we can't be doing with all that sectarian shite,' said the Celtic man. 'I can't stand all that. It's just about the football for me, always has been. We used to have a coach that would go from Wick for every Rangers v. Celtic game and half the people on it were Celtic supporters and the other half were Rangers fans. There was never any trouble. We were all united by one thing – we all hate religion.'

Indeed, there was a time when Rangers and Celtic were good pals united by their hatred of another Glasgow team, Queens Park. The big guns of Scottish football in the late nineteenth century, Queens Park still play their league matches in the vast surrounds of the national stadium, Hampden Park, even though they attract crowds in their hundreds rather than thousands. They were Scotland's first football team and, as such, they made up the rules as they went along. When they hit on the idea of playing the first international match against England, they picked a team full of their own players. This, not surprisingly, baited the other clubs and the rise of Rangers and Celtic began.

The *Scottish Spartan* newspaper dubbed a Rangers v. Celtic match in 1900 'the auld firm' in recognition of the fact that here were two clubs with their business heads screwed on tightly, and the historical religious divide of Celtic's Irish Catholic roots and Rangers' Scots Protestant beginnings set a clear dividing line that's plagued the fixture ever since. It's the difference, they say, between the loyalty of Rangers fans and the faithfulness of Celtic supporters.

While Rangers marched on to loyalist anthems like 'The Sash', 'The Orange and the Blue', 'The Green Grassy Slopes of the Boyne', 'The Old Orange Flute' and 'The Billy Boys', Celtic had a broad range of Catholic and anti-British songs to choose from as well as the famous 'Celtic Song':

Hail hail the Celts are here, what the hell do we care?
For it's a grand old team to play for, for it's a grand old team to see
And if you know the history it's enough to make your heart
    go … nine in a row.

Now their most prized anthem is 'Fields of Athenry', which is practically the Irish national anthem. Go to any tourist pub throughout Ireland and you will hear some bar singer belting it out. You'll hear it sung at most Celtic matches, quite a few Scotland games (rugby, as well as football), and these days at Liverpool too. Nobody's more amazed by this turn of events than Pete St John, the Dublin man who wrote it in 1979 and still can't believe it got him an invite to sing it live at Celtic Park.

Originally an electrician, St John spent much of his youth travelling, living in various parts of Canada, the US, Central America and the West Indies, paying his way with any number of jobs from truck driver to author and singer while also being actively involved in the Irish peace movement. When he returned to Dublin in the late 1970s, he started writing songs seriously and became fascinated by the 1840s potato famine and the human devastation caused in Ireland by the perceived British indifference to the disaster.

Set in Galway, 'Fields of Athenry' created a tragic love story within the horrors of the famine – namely, a desperate husband transported to Australia as punishment for trying to steal some corn so that his family could eat. British Prime Minister Robert Peel had imported large quantities of corn from India to alleviate the crisis but the baddie of the saga, a certain Lord Trevelyan who was put in charge of its distribution, decreed the corn was too hard to be milled and refused to release it. It was this corn that the hero of the song was trying to liberate.

The quietly infectious chorus, the sentimental nature of the song and the painful sense of injustice it evokes brought an extraordinary response in Ireland, where Paddy Reilly turned it into a hit single. There have been more than 400 cover versions and five million copies have been sold. It featured in the movie *Veronica Guerin* and has been round the block so many times that few in Ireland still take it seriously, let alone think about its emotional content. But 150,000 starving Irish men, women and children emigrated to Glasgow in 1846 to escape the famine, and as the strains of 'Low lie the fields of Athenry/Where once we watched the small free birds fly' float out from Parkhead, the effect is still mesmerising.

'It could be about Scots, Irish or English; it's a song about poor innocents who get caught up in a disaster,' says Pete St John, bemused to find himself accused of sectarianism with active attempts to get it banned in some quarters of the Glasgow divide in the light of the song's unexpected career as a Celtic terrace anthem. 'Believe me, it's about as sectarian as "I'm Forever Blowing Bubbles".'

In truth it's probably best not to probe too far into the Rangers/Celtic songbooks. Some pretty horrendous sectarian poison lurks within. We've all heard the joke about the definition of a Glaswegian atheist being someone who goes to a Rangers v. Celtic match to watch the football. However, there are some fine examples of wit. A Rangers legend, Ally McCoist, was greeted with chants of 'There's only one John Parrott' (his nemesis on TV show *A Question of Sport*) on his last appearance playing for Kilmarnock. And when Rangers striker Duncan Ferguson faced prison after headbutting Raith Rovers defender John McStay, he was taunted with chants of 'He's tall, he's skinny/He's going to Barlinnie!'

Ferguson did, indeed, serve 44 days in Barlinnie Prison for assault and was banned for twelve matches by the Scottish FA, an incident that inspired a curious offshoot: a symphony, *Barlinnie Nine* by Finnish composer Osmo Tapio Raihala, that premiered in Helsinki in 2005 on the same day that Ferguson scored the winner for Everton in a 1-0 victory over Manchester United. By way of explanation for his symphony, Osmo said: 'It takes into account the contradictions in him: he has an aggressive side but there is a lyrical undertone to him, as the fact that he keeps pigeons shows.' Eh? Run that by me again, Osmo? If pigeon-keeping reflects lyrical undertones, Andy Capp should have been Poet Laureate.

Alberta guides me into Glasgow city centre at 12.20 p.m. but the friend of a friend's mate's girlfriend's uncle's next door neighbour who drinks with a bloke who'd sworn blind to get me a ticket for the match, no problem at all, appears to have gone to ground. I park up and dive into the nearest bar, which happens to be in Sauchiehall Street. A voice from last night dances in my head: 'Don't worry aboot a ticket – you're better off watching the match in a bar, the atmosphere's much better.'

Not this bar, though. There are two tellies showing the match with a dozen or so early Sunday drinkers gathered round each one, staring listlessly at the screen. There are a few green-and-white scarves indicating where their loyalties lie but little of the intense partisan tribalism I was frankly hoping for. I blame Sky, or the police, or whoever it is insists this match takes place on a Sunday lunchtime before anyone has a chance of overcoming last night's hangover, let alone getting tanked up for this particular battle.

I order a pint of foaming lager and try to engage the guy on the next stool in jolly banter. 'What you reckon the score will be then, mate?' He stares at me in silence. 'You a Celtic man, then?' He looks at me blankly and stares back at the screen. 'Looks like Strachan's got this one sorted ...' Not so much as a glimmer. 'You're wasting your time, pal,' says the barman. 'He's Russian; doesn't speak a word of English. It took him 20 minutes to order a vodka.'

There is scattered banter in the bar but it's a long way from the heaving, seething mass of ranting and roaring I'd been hoping for. Even when Celtic score – a quality strike by Maciez Zurawski, a Pole from Wisla Krakow – there's none of the dancing on tables, ripping off of shirts and drinks on the house I had felt would be appropriate. A few fists in the air, some cracks about battering the Hun and a swift round of OJs and that's your lot. I watch for a few more minutes just in case any fights start but the match is boring and the pub almost comatose. There's got to be more fun to be had in Glasgow on an Old Firm derby day than this, so I head off into the street and catch a subway to Ibrox.

You can hear the crowd inside the stadium the minute you step outside Ibrox station. It's a strange and eerie sensation to stand in complete stillness among the debris of chip papers, discarded copies of the *Daily Record* and various sweet wrappers listening to the distant roars. A few dishevelled lost souls wander purposelessly through the muddle of the empty street while those manning the many burger vans listen to the match on their radios, gearing up for the big rush, and a couple of police stand chatting outside the chippy surveying the scene. Around the corner a line of resting coaches lurk from Alloa, Auchterarder and Airdrie, their drivers dozing in their cabins or listening to their radios and wondering what mood their charges will be in on the way home.

I take a second to absorb the sight of Ibrox and the sense of history that it embodies. There have been all those fierce Old Firm epics through the years. There was the death here in 1931 of Celtic's brilliant young keeper John Thomson, who fractured his skill diving at the feet of Rangers forward Sam English, who was on his way to a club record 44 goals that season. A devastated English was cleared of all blame but was still chased out of Scotland by the merciless taunts of fans. He tried to resurrect his career at Liverpool (and Queen of the South and Hartlepool), but ultimately returned home to Northern Ireland a broken man. He died of motor neurone disease at the age of 58 in 1967.

Close your eyes and the Old Pulteney still surging through the veins stirs some of the ghosts drifting round the old place. Frank Sinatra sang here, *Chariots of Fire* sprinter Eric Liddell trained here, and Jim Watt sang 'Flower of Scotland' in the rain here before beating Howard Davis, the cocky American in the pink salmon trunks, to retain the lightweight world title in 1980. And the list of footballing greats who trod the turf here is endless.

There was Jim Baxter, still remembered for his audacious 'keepie-uppies' designed to humiliate England, then world champions, when they played Scotland in 1967. He even took bets before the game on how many times he could nutmeg England defender Ray Wilson. John Greig, whose statue stands tall and proud outside Ibrox; the much-loved winger Davie Cooper, who died of a brain haemorrhage in 1965 at the age of 39 while still playing for Clydebank; Alan Morton, the 'wee blue devil' of the 1920s; the striker Robert Smith MacColl, who scored six goals for Rangers in the last match of his career against Port Glasgow Athletic in 1912 but is now better remembered for the chain of newsagents he helped set up; larger than life goalkeeper Andy Goram; the sublime Danish player Brian Laudrup; flute-playing Paul Gascoigne; oh, and Ally McCoist, who scored a club record 355 goals for Rangers before making an arse of himself on *A Question of Sport*.

Then there is Iain Durrant, the twinkle-toed golden boy of Scottish football who was put out of the game for over two years by a tackle from Aberdeen's Neil Simpson in 1988, which provoked an ongoing Aberdeen-Rangers enmity that almost rivals Rangers-Celtic. One Aberdeen pub stuck a TV screen in the urinals showing Rangers games so that Aberdeen fans could pee over them, and objectionable songs recalling the infamous Durrant incident are still sung at matches between the two clubs.

Oh, and let's not forget Graeme Souness. Graeme was sent off on his Rangers debut against Hibs, inspiring a mass brawl after a series of horrendous challenges, a moment he's described in the biography *A Soccer Revolutionary* as his lowest point in football: 'I remember seeing the red card and looking up. There were 30,000 people jeering and I could see my dad in the front row of the directors' box. I can still feel the shame now. I'd let my dad down; humiliated him in his own street.'

Souness, of course, was never one to knowingly avoid confrontation or controversy. While managing Galatasaray in Turkey he nearly caused a riot by marching on the pitch at the end of an away cup victory over their most hated rivals Fenerbahce to plant a Galatasaray flag in the centre circle. In the first match of the 1987–88 season playing for Rangers against Celtic he was said to have been given three red cards by the referee for different offences. But when he became player-manager of Rangers Souness was credited with changing the whole culture of Ibrox, signing a succession of English players like Chris Woods, Graham Roberts, Ray Wilkins, Colin West, Trevor Francis and Terry Butcher.

The arrival of the supposedly civilised English players was widely expected to dampen the traditional gladiator show-downs of Old Firm derbies, but it didn't quite work out that way. With an inflammatory opening battle cry of 'No Surrender', Butcher led Rangers into one of the most vicious confrontations of them all in 1987. Frank McAvennie of Celtic and Rangers' English goalie Chris Woods had a fight and were sent off as the match erupted into a free-for-all. Butcher was also red-carded for punching the Celtic keeper. Nine-man Rangers clawed back to an unlikely 2-2 draw with a last-minute equaliser and three English players, Graham Roberts, Chris Woods and Terry Butcher, all ended up in court, charged with causing a breach of the peace, along with McAvennie. In the event, only Woods and Butcher were found guilty and received fines. Roberts, who took over as emergency keeper after Woods was sent off and was at one point observed to be conducting the Rangers crowd in their sectarian singing, later described the game as one of the highlights of his career.

In late 1987 Souness also signed Rangers' first black player, another Englishman, Mark Walters (whose middle name, triv fans, is Everton). However, Rangers were well behind Celtic on this one. In the 1950s an Afro American serviceman stationed in Glasgow, Giles Heron – father of the singer Gil Scott-Heron – had played briefly in the green and white hoops. Scotland's first black player was even earlier. Back in the 1870s, Andrew Watson, the son of a Scottish sugar planter born to a local girl in British Guyana, was studying engineering in Glasgow when he was signed up by Queens Park and capped three times by Scotland. He even captained them to a 6-1 victory over England in 1881. Reports from the time found nothing strange or comment-worthy about his colour; they thought the only odd thing about him was that he wore brown boots instead of the customary black ones.

Yet the arrival of Walters still raised a few eyebrows, especially when he was photographed at Ibrox wearing a kilt, sporran and black bow tie. His first match was a New Year's

Day clash with Celtic when he was predictably bombarded with bananas and boos, some of them emanating from Rangers' own supporters. But if nothing else Scots love a player with a box of tricks in the locker, and the flamboyant Walters really won over the fans when he earned his spurs with a red card in an Old Firm derby.

The shock when Walters joined Rangers, however, was nothing compared to the outrage when Souness confronted the last taboo and signed a Catholic, ex-Celtic hero Mo Johnston. Souness, who was married to a Catholic and had no time for religious bigotry, had previously tried to sign Catholic Ray Houghton from Oxford, but Houghton rejected the move, fearing the reprisals. When the transfer of Johnston was announced there was anger throughout Glasgow, not least from Celtic, who had been carrying out their own negotiations to bring Johnston home from French club Nantes. Celtic supporters chanted 'Judas', 'Quisling' and 'Brutus' while Rangers fans queued up to burn their season tickets and scarves, vividly recalling the time when Johnston scored for Celtic against them and crossed himself in front of them.

Johnston held his head high and went on to have a decent career with Rangers, trying to ignore the ritual abuse that followed him even as he later saw out his playing days at Everton and Kansas City. But the great religious divide had been well and truly crossed, and it's worth noting that out of the 27 players who play a part in the Old Firm match at Ibrox today, only 10 are actually Scottish and there are more Catholics than Protestants in the Rangers team. At least Mo Johnston wasn't spat at in vain.

You wonder what Bill Struth would have made of it all. A disciplinarian and fitness fanatic credited with revolutionising training methods in football, Struth was Glasgow Rangers' second manager, appointed in 1920 after his predecessor William Wilton had died in a boating accident the day after Rangers had won the Scottish League title. Struth reigned for 34 years, not only presiding over the club's first League and Cup double, but many generations of tomatoes, which he painstak-ingly grew in a greenhouse right next to the away end. They came under constant threat from the feisty Celtic supporters who habitually gathered there, but not one pane of glass was broken and not one tomato was injured during Struth's long spell as manager. He also kept a budgie in his office along with half-a-dozen snazzy double-breasted suits plus a collection of bones: he was fascinated by surgery, often accompanying his players to the operating theatre to watch the surgeons at work.

Struth instituted the practice of players turning up for training in shirt and ties and would watch through binoculars as they arrived at the ground. If any had their hands in their pockets he would send them out again to walk into the ground with their hands by their sides. Even after half of his leg was amputated as a result of gangrene he soldiered on at Rangers, methodically building the club's mythical 'Iron Curtain' defence, and won 18 Scottish League titles before finally retiring in 1954 at the age of 79. He was succeeded by Scott Symon, who was so houseproud about Ibrox that he had an air rifle in his office to shoot at any seagulls that dared to fly on to the pitch.

I cross the road, take a deep breath and enter the lion's den – the Stadium Bar.

The mood of blackness and despair hits you the instant you step inside the closest pub to the Rangers ground, a vast, tacky, soulless place with the strangely disengaged ambience of a 1950s swimming bath. Gaggles of disconsolate men and women wearing the blue shirts and scarves of Rangers sit on scruffy seats around the edges of the pub nursing bottles of lager, faces like thunder, heads in hands. Nobody says a word. A couple of toothless elderly men appear to be playing pool without any balls. It feels like the waiting room for hell. So Rangers are still losing, then …

The commentary blares out through the pub confirming their woe and I search the bar vainly for the television screen. There isn't one. With some amazement I realise that in an era where you can't set foot in a pub in a remote corner of Cornwall or

Cumbria without a live match on Sky on the telly in the corner, here's a pub directly outside the Glasgow Rangers ground on the day of the Auld Firm derby and you have to listen to the match on the radio. And worse, a radio turned up so loud the sound is distorted and you don't have a clue what's going on.

Cunningly disguising my English accent to assume the persona of a passing nonplussed Albanian, I order a pint and sit next to three mountainous tattooed women in 'Loyal Rangers Supporter' T-shirts, slumped in their seats slurping down pints of cider. They are suddenly up in the air shrieking as a shrill lurch in the commentary indicates a Rangers scoring attempt, but the chance is missed and they sink back into their seats as one, depositing an ocean of cider over an already sopping floor. One of them looks at me, says 'Yefickaybastardsoddingballbuggerlightfickyboggywillye ...', and raises her eyebrows as if she is making me an offer I can't refuse. I raise my eyebrows back. She repeats the impenetrable comment, a bit more loudly this time. I smile doubtfully and shake my head. I think it's for the best. Me no understand, me from Tirana. She gets up, spilling yet more cider everywhere, says the exact same thing to a bloke at the bar and cadges a ciggy off him.

There are some interesting fashion statements in the Stadium. One burly, muscular guy in a Rangers shirt is prancing around in the skimpiest kilt imaginable, while a Boy George lookalike lurches around the place in tight tartan top and dangly earrings. There's even a brave soul wearing an England shirt, but he also has a Rangers shirt underneath it so he escapes with his life. I vaguely wonder what this place would be like if Rangers were winning but decide to perish the thought.

The match ends at 1-0 to Celtic and the fans swiftly come piling in, swearing abjectly about the team, the manager, the captain, the tactics, the referee, the groundsman, the weather, the singing, the programme sellers, the pies, the bogs, the price of a pint, the price of holidays in Marbella and the weird Albanian bloke sitting in the corner. They are unanimous on one thing – they have just lost to the worst Celtic team that's ever set foot on the sacred Ibrox turf in what has been the worst football match ever staged in Scotland. Oh, and the referee's a wanker.

I fall into conversation with three disgruntled guys. One's a Dutchman, one's a Cockney and one's from Belfast (no, it's not a joke). 'Far-kin tosspot weekend this turned out to be," says the Cockney bitterly. 'I'm a Chelsea fan, ain't I? Got up at six yesterday to go to Middlesbrough and saw the Chelsea get beat 3-0 by the northern gits and then came up here to see Rangers and they get beat too.' 'It could be worse,' consoles the Dutchman. 'We could be watching Ajax – they also got beat.' 'The way my luck is going today, the friggin' boat will sink on the way home,' reflects the Belfast guy. 'Tell you what,' says the Cockney. 'Let's just stay here and get ratted.'

A guy comes in trying to flog posters of the Rangers team (£1 a poster, 50p for the rubber band) and vanishes deep into the heart of the now-packed pub only to re-emerge, several minutes later, looking slightly the worse for wear. 'So that's 35 fuck offs, 11 up-yer-wee-brown-holes and one sale,' he reflects. 'Nae bad, nae bad at all …' Meanwhile, a couple of young blondes flirt with the drinkers, cavorting around in their undies and giving out flyers for a lap-dancing club.

I escape outside fully expecting to see carnage but instead there's just a lot of swearing and disillusionment, some of the fans even finding solace from gently patting the heads of the police horses as they are herded into Ibrox station, their sagging flags and Union Jacks looking rather sorry. There is not a whiff of a green-and-white hoop, though, as the jubilant Celtic fans have seemingly been spirited magically away. I saunter off through the police cordons in search of them, wondering if all the fuss about sectarianism is just a media fabrication after all.

That's when I find the wall. Recently signed by Celtic from Manchester United, Irishman Roy Keane has reportedly just marked his first Old Firm match with a Man of the Match performance. But there, painted on the wall outside Ladbrokes, is the message 'Roy Keane – RIP'. That, however, is relatively mild compared to slogans about the late IRA hunger striker Bobby Sands, anti-Fenian slurs and obnoxious racist messages that are also daubed on the wall. I flee to the club shop and decide that while they may have lost the Old Firm match, Rangers win the prize for the most original merchandise – 'Rangers Hot Chilli Sauce: £4'. At least supper will go with a zing.

The next morning I make a pilgrimage to Scotland's home of football, Hampden Park. My initial reaction is crashing disappointment. It's a grey old day and the old stadium looks bleak and unimposing, blending uneasily with the surrounding buildings. It's hard to imagine the famous Hampden Roar and the thrills and spills it has accommodated over the years. There was the famous European Cup Final in 1960, when legends like Puskas, Di Stefano and Gento took Eintracht Frankfurt to the cleaners as Real put on a masterclass in front of a crowd of 136,000. The 1937 Scottish Cup Final when 146,000 crammed in to see Celtic beat Aberdeen 2-1, still a record for a club match in European football. Then the following year produced one of the greatest shocks in Scottish Cup history when Second Division East Fife beat Kilmarnock 4-2 in extra time after a replay.

When Rangers and Celtic met in the final here in 1909 they played out two draws. At the end of the second game the crowd hung around waiting for extra time, only to be told there would have to be a third match. Suspecting they were being fleeced for yet more money and the two previous draws had been stage-managed, the crowd rioted. They swarmed on the pitch, uprooted the goals, cut up the turf and set fire to the place, even making the ultimate sacrifice of pouring whisky on the fire to keep the flames going. A number of police and firemen were injured and the Scottish FA decided to cancel the Scottish Cup that year amid calls for soldiers with fixed bayonets to take charge at future Hampden matches.

I follow a family into the Scottish Football Museum. They are all wearing Valencia shirts and the guide at the door gives them a warm welcome. *'Buenos dias – como estas*?' he asks. They look at him blankly. 'Come again, mate?' 'Oh sorry, I thought you were Spanish.' 'Nah, we're from Southend. Just been to Valencia on our holidays. We couldn't get tickets to see an Inter-Toto Cup match while we were over there so I had to buy them all shirts instead, ha!'

The first thing that greets you inside the museum is the famous picture of Dave Mackay collaring Billy Bremner. Well, that and the constant re-runs of Archie Gemmill's wonder goal against Holland in the 1978 World Cup, although some of us recall Scotland's World Cup effort more for the misguided triumphalism of their 'Ally's Army' anthem:

> We're representing Britain and we're ganny do or die
> England cannae dae it 'cos they did'nae qualify
> We're on the march wi' Ally's Army
> We're going tae the Argentine
> And we'll really shake them up when we win the World Cup
> 'Cos Scotland is the greatest football team …

Yet despite Gemmill's moment in the sun, Scotland were eliminated in the first round that year. Business as usual, then …

As we head through the museum, pretty soon we're into a section devoted to Jim Baxter and the mad celebrations at Wembley in 1967 when the Tartan Army danced on the pitch to celebrate their 3-2 victory over England, collapsing the goals by swinging on the crossbars and digging up huge lumps of turf to take home as souvenirs. This and other Scotland visits to Wembley inspired a fine song by Gordon Menzies of the band Gaberlunzie:

> When Scotland's playing England oh it really fills my heart
> Wi' a' the flags and banners aye we surely look the part
> But win or lose it's aw the same
> We did'nae come tae see the game
> We're just the happy hooligans of Wembley …

I learn a lot wandering round the museum. It's exciting to discover that Dumbarton are sponsored by my favourite whisky, Laphroaig, Kilmarnock have won awards for their pies, East Stirlingshire once fielded four different goalkeepers in one match against Albion Rovers, and Andy Goram was the last man to represent Scotland both at football and cricket. There's also the sad case of Renzo Serafini, a decent player from Inverness who was imprisoned during the war simply because of his Italian background; and Willie Woodburn, a Rangers centre half who was banned for life after headbutting a Stirling Albion player. It seems Duncan Ferguson got off lightly.

In the coffee shop afterwards I share platitudes with my new friends from Southend in the Valencia shirts and we discuss the respective merits of Rangers and Celtic. Overhearing us, a voice pops up from behind the cappuccino machine: 'There's only one team in Glasgow!' I brace myself for a pile of sectarian bile. 'It's Partick Thistle.'

Well, it's an interesting concept. By an amazing coincidence, Patrick's first ever match (in 1876) was against a Scottish junior team called Valencia and, while never a threat to either of Glasgow's big two, they seem to be regarded with affection by both. Partick inevitably respond by slagging them both off and singing songs like: 'We hate Roman Catholics, we hate Protestants too/We hate Jews and Muslims/Thistle we love you!' Not to mention: 'Hello hello, how do you do?/We hate the boys in royal blue/We hate the boys in emerald green/So feck the Pope and feck the Queen!' What could be more even-handed than that?

My fascination with the mores of Scottish football is further galvanised by a man who invites me to accompany him on a 5 a.m. trip to Glencoe to commemorate the massacre of the McDonalds by the evil Campbells. See, Phil Fox is from Clacton in Essex. As a kid he was always into Ipswich Town, regularly making the trek to Portman Road to see his brave heroes in blue. Dismayed by their indifference as the Scottish football results were being announced on the radio every Saturday night, Phil and a mate decided that they should each adopt a Scottish team to spice up the Scottish results sequence. So they put all the names of the Scottish clubs in a hat and each pulled one out. His mate got St Mirren and Phil pulled Greenock Morton.

At this point most of us would have been tempted to have another go, or maybe just forget the whole idea and concentrate on Ipswich. Not Phil Fox. He took fate too seriously. From that point, around 1968, he became a committed Morton fan with all the blind devotion and ludicrous sacrifices of time, money and effort that entails.

Three decades later, Phil Fox is still making the 1,000-mile round trip to most Greenock Morton home matches, occasionally flying or catching a series of coaches but mostly driving up overnight on a Friday and power-napping in service stations ('If I get tired I just kip in the car for 20 minutes and it soon perks me up again') to arrive at the Spinnaker Hotel at Gourock in time for Saturday lunch, where a succession of admiring Morton fans line up to buy him whisky.

'I usually start about 10 p.m. and it's a fantastic feeling coming into Scotland as the dawn breaks,' he says. 'You get some lovely rainbows coming through Lockerbie and when I get on that M8 from Glasgow and hit Dumbarton Rock, I start feeling excited. It's like coming home. Mind you, three weeks on the trot I drove up through ice and snow and the match was off every time. I just turned round and went home. Three weeks in a row.'

Phil isn't merely a long-distance lover. His commitment to Morton is so total that he is actively involved with fund-raising for the club via sponsored walks, booze cruises and the like. He talks knowledgeably of the slum areas and associated drug problems in Greenock and how they can best be resolved, and tells of his pain at arriving for Morton matches to see dozens of coaches moving out in the opposite direction full Greenock-based Celtic fans: 'I just can't stomach all that bigotry you get with Rangers and Celtic fans and all the hatred involved. You wouldn't believe the bile that comes out of their mouths.'

Phil runs a sand blasting company and has a partner, Sue, of 13 years who occasionally accompanies him on his weekly rituals, basically because she'd never see him if she didn't. 'Oh, I love her to bits,' he says, suddenly sentimental. 'She understands. She knows it's in my blood.' Traces of an acquired Scottish accent even emerge when he gets animated. 'Going to the wee away grounds is fantastic,' he says. 'They've all got good social clubs. Last year we went to Stranraer and had to beat them to go up. In the end we drew 1-1 and did everything but score the winner. I got paralytic that night. That's the thing about football up here – everyone knows you. Dougie Rae, who owns Morton, sometimes comes up the Spinnaker with us and we all get pissed together. You don't get that in England. Well, you might do at Ipswich, but most of the big clubs don't want to know.'

A by-product of his Morton obsession has been that Phil has immersed himself in Scottish history, making extensive studies of the Highland Clearances, Rob Roy, clan warfare and the rest of it. That is when he starts talking about the McDonalds and Campbells and the massacre of Glencoe. I tell him that my grandmother was a McDonald and I know all about it: I wouldn't trust Sol Campbell for a second. 'You should come up to Glencoe then,' he replies. 'We go up in our kilts at 5 a.m. when it's pitch black to commemorate the anniversary of the 1692 massacre. You should come, it's great.' A couple of glasses of Old Pulteney later, I'm seriously considering it.

I tell him that if he loves Scotland so much he should come up here to live. 'Oh I will,' he says, 'I definitely will. See, I feel more Scottish than English. I'm a Scotsman trapped in an Englishman's body. Scotland means more to me than life itself. I'm not anti-English; it's just that I am very pro-Scottish. I will move here in a few years. I don't want to die in England.'

So what's it to be? Do I go to Glencoe in the middle of the night with a Scotsman trapped in an Englishman's body? Or shall I find another football match? Mountain, or football? Sorry, Phil, but it's football, football, football, every time. Football's the winner.

The big shock I get when I arrive at Dundee's Dens Park stadium is that there is another, even bigger stadium directly next door. I wonder if it's a mirage. The fans in their dark blue scarves file past without giving it a second glance as they pour into the Dens, but I just stand there gawping at it as it seems to scowl at the passing fans through the darkness. It's Tannadice, the home of Dundee United, slap-bang alongside the home of their local rivals. It's a pity they haven't got a Scottish Cup replay tonight too: I could have hopped to and fro between the two games.

Still trying to get my head round the idea of two big clubs nestling so intimately alongside one another, I join the noisiest mob queuing to get into Dens Park. I'm inside before I realise they are wearing not the dark blue of Dundee but the red of – who is it? *Airdrie*. I have come on a whim after noticing Dundee had a home game and I barely noticed who they were playing, but I quickly settle among my boisterous new chums in red.

Tam, decked head to toe in Airdrie paraphernalia, is only too pleased to bring me up to speed with the state of play between the two teams. This is the sixth time they have met this season in various competitions and Airdrie haven't lost yet so Tam and his mates are confident, launching into an adaptation of the Spurs song 'Ossie's Dream': 'Airdrie's on their way to Hampden!' they bellow in my ear.

Well, why not? Rangers and Celtic are both out of the cup already and several other fancied teams have bitten the dust, so the odds on a First Division club taking the trophy are shortening. Tam is certainly convinced this will be their year – or, at least, that's what I think he's saying. The more animated he becomes the more impenetrable is his accent, but I like Tam. He keeps talking to me and I nod and grin and put my thumb up, though he could be inviting me to join the Foreign Legion for all I know. Tonight, though, *ich bin ein Airdriener*.

Airdrie play in a rather fetching kit, their red shirts decorated with a deep white V shape. Dundee are sponsored by the Forfar Roof Truss Company Ltd (just in case you need a truss for your roof), although both kits look positively dowdy compared to the garish yellow day-glo shirts and socks worn by the match officials. If you saw the ref running towards you, you could easily mistake him for one of the emergency services.

From the start it is pretty obvious that Dundee are the better team. They are quicker, hungrier and, unlike Airdrie, seem to have grasped the idea that when you get the ball you stand a better chance of winning if you pass it to someone on your own side. They have a midget striker called Deasley who wriggles between the legs of two Airdrie defenders, scampers away from them and chips the ball expertly past the balding Airdrie keeper Robertson right in front of us. In truth, it's a quality goal, but I loyally stand to shake my fist and shout obscenities, claiming foul, offside and general skulduggery.

Suddenly police in yellow coats surround us and start lifting people out of the crowd seemingly at random. Chants of 'fuck the polliss' and 'fascist wankers' break out all around, inciting the polliss to dive in to pluck out more of our barmy army. The incursion gets passions going in a way that nothing on the pitch seems able to do.

At half-time I learn more fascinating facts about Airdrie. They're called the Diamonds, their home ground is exotically named Shyberry Excelsior and, most excitingly of all, the late Justin Fashanu, Britain's first openly gay player, once played for them. By the second half, with Airdrie kicking at the goal in front of us, I'm consumed by the frenzy of it all. I draw the line at holding up my arm in something reminiscent of a Nazi salute to sing 'Can't Help Falling In Love' but I'm up and down like a yo-yo at every chant of 'Stand up for the Air-der-ree', even though I can't understand a word anyone is saying and couldn't pick out Airdrie on a map of Scotland even if it leapt up and bit me on the roof truss.

We play with more determination in the second half but the midget in the blue escapes again, this time crossing for Lynch to tap in the killer Dundee goal. The Dundee fans belatedly wake up, realise they are going to win and wave cheerio to the regular succession of our fans being bundled out by the polliss. In no time at all, there's only a few of us left. I turn to Tam to see what he's made of it all but he's gone too.

By the time the match ends I'm the sole remaining fan chanting 'Airdrie till I die' and clapping the brave fallen as they shuffle shamefacedly off the pitch, clapping me in return. Outside the polliss still seem to be arresting Airdrie fans for no reason whatsoever, and I slide off into the night. Dundee United's Tannadice Stadium smirks in the shadows as I pass.

— CHAPTER 10 —

We All Agree, All Stewards Are Tosspots

'So here's to you Mr Ridsdale
Your team's a joke and you're all broke
God please you please, Mr Ridsdale
Viduka's fat and Alan Smith's a twat'

Visiting fans serenading Leeds United, to the tune
of 'Mrs Robinson', in their times of trouble

'Hand it over.'
Yer wot?
'Give me the camera.'
Bog off.
'Gimme it.'
Why?
'You're breaking the rules.'
What rules?
'Taking photographs of stewards without their consent.
Gimme it.'
Piss off.
'I am afraid we will have to remove you from the stadium.'
Bollocks!
He grabs me and tries to take the camera. Other stewards
appear but the Leeds fans see them coming and block them and
I wrench clear. There is a momentary stand-off as we glare at
each other and it threatens to turn ugly and then I summon up
all my fury and *really* give to him: 'I am writing a book and you,
sunshine, are going to be in it!'

I shrink back in shame and embarrassment, scarcely believing that I have said something so naff while the stewards are completely flummoxed and retreat to their holes in the ground to await further instructions. God, I love being a football fan …

All supporters have to leap through hoops at regular intervals; it goes with the territory. However, if there's one team you really don't want to have supported in recent years, it's Leeds United.

At the turn of the twenty-first century you must have felt like you were king of the world when you came to Elland Road. Third in the Premier League in 2000, they lit up Europe the following season with a superb run that took them to the UEFA Champions League semi-finals. With a whole crop of exciting young players bursting into the team like Jonathan Woodgate, Harry Kewell, Alan Smith, Lee Bowyer and Rio Ferdinand, a personable young manager David O'Leary talking fetchingly of his 'naïve' team of 'babies' and a seemingly endless well of funds to dip into whenever the fancy took them, Leeds were surely on the crest of greatness.

They'd touched on it in the 1970s, but uncompromising players like Billy Bremner, Jack Charlton, Johnny Giles, Paul Reaney and Norman Hunter were fashioned with such ugly, ruthless efficiency by the shifty-looking manager Don Revie (an *EastEnders* extra before his time) that they were widely reviled outside Leeds. A violent and obnoxious band of supporters did nothing to help their cause.

This time around it seemed different. Leeds were young, exciting and cavalier and, after the stultifying tactics of previous manager George Graham, O'Leary and his young forward-thinking, publicity-friendly chairman Peter Ridsdale seemed like the future. On New Year's Day 2002, Leeds were top of the Premier League and looking at the stars. Stars which ended up blinding them.

Even while they were flying high, the wheels were coming off. Woodgate and Bowyer were embroiled in an unsavoury assault case (Bowyer was later cleared), two Leeds fans were stabbed to death in Istanbul before the European tie with Galatasaray and there were intermittent crowd disturbances at matches. And someone, somewhere, didn't get their sums right. Leeds United were living on borrowed money, and they ended up finishing fifth and being denied the Champions League qualification that was essential to keep them afloat.

The subsequent tumble was messy. O'Leary went and Terry Venables came in, which is never something to be recommended for peaceful equanimity. Players came in and went out in rapid succession, Venables didn't hang around long in the rubble and eventually Ridsdale went as well. When the music stopped, Leeds were in the Championship, all their favourite players had gone and the club was in financial ruin.

Just a Ridsdale's throw from Elland Road, Soccer City is alive with the sound of football. The smell of sweat blends sweetly with the nectar of lager as a procession of thin blokes, fat blokes, medium-sized blokes and movable mountains jog in and out of the place heading for the impressive array of indoor pitches. They look like five-a-side pitches, but here the custom seems to be 35-a-side where teams with names like Everything But the Goal and Young, Gifted & Broke gather to do battle.

People are spilling from the innards of the Magic Sponge bar, arguing over team selection for today's match while keeping a casual eye on the screens that are showing the Sky lunchtime match that's become a key part of the pre-match ritual these days. I'm here to see a football match that kicks off at 3 p.m. on a Saturday afternoon – now *there's* a novelty.

In a funny little alcove opposite the main bar, a man in tinted glasses has a wad of tickets for today's game and is painstakingly trying to work out who has paid for their tickets and who hasn't, who hasn't turned up, and why has he got a dozen tickets spare? And there's the problem of the upcoming away game at Coventry, where they have been told that police will go on the coaches before they get to the stadium and if they find any alcohol on board they won't let them in. That's the way it is if you're a Leeds fan on the road: policed in, policed out, not a sniff of alcohol, no swearing, one glare in the wrong place and you're out, chum. Leeds fans are treated like pariahs wherever they go.

But as that great philosopher Sir Billy Ocean once said, when the going gets tough the tough get going, and a hardcore group of fans have set out to actively demonstrate their love, loyalty and devotion to Leeds with positive action. They've formed the Leeds United Ultras, a group of supporters dedicated to restoring pride in the club and passion in the players on the pitch, setting themselves the task of lifting the team with a rigid policy of singing at all times.

It's a continental idea and one that's been devalued by association with right-wing extremists in Rome and the execrable Paulo Di Canio's infamous fascist salutes to the Lazio Ultras. However, the Leeds lads and lasses gathering in the Magic Sponge are appalled by the very notion that *their* group could be construed as having any racist or violent connotations. 'We may be a bit politically incorrect sometimes, though,' says one, recalling the match against Brighton when their keeper foolishly took his shirt off in front of the Leeds fans and was immediately hit by a fusillade of chants aimed at Brighton's reputation as the gay capital of Britain.

He may have been born in Lincolnshire, but Clive Miers is steeped in Yorkshire culture. After three centuries of Miers living in Leeds, his father moved the family to Lincoln for business reasons but ensured they were raised on Wensleydale cheese and Yorkshire cricket. Clive saw his first Leeds match away at Leicester in 1968. In 1975, he hitchhiked to Paris to queue for tickets to see Leeds go down 2-0 to Bayern Munich in the European Cup Final, and he is so fanatical that he chose Bradford University ahead of Oxford just so he could be close to Leeds. When Clive had the opportunity of setting up his own business he made sure it was in Leeds: not for commercial opportunities, but purely for better access to Elland Road.

The managing director of Miers Mortgages, Clive is one of the prime movers behind the Ultras. He initially wanted to replicate the continental template with huge banners and all the rest, but soon found that British laws wouldn't allow it. Traditionally the hardcore Leeds singers of the 1980s and 1990s congregated in the north end of Elland Road, so the Ultras decided to set up base in the South Stand to create a 'wall of sound'.

'We're very committed to the ideal of creating an atmosphere,' Clive tells me between trying to distribute tickets, swap banter with other fans and discuss strategy over the Coventry coach problem. 'We actively try to recruit people and we've got a lot of songs.' I wonder if they're all written in advance and carefully rehearsed beforehand, but apparently not. 'No, we just make them up on the hoof and if they're any good everyone else will join in. They're not necessarily original but they'll be reacting to the match. When we played Crystal Palace the keeper was wearing a particularly natty pair of tracksuit bottoms and someone just started singing the old Madness song "Baggy Trousers". It's very spontaneous.'

The traditional Leeds fans' song is 'Marching On Together' which, unusually, became a terrace anthem on the back of a commercial pop release by the team. Officially titled 'Leeds Leeds Leeds', it was written by two of the most successful pop songwriters of the day, Les Reed and Barry Mason, and originally recorded by the Leeds team for the 1972 Cup Final (when they beat Arsenal 1-0) as the B-side of a song called, without an ounce of imagination, 'Leeds United'.

Most FA Cup Final songs sung by the teams disappear before they get to the royal box to pick up their medals, but the supporters took 'Marching On Together' to their hearts, primarily because it was a song for the fans. And through blood, sweat, pain, tears, relegation and Ridsdale, they've been singing it ever since. When Vinnie Jones made a triumphant return to Elland Road to play in Lucas Radebe's testimonial in 2005, he took the mic, said, 'I've only got one thing to say to you lot,' and launched into 'Marching On Together'. It's said that only two ex-players ever returned to play against Leeds at Elland Road and got a standing ovation. One was John Charles and the other was Vinnie Jones.

Leeds fans the Kaiser Chiefs, who are famously named after Radebe's former club in his native South Africa, predictably bag a lot of tannoy action as we arrive at the stadium to see Leeds take on Norwich City. 'I Predict a Riot' booms out and the crowd sings along. One of their finest recent moments came when a wobbly fat guy from Preston North End started to try and wind up the Leeds fans, who responded with a rousing chorus of 'I Predict a Diet'. It's genius, I tell you.

All seems well as we enter the South Stand. The snow has stopped, Leeds are on the up again and the play-offs are beckoning. The 100 or so Ultras gathering in their allotted section have got official recognition by the club now and there's a mood of optimism about the place that they haven't experienced here for a few years. All their prime assets – Alan Smith, James Milner, Paul Robinson, Harry Kewell, Aaron Lennon et al – have been long flogged off and, worryingly for some, Uncle Ken Bates has turned up as chairman. Yet manager Kevin Blackwell has kept a level head to steady the ship, they are no longer haemorrhaging money, and in their more fanciful moments in the Magic Sponge earlier, some were contemplating a late dash to steal an automatic promotion spot back to the Premiership from their deadly rivals Sheffield United.

'It's all relative,' says Clive Miers. 'My personal low point was losing 5-1 away to Shrewsbury in the 1980s. But by the time we reached Birmingham on the way back we found it funny. We've seen lows before. That's what that song "Marching On Together" says. "We've been through it all together and we've had our ups and downs. We're gonna stay with you for ever, or at least until the world stops going round."

'The season that we went down we actually had a really good time. It's not just about results and watching the football or just about the team; Leeds has always been about the supporters. It's a much broader thing than watching Man Utd. We're not well liked, we know that, but ...' But you don't care? 'That's right! When we were everyone's second favourite team and it was O'Leary's young babes or whatever it was, it pissed a lot of us off to be perfectly honest – we don't like being *liked*. We love it that people don't like us.'

And it seems that regrouping in the Championship hasn't done them any harm at all. 'No, it's good. We've visited a few grounds we've never been to before and we've found the fans of other clubs very friendly. I know there's always a sense of trepidation whenever Leeds United are in town but the hooliganism problem has gone now. There are so many people with banning orders, and the prices have forced people out as well.'

I also talk to Kjell Skjerven, who is one of an astonishing 3,000 members of the Norwegian branch of the Leeds United Supporters Club. Kjell, who's 38, is more serious about it than most, though – he gave up an idyllic life living by a Norwegian fjord to spend a year working in a Co-op in Yorkshire just so he could see his beloved Leeds every week. 'The best year of my life,' he tells me breathlessly. 'I lived ten minutes from Elland Road, I went to all of the home and away matches, and on the pitch at the Burnley game I was presented with a signed shirt and treated as a VIP.'

Kjell adopted Leeds in the 1970s in a typically random fashion familiar to other uber-fans like Dave Burnley with Burnley and Phil Fox with Morton, after watching them on Norwegian television. He first came to England to see them in 1993. 'We lost 1-0 away to Wimbledon, drew 0-0 at home to Manchester United and then beat Oldham 2-0,' he recounts, faithfully. 'But of course we get a lot of English football on TV in Norway so I was able to see them quite a bit anyway when it wasn't possible to travel across.'

He does go and watch Norwegian games too, but prefers the cut-and-thrust of English football. 'It's so great to be singing with other Leeds supporters,' he says. 'In Norway they sing the same songs you have in England except they are sung in Norwegian and they are much *quieter*.' Kjell is back living in Norway now but returns to Elland Road on a regular basis, and when he can't make the trip he is glued to a telly or the internet to follow the matches. So are Leeds going to make the play-offs this season, Kjell? 'Oh yes! I've already booked my hotel in Cardiff.'

We take our seats at the back of the lower tier of the South Stand, and true to their word in the Magic Sponge the Ultras launch an avalanche of song as soon as the players run out to 'Marching On Together'. I have to hand it to Les Reed and Barry Mason, they knew their way around a good chorus (well, they did also write 'The Last Waltz', 'Delilah' and 'Les Bicyclettes de Belsize'), and before I know it I'm caught up in the frenzy of it all and joining in with the 'Leeds Leeds Leeds' bit.

We stare across at the Norwich supporters hemmed in the enchantingly named 'Cheese Wedge' close by and don't hear a peep out of them. They may have sung 'On the Ball City' at Wembley and the San Siro, but there's not much evidence of it at Elland Road, nor of 'The Ballad of Crossan & Bly'. Come on! Let's be 'avin' yer!

We sing,'Small town in Ipswich, you're just a small town in Ipswich' at them, thinking that will *really* annoy them, but they don't even blink. So then it's the charming 'Yer mum's yer dad, yer dad's yer mum/Yer interbred, yer Norwich scum.' And then the guy in front of me ups the stakes: 'Three humps, you've only got three humps'. The theme is taken up all around me as people offer suggestions of increasingly grotesque hypothetical body parts for the Norfolk contingent: 'Four tits, will you marry me?' Then it's 'You're going home in a Massey Ferguson' followed by 'Does your girlfriend wash your hair?' *That'll* teach Delia for not returning my calls.

However, when they were fighting for their lives in the Premiership Norwich did come out with one of the best responses to an opposition heckle that I've ever heard. They were playing Chelsea shortly after Norwich director Delia Smith's famously tired-and-emotional half-time exhortation for the crowd to get behind the team (which led to some outrageous allegations that Delia may have been at the cooking sherry). The

Chelsea fans chanted 'We've got Abramovich – you've got a drunken bitch'. Norwich came back instantly with an even more dastardly insinuation: 'We've got a super cook – you've got a Russian crook'. We are, indeed, not worthy.

It's frighteningly easy to get caught up in the mass frenzy today. I mean, I've never had much truck with Leeds since Revie's team cruelly humiliated a wretched Southampton side 7-0 in 1972, at one time making 25 passes amid an arrogant exhibition of flicks and ball-juggling that seemed to go on for about 10 minutes without a Saints player touching the ball, and is still shown on TV ad nauseam. But here I am on my feet with the rest of them dancing, singing, clapping and hurling abuse at the opposition like I'm watching a team I really care about like, I dunno, Airdrie or Total Network Solutions.

Halfway through the first half there's a bit of pinball in the Norwich box in front of us and the ball falls for blond bomber Rob Hulse to bang into the net. We're up on our feet again and a couple of stewards pass among us as they do every time we stand to sit us down again. The half-time beers taste especially sweet as we continue our debate about the direction of football and the impersonal new 'flatpack' stadiums of Reading and the like. 'Have you been to Brighton?' asks Clive Miers. 'It's a weird place that Withdean Stadium. You're so far from the pitch it's impossible to engage in the match. The highlight was a fight between the ball boys.'

I confess my allegiance to Southampton. It's a bad move. 'Our best day of the season was going down there,' gloats Clive. 'We were 3-0 down and dead and buried at half-time, so we all thought to hell with it, we're here now, we'll just have a ball. So we sang our hearts out and had a laugh and then we scored and the momentum grew and we ended up winning 4-3. The players said afterwards that they were inspired by the fans.'

Halfway through the second half at Elland Road things take an unexpectedly sour turn. Andy Hughes equalises for Norwich and then an ex-Leeds player, Darren Huckerby, takes off like a whippet, knocks the ball across and Paul McVeigh gets on the end of it to put the Canaries 2-1 up. Ah, *now* we can hear 'On the Ball City'.

The Ultras around me aren't happy. Some are trying to rustle up the old anthems to get the team going again, others want Blackwell to make changes and some just start yelling abuse at the players. The stewards keep pushing in front of us, obscuring our view, telling people to sit down, but as soon as Leeds mount a meaningful attack they're back up and we go through the whole tedious process again. It's a fact of life at football. People stand when something exciting happens and when the excitement passes they sit down again. They don't require a bunch of little Hitlers telling them to do it.

Next to me is Martin Brown, who has his six-year-old daughter Mia with him, and in an attempt to see the action above the constant irritating flow of stewards we remain upright, leaning against the wall behind our seats. It's the last row, we're in nobody's way, we're not being abusive and we're no danger to ourselves or anyone else. But along comes An Important Steward – we know this because he doesn't have an orange waterproof but a smart civvy coat and a smug swagger – to tell us to sit down.

Martin's had enough. 'What's your problem? What's the issue?' 'It's an all-seater stadium.' 'But we're not causing a problem. If you get out of the way I'll sit down.' 'But it's an all-seater stadium.' 'I've paid £25 for a ticket to see the match, not watch you getting in the way.' 'There's no need to take that tone – sit down.' 'Get out of the way and I will.' Suddenly the two are eyeball-to-eyeball and there is real menace in the situation.

I'm wondering if the steward wants to be a traffic warden when he grows up but as the argument erupts again, the frightened Mia starts sobbing her eyes out. Martin tries to comfort her and the other Ultras in the vicinity are outraged that the aggressive tone of the steward has caused the little girl such distress and turn on him. 'Are you proud of yourself?' one yells in his face. Other stewards pitch in and the incident looks like it could escalate into violence. That's when I start taking photographs.

That's when the stewards turn on me. That's when they try to take my camera and throw me out. That's when I tell them I'm writing a book and they'll be in it.

The arguments continue but Mia's tears dry and the rage subsides. By this time we've completely lost touch with events on the pitch but Leeds are putting in a grandstand finish. In the last minute they get a free kick just outside the penalty area and the American Eddie Lewis steps up to send a swirling shot past Robert Green in the Norwich goal. That puts a smile back on Mia's face, and if Mia's smiling the whole world smiles too.

Back in the Magic Sponge, though, attitudes harden again. Martin says he's writing a letter of complaint to Ken Bates and others want to raise the whole question of the problem of insensitive stewards with club officials. I end up writing to Ken Bates myself and several weeks later get a reply (though not from Ken) along the lines that the situation has been monitored and now everything in the garden is lovely. Clive Miers' response to that is 'Laughable! Bearing in mind we had one arrested and two thrown out a couple of games ago. For singing too close to the away fans!' Maybe the man who wanted to introduce electrified fences may not be the most sympathetic person to complain to about mistreatment of supporters.

Given their track record, it's perhaps understandable that Leeds are hyper-sensitive to the potential problems of excitable fans. However, anyone with a modicum of common sense would have resolved the situation before it began with a friendly nod and wink. Or maybe stewards as a breed apart are just not at the races.

The whole crowd stood on the Kop at Anfield for the entire of the England v. Uruguay game and no stewards bothered us. But the Leeds stewarding problem (which, incidentally, is far from exclusive to Leeds) is endemic of the way that clubs generally treat the fans. Clive Miers tells me about the away match at Hull City, a game with no history of trouble, where they had 300 police around them, an alcohol ban, ticket restrictions and a midday kick-off. 'If this had been a political march then the mantra of human rights violations would have been trotted out,' he sighs. 'But we're football fans ...'

What we need is a fans' representative on the boards at football clubs. Oh, hang on; there is one. In 1984, many years of decline on the pitch and the financial pressures which came with it resulted in Charlton Athletic going into administration. With their ground, The Valley, falling apart and no money to mend it, they had to groundshare with Crystal Palace. Support dwindled, results on the pitch were poor and they were a club ready to die.

Except their fans weren't prepared to let it happen. They were determined to make the club solvent again, go back up the leagues, restore Charlton to their former glory and – this was the *real* Holy Grail – take them home to The Valley. Getting little support from the London borough of Greenwich, they formed their own political party to make noises in the corridors of power and, with a 15,000-vote mandate from the electors, The Valley party were able to apply pressure on the council to approve plans to renovate the old ground.

It was still a long haul and Charlton also had a spell playing at West Ham's Upton Park. But with fortunes also reviving on the pitch, the fans committee achieved their miracle and in 1992, eight years after they'd left, they made an emotional return to The Valley. With Alan Curbishley in charge of matters on the pitch, a return to the top division followed soon afterwards.

Charlton fans had played a very special part in keeping the heart of Charlton Athletic beating and, after such a close involvement with the club's survival, it seemed a logical step for the board to create the first supporters' representative director. The person voted in was Sue Townsend, a season ticket holder and Charlton regular for 24 years, who runs the Maidstone branch of the supporters club.

'I think that more clubs should have fans, representatives on the board to give the fans' perspective on any issues that arise and give them a voice,' she says. 'It helps the club, too, to know there is someone the supporters can go to if there's a problem or an issue that needs sorting out.'

Charlton have always been a fan-friendly family club and Sue says that in her three years on the board (she left in 2006) the other directors were always very considerate and proactive in trying to facilitate the concerns of the fans, 'although we didn't have too many problems and I didn't have to bang the table or anything'. You can bet your life there would be plenty of action if Leeds ever entertained the notion of a fans' representative on the board, but somehow you can't see Ken Bates or Abramovich or the Glazer Brothers or any of the other big shots entertaining such a notion.

'Oh yes,' continues Sue, 'there are a lot of issues in the way football is going that affect a lot of us. The cost, for one thing – you do wonder how much consideration they give the fans. Take the whole business of the fixtures. On December 28, we had a Wednesday night game at Newcastle. We got all the way up there in the snow, and 25 minutes before kick-off the match was called off, not because of the state of the pitch but the condition of the roads outside the ground. Who considered the fans that day? *Anybody*?

'And in truth, how many really exciting matches are there in the Premiership now? We had some fantastic matches in the old First Division, and in many ways it was more enjoyable in those days. It's great to see players like Rooney but the costs are getting ridiculous now and the number of fans travelling away has dropped tremendously. The man in the street is being priced out and it may be time to form a supporters union to try and do something about it. What would happen if we all said we're going to boycott all matches this week and nobody went? That would make them think, wouldn't it?'

I've written Hull City into the equation here. They have got a grudge match coming up at Leicester City, once the domain of their manager Peter Taylor, and the plan is to travel on a coach with a load of Hull supporters, watch their own match against the Leicester fans and then drink in the animosity at the Walkers Stadium. So I book a weekend in Hull. *A weekend in Hull*! Just writing it now makes me go all quivery. The very same Hull nominated at No. 1 in the book *Crap Towns: The 50 Worst Places To Live in the UK* with a description from a former resident of 'a sad story of unemployment, teenage pregnancy, heroin addiction, crime, violence and rampant self-neglect'.

I'm looking forward to discussing this on the road to Leicester with my new chums, but unfortunately my contact at Hull Supporters Club seems to have gone AWOL. I'm standing around Hull waiting to be mugged on Saturday morning when I finally get a phone message from him saying the supporters' club match is off so therefore there's no coach, and therefore there's no lift for me, and therefore they'll meet me in Leicester.

With no wish to drive back down to Leicester on my own and certainly no wish to hang around in Hull without armoured protection, I make a late decision to change plans and drive to Newcastle to see their match against Bolton. The weird thing is that it doesn't look very far on the map. Whip up the north-east coast, round that funny bit at the top, turn right and there you are – the fog on the Tyne's all mine, all mine. Two hours tops, I would say.

Four hours later I'm still ploughing through snow and sleat and horrendous traffic jams wondering where the hell they've moved Newcastle. When I pass Middlesbrough and see the fans rushing to the game for fear of being late I realise that it could be tight making St James's Park in time for kick-off. For the first time I wish that the ground was a flatpack job stuck on an out-of-town trading estate, but St James's, of course, is right slap-bang in the centre of Newcastle and you have to wade through the city traffic and then find a car park which hasn't already got a queue of vehicles round the block waiting to get in.

By the time I make it through Chinatown to the imposing stadium, fifteen minutes after kick-off, everything seems firmly shut. I'd booked a ticket on the phone before leaving Hull but nobody seems to know where it is. The man in the penguin suit guarding Shearer's Bar sends me on a long climb up to the ticket office, the man in the ticket office sends me to a hole in the wall, the woman at the hole in the wall tells me to bang on the gate and wait for one of the stewards to let me in, and the steward sends me back to the man in the penguin suit. He tells me to go to the ticket office and I tell him Shearer was rubbish after he left Southampton. Oh, and that I'm writing a book and he's going to be in it.

Is there anything more frustrating than being outside a football ground listening to the gasps and roars of those inside without a clue what's happening? Although after frustrating afternoons spent listening to Burton Albion, the Manchester derby and the Old Firm match I should be getting used to it now. Eventually the man in the ticket office finds my name in a little black book somewhere, I knock on the back gate three times and ask for Alice, and the canny Geordie steward lad lets me in. I give him a kiss and bound up the stairs to find my seat.

Whoosh! The view at the top, the atmosphere, the *sensation* of the place takes my breath away. I'd been here before, years earlier, to interview an entertainingly indiscreet Kevin Keegan laying into the FA, Manchester United and Arsenal, but to suddenly arrive here in the centre of a vibrant cacophony of noise, colour and excitement is something else. It feels like walking into a painting that has suddenly come alive and I stand for a moment on my ledge gulping it all in, gazing down at the play below me.

There's a crescendo of noise immediately behind me and I wonder for a second what it is, until one of those voices arrows into focus: 'Get oot the way ye bloody moron you're blocking the view – ah canna see the game!' At that precise moment Nolberto Solano sends an exquisite free kick hurtling into the corner of the Bolton net. I turn to see a man the size of Gateshead marching purposefully out of his seat to hurl me over the balcony on to the pitch, and I make my excuses and leave.

It turns out to be a cracking match. Shearer heads a second goal on the stroke of half-time, igniting a mass chorus of 'Hey hey Shearer! Ooh aah! I wanna know-ow-ow/How you scored that goal' to the 'Hey Baby' tune. With half an eye out for the man-mountain who is still baying for the blood of the fool who made him miss Solano's goal, I engage in merry banter with the guy I've been hiding next to ever since. 'Oh aye, I'm glad we got rid of Souness, like,' he says. 'I can't think what they were doing appointing him in the first place. I never liked him since he had that perm at Liverpool.'

In truth, the Toon Army isn't on top of its game today. Pete Boyle's words ring round my head: 'Oh aye, Newcastle and Liverpool can make a lot of noise when they feel like it, but half the time it's like a museum and you can hear a pin drop.' Yet I am still seduced again by the majesty of St James's Park and its traditional role in the very heartland of Geordie culture. When the crowd starts to sing 'Blaydon Races', it gives me goosebumps.

A Gateshead man called Geordie Ridley first sang the song in 1862 at a testimonial dinner for a Tyneside hero, rower Harry Clasper. The Blaydon Races were a real event that took place on an island in the middle of the Tyne but were aborted in 1916 following a riot after the winning horse was disqualified amid allegations of all manner of skulduggery. Ridley, who began trying his hand at writing songs about local events and characters after an injury curtailed his career at the local iron works, achieved little acclaim for the song in his own lifetime but it came into its own with the advent of music hall and was popularised by a Newcastle comedian called Scatter:

> O me lads, you shoulda seen us gannin'
> Passing the folks along the road just as they were stannin'
> Aal the lads and lasses there aal wi' smilin' faces
> Gannin' along the Scotswood Road to see the Blaydon Races.

Like West Ham blowing their bubbles, 'Blaydon Races' has been part of the furniture at St James's Park since anyone can remember, and when the fans start to sing it seems to conjure up the ghosts of all the legends towering over Tyneside footballing folklore: Wee Hughie Gallagher, Jimmy Scoular, Bobby Mitchell, George Robledo, Joe Harvey, Bobby Moncur, Malcolm

Macdonald, Pop Robson, Ivor Allchurch, Kevin Keegan, Peter Beardsley, Chris Waddle, Paul Gascoigne, Len Shackleton ... well, maybe not Shackleton, the self-styled 'Clown Prince of Football' who blotted his copybook by signing for Sunderland and then proceeded to slag off Newcastle: 'I've nothing against Newcastle, I don't care who beats them.'

And let's not forget 'He's fat, he's round, he scores at every ground, Mickey Quinn, Mickey Quinn', whose own richly entertaining autobiography *Who Ate All the Pies?* is not only a fantastic belly laugh (if you'll pardon the pun) but provides some telling insights into the Geordie psyche, particularly as regards their attitude towards their centre forwards. A gobby Scouser from an unsalubrious council estate, Quinn was dancing on air the day he signed for Newcastle in 1989. As he walked into the city for a celebratory snifter he told his girl-friend, 'This is one of the proudest moments of my life. It's what I've been struggling to achieve since I practised kicking a tennis ball against a wall every night when I was a kid.'

It was at that exact moment that a large, angry-looking demonstration came marching towards them, most of them wearing Newcastle United shirts and waving a huge banner. It said: 'WHO THE FUCK IS MICK QUINN?' Yet amazingly, it all ended happily. As he completed a hat trick on his debut, Quinn ran to the Gallowgate end, arms aloft, screaming, '*That's* who the fuck Mick Quinn is!!' He never had to buy a drink on Tyneside again.

The greatest legend of them all in these parts, though, is 'Wor' Jackie Milburn, who answered an ad in the *North Mail* and turned up for a trial match in 1943 with a pair of borrowed boots in a brown paper bag clutching a pie and a bottle of pop. He scored six goals in that trial and was signed on the spot. When he left, 14 years later, he'd scored a club record 200 goals in 395 games, won 13 caps for England (scoring 10 goals), led the Magpies to three FA Cup Final victories in 1951, 1952 and 1955 and turned the already hallowed black-and-white striped No. 9 shirt into something akin to a sacred monument.

Wor Jackie, a shy man from the coal mining community of Ashington, had no time for the trappings of fame and celebrity and seemed to live on another planet entirely to the overpaid party animals that have represented the city in recent years. What would he make of two Newcastle players, Kieron Dyer and Lee Bowyer, getting sent off for fighting one another? Or the rebellious strops of Craig Bellamy, or the preening self-regard of David Ginola and Lauren Robert?

Jackie Milburn never made a fortune out of football and when Newcastle offered him a testimonial a decade after he retired, he didn't think anyone would remember him. He thought wrong. Over 50,000 turned out at St James's Park to chant his name at an all-star match that included his famous nephews Bobby and Jackie Charlton and the great Hungarian Ferenc Puskas. Now there are two statues of him on Tyneside, the West Stand bears his name, and when he died of lung cancer at the age of 64 in 1988, over 30,000 filled the streets around his funeral.

He kept it quiet, but Wor Jackie was a bit of a singer too. After he'd died the family found tapes of him as a very passable tenor and you wonder how different his life would have been had he lived in a later age. As it is, Jackie's – quite beautiful – singing of 'Love Is a Many Splendoured Thing' has been set to a rap telling the story of his career, which is included on a CD, *Howay the Lads: Classic Newcastle Songs*.

Now another local boy made good, Alan Shearer, has just broken Milburn's goal record and the No. 9 shirt has shifted up another notch in the annals of Tyneside folklore. Unlike Milburn, though, Shearer has never won a rusty screw in all his time in that shirt and after all those years of disappointment, under-achievement and frustration it's small wonder the Toon Army goes a bit quiet from time to time. A fan can't live on sentiment alone.

So there are no big booming choruses today. There is no sign, either, of Harry Palmer. In 1992 Harry, an unemployed painter and primitive acoustic guitarist, sent a tape of his punky alternative versions of Geordie classics and terrace anthems to St James's Park. The tapes were played at half-time during a match against Luton Town and caused a sensation. Harry became a terrace cult hero, with TV appearances, newspaper interviews and the VIP treatment from John Hall and Kevin Keegan. His charmingly makeshift interpretations of Leazes End chants and fan songs even made it on to record and got him a few gigs in a Pete Boyle style.

Back on the pitch, Bolton make a game of it in the second half but there's little action from their fans – not even from Vernon Kay, the kids' TV presenter who spent the first day of married life with his bride and fellow micro-celeb Tess Daly watching Bolton. Not that his fellow supporters were impressed: they all chanted 'You're not as good as Ant & Dec' at him.

There's a battle royal between two outstanding English midfield players – Scott Parker for Newcastle and Kevin Nolan for Bolton – before Ameobi bangs in Newcastle's third. Kevin Davies scrambles in a goal for Bolton which stirs them into a last-gasp onslaught, but goalkeeper Shay Given keeps them at bay and the Magpies run out 3-1 winners. We flock out contentedly at the end, the Geordies rehearsing the stories to tell their grandkids about the heroics of the great Alan Shearer while I wander round the unfamiliar streets that are already thronging with bright young things prancing around in their undies as the city's legendary Saturday night shenanigans get underway.

Completely lost in the back streets and wondering where I've left my car, I stumble across a couple of kids kicking a ball against a wall. It feels like I've suddenly been transported back to a bygone age: the kids are in short trousers with grazed knees and scuffed shoes pretending to be Milburn and Shackleton. Then one of them dribbles and impersonates John Motson: 'Shearer's on the ball, he shoots ...' As he lets fly the other kid sticks out a foot to divert the ball, then raises his arms and punches the air. 'Great ball from Shearer, and Ameobi scores!' I feel strangely emotional.

You won't find any sympathy in Newcastle for the plight of

their deadly rivals eight miles away in Sunderland. Doomed to relegation almost from the first day of the season, a visit to the Stadium of Light seems like an official observation of the last rites. But I can't think ill of Sunderland, who are the only Premiership club to respond to my plea for information, encouragement, tickets and dusky handmaidens when I am researching this book. They return phone calls, emails and convivial banter and furnish me with a press pass for their local derby with Middlesbrough.

The days of the Roker Roar are long gone since Sunderland moved into this gorgeous space age stadium on the outskirts of town, so close to the Wear that you fear it may topple in and get us all wet. The surroundings are bleak but the stadium itself is a remarkable construction, incorporating sculptures and architecture that honours the site's history as a colliery. It's just a shame about the team, really.

After wandering the wrong way along plush corridors into executive suites, board rooms and at one point nearly the changing rooms, I finally locate the vast press room where a large gaggle of earnest young reporters with spiral notebooks are discussing systems and body language and missed deadlines and rude managers. We are also served soup, a rather fine curry and as much coffee as you can drink (which, in my case, is lots). I'm starting to wonder if it hadn't been a mistake to abandon that job on the local paper sports desk covering Slough Town matches all those centuries ago. I mean, this is the media, and they're being treated like royalty. That can't be right, can it? They'll still slag you off at every turn.

Rob Mason, the personable programme editor and club historian, introduces himself and starts talking about Charlie Hurley, an iconic former Sunderland captain. 'As well as being a great centre half he was dominant at corner kicks,' he says. 'When Sunderland got a corner the whole ground would sing "Charlie! Charlie! Charlie!" They wouldn't take the corner until he was in the box, and then he would either head it in or head it down for someone else to get a chance. He left here in 1969 but you just mention the name Charlie around here and everyone knows exactly who you're talking about. He still comes to games from time to time and whenever he comes on the pitch he gets a standing ovation.'

It's a shame you can't bring on Charlie for corners now, eh Rob? He smiles benignly and talks more of the passion for the game in this corner of the country. 'In my opinion, Sunderland and Newcastle supporters jointly are the best supporters in the country. We've hardly won a game this season, last time we were in the Premier League we had the worst record ever with just 19 points, we've only won one trophy since the Second World War, and yet we haven't had an attendance this season under 30,000. No way would Manchester United or Liverpool have crowds like that if they had our sort of record.

'Nobody's happy getting beat, but just because you're getting beat doesn't mean you stop supporting your club. The way it works up here is if you go out there and give it your all, people will back you. If you don't give your all they'll crucify you. And if you give your all and you're a decent player they'll worship you. That's why Julio Arca is worshipped up here.'

Sunderland were actually founded in Glasgow by an Ayrshire man, James Allen, in 1879 and their current travails are nothing new in the long and winding road that's brought them to the Stadium of Light. One of the giants of the early years, they hit the rocks after the Second World War. Blighted by an illegal payment scandal, they slithered down the league and in 1958 were relegated from the top flight for the first time in their history.

They restored some pride, of course, in 1973, with one of the most startling FA Cup Finals ever. A mediocre Second Division team pitched against Don Revie's coldly invincible Leeds United, people were talking openly of a cricket score against them. Laughing and joking on the Wembley pitch beforehand in their ludicrous perms and mad 1970s flares, the players even seemed to know it themselves and displayed a casually resigned attitude to the fate that awaited them.

But once the match started Sunderland turned into rampaging

lunatics, charging around the field, launching themselves at the Leeds players, hoofing the ball into orbit every time it came near their goal and generally unnerving Leeds with their cavalier spirit. The subsequent images still swim easily into focus: Ian Porterfield's low strike into the net to give them an unlikely lead after half an hour, and fearsome all-hands-on-deck, we-shall-not-be-moved defensive resilience for the next hour. Balls pinging around the Sunderland area, last-ditch tackles from captain Bobby Kerr's inspired troops, Jimmy Montgomery's gravity-defying triple save from point blank range in the dying minutes, and manager Bob Stokoe's comedy dash to embrace his heroic keeper at the end as the Cup went to Wearside.

In 1987 they slid to their lowest ebb with relegation to the Third Division and it has been a long haul back to re-establish themselves as one of the country's premier clubs. And fancy new stadium or not, it's not going to happen this year as once more the trapdoor gapes open below them. Yet in the midst of it all, 'The Continentals', a fan group from Holland who come over on the boat to take in matches all over Britain, took a particular shine to Sunderland. There are now 30 or so Dutch season ticket holders, including some with dual season tickets for Feyenoord.

A couple of Dutchmen, Leo Meijer and Hans De Roon, had such a thirst for the British game that they once travelled from the Netherlands just to see a match between Middlesbrough Reserves and Liverpool Reserves. De Roon, in particular, was so smitten by the North East that he upped sticks and left Holland completely to buy a house next to Roker Park and see Sunderland every week without that inconvenient boat ride first. He's back in Breda now playing trad jazz, but he remains a Mackem at heart and still makes regular pilgrimages across to cheer on Sunderland.

Tonight's match really isn't pretty. How could it be? Local derbies rarely are. Besides which, one team is already virtually doomed to relegation and the other is fighting for its life. But I sit back in my press enclosure splendour, admiring the desk they thoughtfully provide for note-writing, occasionally glancing at the television monitors that replay the major incidents, listening to the various radio commentators around me chattering into their mics and looking at the anxiety etched on the faces of both sets of fans hoping for a miraculous turn around.

Not that the nail biting lasts for long. Sunderland forget that Emanuel Pogatetz, the big lad strolling into their penalty area when Middlesbrough are awarded a free kick just outside the box, isn't there to discuss the latest bargains at B&Q and may have evil intent. A free header, back of the net, and Sunderland are in trouble again. A few more minutes go by then young defender Stuart Parnaby robs the Sunderland crowd's darling Julio Arca, waltzes through some half-arsed tackles and drives in Middlesbrough's second. We are less than 20 minutes into the game and it's effectively all over.

Sunderland do come out for the second half with a bit more fire in their bellies, which briefly inspires their fans to a few choruses of Elvis's 'I Can't Help Falling In Love', one of several songs they claim to have introduced to matches and subsequently seen adopted by the rest of the country. Another is the old Monkees hit 'Daydream Believer', which Newcastle fans savagely turned against them when Peter Reid was the manager by singing, 'Cheer up Peter Reid, oh what can it mean/To be a sad Mackem bastard with a shit football team'. This was invariably followed by 'Peter Reid's got a fookin' monkey's heed' to the tune of 'Yellow Submarine'.

Twenty minutes from the end, Jimmy Floyd Hasselbaink puts Sunderland out of their misery with a stunning 25-yard shot. Still, they've been here before and they mostly try to retain a sense of humour about it. When Newcastle came recently and started singing 'Going down going down going down', the Sunderland fans responded with 'So are we so are we so are we'.

There's a kerfuffle behind me as a man in a Sunderland top tries to get through our press enclosure, which is directly behind the dugout. A steward stops him. 'I just need to give something to someone,' says the guy, all red-faced and worked up, waving a small ticket wallet. 'It's me season ticket!' The steward is momentarily perplexed and almost lets him through. 'Who do you want to give it to?' 'That twat down there!' He's pointing to Sunderland manager Mick McCarthy. Bizarrely, an identical situation arises at Middlesbrough the following week, when a Boro fan does make it on to the pitch to toss his season ticket at manager Steve McClaren.

There are long faces all round back in the warmth of the press facility, where microphones are set up for the post-match press conference. Steve McClaren soon skips among us with a smile as big as the Wear and such a spring in his step I'm convinced that when he moves in front of the mic he's going to give us a round of 'There's No Business Like Showbusiness'. He doesn't stop beaming throughout the conference, praising his boys to the skies, cracking jokes and talking animatedly through every nuance of each goal. The press boys soon run out of the questions, but perhaps thinking of his next job as England manager, Steve is reluctant to leave.

And then comes the long wait for the Sunderland manager. Rumours fly around. He's already resigned. He's still got the team locked in the dressing room throwing teacups at them. He's too upset to talk to the press. He's currently standing on top of the stand and a groundsman is trying to talk him out of jumping into the Wear. But eventually Mick McCarthy appears, looking haggard, worn and beaten. He slumps into a seat in front of the mic and stares across at us. We all avoid his gaze, looking at our feet, shuffling our notebooks and coughing nervously. After a painful silence, McCarthy speaks in that wonderfully broad Yorkshire monotone that used to wind Roy Keane up so much when they were locking horns for Ireland: 'Christ I don't know what *you're* all looking so miserable about, I'm the one who should be upset! Go on, fire away, give it your best shot.'

Considering their reputation as the most evil creatures on God's Earth, the press are remarkably kind. Even the bloke who asks if McCarthy is going to resign apologises first and puts it in a nice way. No, says Mick, he's not a quitter. But is he resigned to relegation now? No, says Mick, he's not a quitter. I'm starting to wonder if there's a robot malfunction here. Which may explain a lot about the way Sunderland played tonight.

McCarthy is sacked a couple of weeks later and Sunderland are down by Easter, while Middlesbrough recover and not only survive, but go on a remarkable run in the UEFA Cup. Meanwhile, I leave the North East stinking of curry and wondering if the Dutchmen are getting the ferry home tonight.

— CHAPTER 11 —

It's All About the Bovril

'Let all tonight then drink with me
To the football game we love
And wish it may successful be
As other games of old.

And in one grand united toast
Join player, game and song
And fondly pledge your pride and toast
Success to the city club!'

From 'On the Ball City'

The key to the search for the soul of British football, I foolishly tell myself, is to be found in Milton Keynes.

Milton Keynes, home of the concrete cows 50 miles north of London, was purpose-built in 1967 to absorb the London overflow in a location equidistant between London, Birmingham and Leicester. It's strange, really, that in the brave new world into which it was foist there was no provision for a football club. If you happened to be relocated to Milton Keynes, the closest professional clubs from which to derive your guilty pleasures were Luton Town or Rushden & Diamonds, affectionately known as the Annies after the name was once misheard as Rushden Anne Diamond.

Well, Milton Keynes never did have its own football team until Wimbledon strayed there in 2001 – the same Wimbledon who rose from the Southern League to the Premier League and were indelibly associated with Dicky Guy, Dave 'Harry' Bassett, mud, hard men, long ball, Wombles, Dave Beasant, Dennis Wise, Laurie Sanchez, Sam Hammam and Vinnie Jones scaring the crap out of Liverpool to win the 1988 Cup Final and mooning at the crowd back at tatty old Plough Lane.

Plough Lane, Wimbledon were fond of saying, was a dump but it was *their* dump. In the wake of Hillsborough, the Taylor Report changed the whole face of football grounds, sparking a mass upgrading of stadiums and the sprouting of a bunch of new ones. It became very clear early on that Wimbledon couldn't play at Plough Lane in the state it was in and after 79 years the club left, supposedly temporarily, to groundshare with Crystal Palace in 1991. Alarm bells were already clanging amid rumours of a complete merger with Palace, and action groups were set up to campaign for a swift return to the borough of Merton.

The optimistic talk of redeveloping Plough Lane gradually began to subside, various representations to build a new stadium in Merton came and went, and support at Palace dwindled despite relative success on the pitch, including flirtations with European qualification. Then two Norwegians, Kjell Inge Rokke and Bjorn Rune Gjelsten, invested £30 million for an 80 per cent stake in the club. According to Sam Hammam, it was to be the salvation of Wimbledon. It turned out to be the destruction.

In one of the maddest schemes ever floated in football, plans were launched to relocate Wimbledon to, er, *Dublin*. The club's internal turmoil was exacerbated by manager Joe Kinnear suffering a heart attack before an away game with Sheffield Wednesday. Some Norwegian in green wellies became manager and Sam Hammam headed off up the M4 to Cardiff despite saying, 'I remain the father of Wimbledon.' In 2000, Wimbledon were relegated from the Premier League.

Widely ridiculed, the Dublin plan was dropped but replaced by another one that initially sounded almost as bizarre – a relocation to Milton Keynes, 70 miles away. Surely the FA wouldn't sanction this idea? As club owner Bjorn Gjelsten commented, 'If it's Milton Keynes, it might as well be Oslo.' In the first match of the 2001–02 season the Wimbledon fans filled the sky with black balloons before their match with Birmingham City to signify their horror at the increasingly dreadful turn of events.

As the proposed move took root, the fans took action, with South African chairman Charles Koppel, a business associate of the Norwegians, now firmly installed as Public Enemy No. 1. Buoyed by Charlton fans' campaign to get back to The Valley, Wimbledon supporters still believed a return to Plough Lane was possible even though the land had now been sold. They staged demonstrations at every home match and during one game against Barnsley they symbolically turned their backs on the pitch. The Milton Keynes move still looked ludicrous and was initially turned down by the FA. However, on appeal a three-man commission was set up to study the case and, to the astonishment of the entire football world, approved the move. A protest was held at the FA and a banner unveiled bearing the words 'WIMBLEDON FC – R.I.P. FA SELL-OUT'. But it was no use – the deed was done.

Yet the fans didn't sit around moping. They didn't slope off into the sunset and reinvent themselves as lifelong Chelsea supporters. They didn't think Wimbledon – *their* Wimbledon – should be allowed to die. So they got off their arses and did something about it.

'Looking back,' says Iain McNay, 'I think the Norwegians did us a favour. I can't tell you how much fun we've had setting up a new club.' Iain, also chairman of Cherry Red Records, which has an impressive catalogue of over 60 CDs of club-dedicated football songs, is a director of AFC Wimbledon, the club that the old Wimbledon supporters built from scratch even while the mother ship was crawling through a traffic jam on the M25 towards Milton Keynes. It seemed like a dream: a club owned and run by its own fans. No fat cat chairman with an ego the size of Herts, no faceless board of directors with their own agendas, no secret deals behind locked doors.

The Dons Trust set the wheels in motion. They had to go right down to the bottom of the pyramid to start, but they found a manager (ex-player Terry Eames), held an open trial for players on Wimbledon Common and, all but using jumpers for goal-posts, began all over again. Their first match, a friendly against local neighbours Sutton in the summer of 2002, attracted a crowd of 4,657 and the new Dons were off and running.

'It's a great feeling to be so involved in something from the start,' McNay tells me over a splendid lunch in Acton, 'although it's not always easy. Imagine all the different opinions that supporters have over one match. Then imagine the different opinions they have over the way the club should be run!' Did any of the original Dons fans stay loyal and follow them into their new identity as Milton Keynes Dons? 'I think there are about 30 of them left,' says McNay with unexpected precision, adding that the majority of those who follow AFC Wimbledon will refuse point blank to set foot in Milton Keynes if, as seems increasingly possible as one goes up the leagues and the other comes down, the two Wimbledons ever meet in competitive action. 'If only they hadn't put "Dons" on the end of their name I think I'd have let it go,' he says. 'But using the name "Dons" really sticks in my throat.'

So I decide there's only one thing to be done: I must venture into the dark side. On a crisp Friday I head for Bucks, where Milton Keynes Dons are playing my old chums from Bristol City. After going into administration in 2003, MK Dons moved into their new ground at the National Hockey Stadium in Milton Keynes the following season and were bought by a local consortium led by Pete Winkelman, a music promoter with long hair and a smooth tongue who used to manage the wondrous 1980s Brummie girl band We've Got a Fuzzbox and We're Gonna Use It. You would like to think the team now run out to the raucous strains of Vickie, Maggie, Jo and Tina banging out 'Love Is the Slug', but sadly this is not the case.

A series of shocks lurk at the National Hockey Stadium, which seems to be in the middle of a trading estate ('Milton Keynes *is* a trading estate, isn't it?' says one of the Bristol City supporters emerging from Burger King). The biggest shock is discovering there are queues everywhere. And not just in Burger King. You queue to buy a ticket for the match ('Sorry, the Cowshed is full up,' says the man in the the ticket office. OK, is there any room in the Pig Sty, then?). Then you join an even longer queue to get into the ground.

The match has already kicked off by the time this laborious negotiation has been completed and I walk towards the tall, strange, roofless monstrosity designated by my ticket, gawping at a scrub of land containing a five-a-side goal and a clutch of plastic cows grazing right next to the League One match that is getting underway. I'm already thinking I've wandered into a strange Kafka fantasy world as I walk around the cows and virtually on to the pitch itself to get to the steps of the long, tall, thin thing that's laughingly called the North Stand.

At this point Bristol striker Steve Brooker ('who ironically used to live in Milton Keynes!' declares an indignant local reporter afterwards) bursts past sleepy Dons defender Ben Chorley and buries the ball in the home net (happily, they're not hockey goals). He immediately swivels in triumph and sprints to the touchline to the exact point where I'm standing. I'm not sure what the protocol is here. Do I jump on his back? Kiss him? Shake him warmly by the hand and say, 'Well played, son'?

We stare at each other in confusion for a second and then the other Bristol City players arrive at speed and we all end up in a rugby scrum. I am involuntarily trapped in the middle of a goal celebration yet the weirdest thing about the hugging and high-fiving going on is that *nobody says a word*. I had kinda thought they would talk each other through the goal as a sort of rehearsal for post-match interviews: 'Great strike, Steve!' 'Thanks mate, the ball from Bradders was a bit special.' 'Cheers, mate: see, I look up, see you make the run and think this one's on your right peg. Different class, mate, different class.'

I climb into the North Stand, which is surely designed to house the giraffes for the next Animal Olympics, and suddenly realise that I am surrounded by squealing teenagers. I'm not sure if I've walked into a youth club outing (where's the vicar, where's the table-tennis?) or a McFly concert. It's a kids-for-a-quid match apparently, which may go some way to explaining the impressive 6,855 crowd, the constant 'Stand up if you love the Dons' chants and the resultant seat motion which is starting to make me feel seasick. Behind the goal in the Cow Shed (and it really *is* called the Cow Shed) they are displaying unexpected passion.

The accepted wisdom of football is that the Milton Keynes experiment is doomed to failure. You can't just artificially stick a football club in an environment without any history and expect it to instantly take root. Footie isn't *Field of Dreams* – if you build it they not only won't come, they won't even take a blind bit of notice. A community will not just suddenly take an alien football club to its heart, and such was the antagonism of the football fraternity in general to the transplant of an already failing Dons to an unattractive new town in Bucks that you could only see it ending in tears.

Yet Peter Winkelman kept insisting that Milton Keynes housed the biggest population in Europe that didn't have a league football team and it was gagging for a club to call its own – even if it had to nick someone else's (Winkelman also had talks about bringing Queens Park Rangers to Milton Keynes), and maybe, just *maybe*, he's right. A brand new 30,000-seater stadium is being built over the way as we speak to welcome these football-thirsty Milton Keynesers.

I had arrived expecting to find half-a-dozen men who had been kicked out of the house by their wives, the complete indifference of the town and the atmosphere of a picnic at the brand new IKEA which the town is also chuffed to welcome to its bosom. Instead, I find the place rammed and raucous with the Cow Shed contingent maintaining a constant noise offensive of 'No One Likes Us We Don't Care', 'Remember You're a Womble,' 'Can't Help Falling In Love' and 'Tom Hark'. I have to admit I'm surprised and impressed. I still want the bastards to get hammered, though.

The Dons still include tales of Plough Lane and the 1988 FA

Cup win in their official history and a fanzine tells the story of one longstanding Dons fan's emotional turmoil as he eventually decided to join the charabanc to Milton Keynes and not go with the rebels. There's even talk of erecting a statue of Vinnie Jones at the new stadium. But they've abandoned the old blue shirts in favour of a pristine all-white strip – *very* Real Madrid – and there is nothing about tonight's experience that offers any remote connection to the old Wimbledon and their dogged, often ugly rise from non-league football to a prominent role in the Premiership.

I sit there freezing in the middle of an army of hyperventilating kids, looking at the strangely random layout of the ground with its empty gaps and its plastic cows and thinking if this is the national stadium then hockey must be a very odd game. It's football, Jim, but not as we know it. Bristol City are still leading 1-0, there are burger wrappers on the pitch, they think it's all over. It is now.

In desperate need of a good old Bovril and Wagon Wheels experience I go to Layer Road, Colchester, very possibly the worst ground in the Football League. In response to a request on a Colchester fans website message board for a United singer, I'm contacted by Lee Clarkson. Yes, says Lee, he'll meet me at the match: come to the Barside. I assume he's talking about a pub but it turns out to be a terrace. I go in the wrong entrance and that most unique of creatures, a helpful steward, escorts me around the ground. I pretend that I'm really hard and am being marched out of the ground for sins against referees.

We get round to the other side and he pushes me into what looks like a large garden shed: 'Here you go – this is Barside.' I put my nose inside and am immediately jolted back by the heat, the stench and the din. It's deafening in here. Chants, songs, shouted conversations and all manner of high jinks collide violently with the tannoy trying to announce the teams and then the roar as the players run out. 'Look out for the loudest singer,' Lee had told me. Fat chance – they're all at ear-splitting volume in here.

I am transported back to another world in a different era long before the Taylor Report, when the crush into grounds was so tight that you were transported without your feet touching the floor, your breath was knocked out of you when the guys next to you started shouting and you had to bob your head to glimpse the action on the pitch. It was madness then and horrendously dangerous, as we were to discover. Yet it was thrilling too. With its low roof, slanting terrace, claustrophobic intensity and jammed bodies, Colchester's Barside feels like that now. The U's are flying, chasing a club record ninth win on the bounce today and, with automatic promotion to the Championship well on the cards, the place is rocking as they charge at Bradford City. Milton Keynes, this isn't.

It's not particularly savoury but it's real. Somehow you entertain different values when you step into a football crowd, where obscenities and filth are the stock in trade and carry little of the anti-social stigma they have outside, and where political correctness is in hiding. Layer Road may be a throwback to the dark ages but it's nice, too, to be able to stand up, to *have to* stand up for a whole game demonstrating solidarity without having some numbskull steward wetting his pants. Layer Road won't be around for long, with plans for a new stadium at Colchester already well advanced, but it is a guilty pleasure being cooped up on the Barside terrace. Sometimes, nothing else will do but to sing 'The referee's a wanker' at the top of your voice, or tell Bradford's Dean Windass that he's a dirty northern bastard (sorry, Dean, nothing personal).

Windass gets his revenge, though, putting Bradford City ahead after half an hour, which suddenly jerks the visiting fans to our left into a bout of naughty hand gestures and a chorus of 'You're not singing any more', which is a bit rich considering that Colchester's supporters have been singing so hard since the match started that they've scarcely noticed Bradford have scored. Still, you can't blame them. Bradford, whose own party-piece for visiting fans when they play at home is 'Here for a curry, you're only here for a curry', have had some desperate times in recent years.

Celebrating winning the Third Division title at Valley Parade on the last day of the 1984–85 season in a match against Lincoln City in front of a packed house, their old stand suddenly went up in a fireball and 56 supporters died. As the millennium dawned they were trading punches with the big boys in the Premiership, spending fortunes on fancy dan foreigners, temporarily wresting the sporting spotlight in a rabid rugby hotspot and boasting a unique identity – the only other English institution sharing their distinctive claret-and-amber colours is Hogwarts School in *Harry Potter*.

But as with Yorkshire rivals Leeds the ambition far outstripped the financial planning and the dream came crashing down from a great height following relegation after two years in the Premiership and the collapse of the ITV Digital deal, which was supposed to make everybody rich. Owing £30 million, they went into administration in 2002 and looked in real danger of disappearing altogether. So yeah, why not enjoy your moment, you Bantams – you only sing when you're winning.

There's barely a chink in the Barside wall of sound and just on half-time Colchester equalise with a powerful strike by Richard Garcia. I'm thrown in the air in the celebrations and when I come down the whole place is going 'Gar-see-yerr/Whooo-ooh-whoo' in a stylee originated by Arsenal fans in praise of their former captain Patrick Vieira. All thanks to that baffling wonder of modern technology, the text message, I fight my way through the throng and manage to locate Lee Clarkson at half-time at the front of the Barside Terrace. 'All right, mate?' he says, beaming. 'A bit cramped in here today, innit? Enjoying the atmosphere?'

I am. And it's about to get even better. With the U's dominating the second half, Garcia heads a second goal and the crowd around me are into their Garcia song again: 'Gar-see-yerr/Whooo-ooh-whoo/Gar-see-yerr/Whooo-ooh-whoo/He scored against the scum, he'll score another one/Gar-see-yerr ...'

'That song's one of mine,' says Lee, proudly. 'I spent a couple of hours at college one day thinking we need to do a song for

Garcia and suddenly it came to me.' Who's the scum? 'Southend,' he spits. 'We all hate Southend here.' After that it's carnival time as Iwelumo volleys a third goal and the arrival of aged Bradford substitute Steve Claridge, socks dangling round his ankles in his usual tramp fashion, is greeted with good-natured abuse about zimmer frames and bath chairs. Then thoughts turn to a forthcoming FA Cup tie with Chelsea. 'Who needs Mourinho? We've got Phil Parkinson!' sings Lee, his face glowing as the blue-and-white stripes around him immediately join in at full volume before erupting into 'Bring on the Chelsea'.

'I started going to games regularly in 1998,' says 21-year-old Lee after the game over a victory pint with his mate Rupert. 'The following season I only missed one game – that was Millwall.' Why did you miss it? 'I was naughty at school and my mum wouldn't let me.'

So have you always been so, er, *vocal*? 'Well, the first few seasons I'd go in the family enclosure but I'd always try and be close to the Barside and sing along with them. After a few seasons I started going in there but some of the regulars stopped going and it got a bit quiet so I thought I'd better start some songs rather than just waiting to join in with everybody else. If nobody else is singing, that's when I start.'

Lee has quite a purist approach to the art of fandom. He believes his role as a supporter is unequivocal encouragement, no matter how badly the team are playing, and he hates it when other fans turn on the players and start booing them. He and Rupert sound like managers as they discuss the requirements to bring the best out of individual players. 'Greg Halford is a really talented player but he can be a bit lazy so we had to give him a kick up the backside,' says Rupert. 'It worked too – he's now one of our best players. Others just need to be encouraged all the time with their own songs.'

Do you plan in advance what you're going to sing? 'No, not really. If things are going well then it's completely spontaneous what we sing, but if we're struggling then I'm thinking in my head what song we can do next that could pick the team up. I don't like singing the same songs over and over again, and sometimes I might write a little list before I go to a game.' Don't you ever worry how embarrassing it might be if you launch into a song and nobody else joins in? 'It's always in the back of my mind but if they don't join in, I don't really care. If it gets drowned out it gets drowned out, but there's usually four or five of us that will try to keep it going.'

They concede that most football songs are recycled. 'Well, it *is* hard to be original,' says Lee. 'You've got to come up with something simple and catchy enough that others will latch on to and join in with, so it's not easy to invent something completely new. We'll go to an away match and if we hear a good song then we'll probably come back and try it ourselves with our own words.' They believe they have a positive effect on the way the team play ('Well yeah, otherwise there'd be no point to us doing it would there?') and like Leeds have drawn inspiration from the Ultras of Europe. On the morning of every home game Lee visits Layer Road to painstakingly set up his banners on the hoardings in front of the Barside as part of his quest to bring the complete fan experience to this unfashionable corner of Essex.

'We sometimes have this discussion: is it the players' responsibility to inspire the fans to make noise or is it up to the fans to inspire the players?' says Lee. 'My argument is the fans can always sing loud but the players can't always play well, but a lot of people argue there is a link with the amount of effort they put in. You never know for sure how much influence you have on the game as a fan, but I think it's a lot. If we go behind, we have more influence than when we're ahead. At the start of the season if we went a goal behind everyone went quiet and we ended up losing. But now, like today, when we go behind everyone sings and we pull it back. I don't think that's a coincidence.'

I like the Colchester lads, their commitment to the sanctity of football and their unwavering conviction about the role they have to play in it. Colchester United are another team whose fortunes I'll follow with avid interest and affection.

This odyssey I've been on which has involved, I don't know, 40-odd games in the last three months or so has made me question many of the sacred laws in the football supporter handbook. You can change your partner, they say, but not your football team. Yet recalling the shots of genuine passion and adrenalin I got roaring on the likes of Airdrie, Stockport County, Total Network Solutions and, yes, Colchester United, I'm beginning to wonder if that's really true. I never thought I'd ever sing at matches but I do, and it feels great to have a real sense of involvement and feel you can touch the players on the pitch.

One week, I even cross enemy lines and sit in the middle of the hated hardcore at Fratton Park to see if the unflinching passion of the fans at Portsmouth touches me in any way. I can even admire the sense of theatre there as they sing the 'Pompey Chimes', one of the oldest of all football chants which reputedly dates from the days when the Royal Artillery, the forerunners of Portsmouth FC, played their games close to the town hall clock with the referee relying on its chimes to indicate the start and finish of matches. The words were originally printed in the Portsmouth handbook in 1900 – 'Play up Pompey, just one more goal/Make tracks, what ho!/Hallo hallo' – and make nonsense of Norwich's claims to have the oldest surviving football song still heard.

They sing it today and I chat quite amiably with the Portsmouth fans around me. Momentarily brainwashed, I admit at one point that I'm a Southampton supporter but they assume I'm joking and let me live. But when it comes to the crunch, I quietly swear when Gary O'Neil scores and they all jump around and dance on my head and sing 'Staying up staying up staying up'. See, the Old Firm, Manchester and Merseyside derbies may be the big ones in public and media perception but some of the parochial ones are just as bitter: Southampton/Portsmouth, Burnley/Blackburn, Kilmarnock/Ayr, Grimsby/Scunthorpe, Brighton/Palace, Norwich/Ipswich, Woking/Stevenage and, possibly at some stage in the future, AFC Wimbledon/Milton Keynes Dons.

I leave Portsmouth depressed by their victory over Fulham, but at least I secure an audience of sorts with Fulham's owner Mohamed Al Fayed, who says their fans are 'the finest in the world'. That's maybe not what the FA thinks when they dance on the pitch after beating Chelsea at Craven Cottage a few weeks later. 'They have supported their club through the dark days of lower league football to the echelons of the Premiership and each step of the journey they have been behind the team 100 per cent,' says Al Fayed. OK, so who are the *second* best fans? 'Newcastle – they are so passionate.'

Do you have a good relationship with the fans, Mr Al Fayed? 'Yes. I was welcomed to the Fulham family with open arms and we have maintained a fantastic relationship ever since. I took them back to their spiritual home of Craven Cottage and I continue to invest to make their home one they can be truly proud of and they continue to show me gratitude for this.' Will you remain part of Fulham's future? 'Of course! I'm a fan just like the supporters who come to the matches and I hope for great things in the future.'

Fulham do, though, come a cropper in the FA Cup fourth round, losing 2-1 at home to Leyton Orient, another club with a high-profile chairman. Snooker, boxing and golf promoter Barry Hearn tells me afterwards this is one of the greatest feelings he's had since being involved: 'Six thousand fans shouting from the rafters at Craven Cottage – magic!'

Unlike Mohamed Al Fayed, who claims never to sing at games, Hearn admits that he does occasionally lose his sense of decorum at matches: 'Oh, I'm always singing along – as long as it's not rude. I don't want to upset the wife!' He'll vent his feelings, too, if the fans are unjustifiably negative. 'I've got angry after a small minority of supporters acted completely irrationally. I understand their frustration when the team doesn't perform, but deep down they know they need to stick with the team to help them.

'The fans are the lifeblood of every club. For whatever reason, be it family, community or something different, people align themselves to a club and stick with it for life. It's your club, you'll back them through thick and thin, and they'll be there for you rain or shine. Like an ideal partner! At Orient we want to be everybody's dream spouse ...' Hmmmm.

I also go into the lions den at Millwall, where the bloke selling fanzines gives me a long lecture about the iniquities of the media who just won't let go of the old stereotypes of skinheads and loutish behaviour which gave birth to the famous chant 'No one likes us, we don't care'. Fanzine Man seems to be holding me personally responsible for every ill that they have experienced over the years: 'We never get any trouble here now. The fans are as good as gold. It's time people like you started giving us some credit.'

So I lean back in my seat to enjoy an afternoon of cultured, free-flowing football warmly applauded by the sporting Millwall supporters. Instead I get a mind-numbingly tedious 0-0 draw with Wolves and the only memorable thing that happens is police and stewards suddenly diving into the back of one of the home stands. Even the innocent Wolves fans look bemused by the activity as reinforcements pour into the trouble area. Perhaps they assume that the Millwall faithful have been pushed over the edge by the stultifying boredom of the match, rebelled against their image as born-again angels and started fighting among themselves.

After the match the rows continue outside the ground where a bunch of supporters are haranguing the police about The Incident. According to the indignant Millwall fan I collar, it arose after the appearance of Wolves' substitute, South Korean player Ki-Hyeon Seol. 'It's crazy,' he tells me in his best South London barrow boy accent. 'Some of the lads up in the stand start calling "DVD" at him when he gets the ball and the next thing we know the police are diving in, barging us out of the way and pulling the lads out.' '*DVD*?' 'Yeah, you know, DVD,' and he mimics the tones of a seedy backstreet Soho salesman offering to sell you a pirate copy of *Asian Lady Boys*. I look at him in bewilderment. 'They say it's racist,' he continues indignantly. What's racist about that? Political correctness gone mad, that's what it is.'

The conclusion of my odyssey, I suppose, is that the true quality football lies in the Premiership; the quality but not necessarily the *fun*, and definitely not the heart or soul. There certainly seems a massive divide now between the top division and the lower leagues, not merely in terms of the football but the whole culture. At Grimsby Town I talk to a local 18-year-old fan, Hannah Cawsey, who puts it all beautifully in perspective.

'I was five when I first started going with my dad and grandad and every season we either seem to be promoted or relegated, but it doesn't matter,' she tells me. 'It's just something that's in your blood. One of my earliest memories is standing on the terraces eating fish and chips, and it just all becomes part of who you are.'

Would you want a Russian billionaire to come along and buy Grimsby and bring untold riches, Hannah? 'No, I wouldn't. We have a chairman who's been a Grimsby fan all his life and he comes among the fans and says "Hi" to everyone and that's how it should be. I don't think it's right that someone like Roman Abramovich suddenly comes along and shoves in a load of money to buy the title. In fact I hate the whole Premier League. It's all about money and that really shouldn't be what football is about.'

Driving home on the M25 on a Sunday afternoon I hear on the radio that Arsenal are playing Charlton at Wycombe in the League Cup Final: the *Women's* League Cup Final. Naturally, I point Alberta the Bold Cavalier straight at Wycombe. The queue along Hillbottom Road, the one route into Wycombe's Causeway Stadium, is so intense that the match is 15 minutes old before I get to hand over my £5 and join the curious mix of families with picnics and yelping teenagers with face paints, most of them rooting for Arsenal. There are ear-splitting squeals every time either team launches a meaningful attack, and it has all the elements of those old schoolboy internationals when kids would be bussed to Wembley from all over the country for perhaps a first taste of the indefinable magic of football. But it's got a lot more credibility than Milton Keynes Dons.

The crowd is 3,506 – predominantly female, many of them wearing track suits bearing the names of their own teams – and the younger element maintains a high-pitched but impressively constant level of chanting, waving their red-and-white balloons above their heads as the match ebbs and flows. Wearing the same redcurrant shirts as their male counterparts, the Arsenal team look far stronger and more sophisticated, and a weakened Charlton team are penned back in their own area for long periods. But in Nigerian-born 19-year-old Eniola Aluko they have a burly, explosive striker who escapes the Arsenal defence twice to score with two quality strikes before half-time.

There's even more fun as half-time turns into a mass karaoke, the girls on their feet singing along in full-throated unison with the likes of 'The JCB Song' and 'I Bet You Look Good On the Dancefloor'. By the time we get to '(Is This the Way To) Amarillo?' Wycombe's ground has turned into a giant under-18s disco, with half of the crowd doing the Peter Kay walk.

The innocence and purity of the occasion feels strangely cleansing after watching the RADA-inspired dying swan acts of Drogba and Robben and the prima donna preening of the other millionaires at the top end of the game. The fact that you're watching women playing ceases to be any kind of issue as soon as the game starts. Tackles are full-blooded, there is no shortage of power, skill or effort, and the players are fully committed. They just don't go into orbit whenever they're tackled or yell obscenities at each other or wave imaginary cards after every foul or go charging after the ref when a decision goes against them. Well, at least not until Arsenal are denied a stonewall penalty late in the second half.

By now, though, the attention of the girls behind me has started to wane and while the squealing has faded I'm now being kicked in the back with regular force as they swing their legs around debating which boys at school they fancy and devise their own alternative entertainment involving staring contests and who's-got-the-longest-tongue competitions. 'Can you turn your eyelids inside out like *this*?' one of the girls asks. The whole crowd in the near vicinity turns around to look. And she does it too. Eyelids. Inside out. Sod the way to Amarillo, *this* should have been the half-time entertainment.

We're suddenly so wrapped up trying to turn our eyelids inside out that we miss Arsenal's goal, scored by Scotland captain Julie Fleeting. Arsenal pile everyone forward in search of the equaliser and our thoughts go to extra time and penalties, but Charlton's experienced keeper Pauline Cope (60 England caps) pulls off a string of immaculate saves and Charlton win the cup.

They are delighted. Arsenal have appeared in twelve cup finals and never previously lost, and at the end the Charlton players come sprinting to the stands looking for their friends and loved ones in a mass hug-fest. But my attention is drawn by a lone Arsenal player who walks slowly to the crowd chatting, signing autographs and posing for pictures. Half an hour later, long after the Charlton players have disappeared inside for their hot shower and maybe a sharp snifter, she's still out there signing autographs.

This is Faye White, the 28-year-old Arsenal captain and central defender who is also captain of England and has clearly assumed a PR responsibility for the wider interests of the women's game. 'Yeah, I was gutted at losing, but if they take the time and trouble to come and support us I'm not going to walk off the pitch and ignore them. It's important to me to go over and say hello,' she tells me later. 'Women's football used to have this image of butch ladies but it's very different now. Football generally isn't as male-orientated as it used to be and people can see from our matches that have been shown on TV that mums and very feminine-looking girls play and watch the game. It can get very competitive and fiery and the tackles really fly in sometimes. But discipline is better than in the men's game and nobody goes down unless they're really hurt. They don't want to be seen as wimps.'

From Horley in Surrey, Faye proved her bottle as a kid prac-
tising with the boys' team that her brother played for and her
dad managed. She wasn't allowed to play in the matches but
she gave as good as she got in training. 'The others just saw me
as one of the boys so it was fine, and when they played matches
I cut the oranges.' She was playing with seniors in her local
women's team Three Bridges (Horsham) by the time she was 14,
and after starring in a friendly against Arsenal three years later,
she became the first player to be picked for England from
outside the national league. Like her dad and brother she was a
Spurs fan, but she didn't think twice about joining Arsenal
when the offer came in 1996.

'It was a big difference,' she says. 'Horsham was a bit of a
social club but at Arsenal the girls were a lot quicker and more
committed. You have to be committed, training twice a week as
a club but doing extra training yourself. Then going to
Liverpool and places like that for matches takes out the whole
weekend, so it is very serious.'

There have been attempts to set up a professional league and
my old mate Mohamed Al Fayed funded a full-time Fulham
side for a while in readiness. In the end it all fell through,
although Faye doesn't discount it happening at some stage in
the future, even if it's a summer league so as not to have to
compete with the men's game: 'There are more and more girls
getting into it all the time and we're fitter and more competitive
than ever. In the 2001 Euros we were a long way off it, but
England are improving very fast. We got 12,500 for the World
Cup qualifier against France at Ewood Park [a 0-0 draw] and it's
growing all the time. We're ranked 13th in the world now.'

Faye's full-time job is at Arsenal where she is involved with
coaching, soccer schools and the centre of excellence, and while
she retains a soft spot for Spurs, she says she's now a Gooner
through and through. 'Yes, we all support the men's team and
they're very encouraging when we meet them, they always ask
how we're getting on. Patrick Vieira was amazingly supportive
when he was here and so is Thierry Henry. They have a

different culture in France and to have a women's side is very natural to them. It would be nice to think it could be like that in England too.'

Face paints, squealing girls, a mass exhibition of the Peter Kay 'Amarillo' walk at half-time and demonstrations of turning your eyelids inside out when the play gets boring? Yeah, Faye, *bring it on*.

With the whole nature of football changing irrevocably before our very eyes, it feels refreshing to have been in the midst of an area of the game that is still in its relative infancy. For in ten years' time the whole feel of places like the Racecourse Ground, Wrexham and Layer Road, Colchester will inevitably be very different. They will have to be, or they simply won't be there at all.

At the top end of the game the big clubs are single-mindedly intent on getting richer and to hell with the greater good of the game. And heaven only knows what will happen if the G14 union of Europe's self-proclaimed elite clubs (from Arsenal to Bayer Leverkusen – er, *Bayer Leverkusen*?) get the sort of control over the way the sport is run that they so desperately crave.

But at some point they will get their bottoms bitten. Maybe it is time for supporters to get angry and fight back against the pricing structures, the indifference of the FA and boardrooms to their concerns, the mad fixture list and the late cancellation of matches they've travelled hundreds of miles to see. A supporters' strike would certainly concentrate a few minds on the truly important elements of a football club.

There is still some poison on the terraces, of course. There are those who hiss at Tottenham games as a reminder to their large Jewish support of the gas chambers; those who chant about the Munich disaster when Manchester United come to town; and the references to the supporters murdered in Istanbul that are aimed at winding up Leeds supporters. Not to mention the pockets of marshmallow heads who are still looking for a fight. But in general the future good of the game lies in the hands of the supporters, just as it always has done.

The enterprise of those founding AFC Wimbledon and FC United offer a beacon of hope that those who truly love football aren't prepared to abandon it and will retaliate against the moneymen. And while there are fans like Dave Burnley chasing round the country in his claret beanie hat and Lee Clarkson bursting his lungs for Colchester United and the Stockport County fans singing their way around the country without a care what league they're in and, yes, Pete Boyle rousing the fans at Old Trafford to sing of old heroes like Busby, Best and Cantona as well as the new ones, then football will still surely be the winner.

And then, in the end, all roads lead back to Bovril and Brentford ...

We are waiting, my dad and I, to meet the vicar to discuss my mum's funeral arrangements when my phone rings. It's Greg Dyke. Well, it's actually Greg Dyke's PA. She says that Greg is willing to talk to me about football. I apologise to the vicar but he's an incredibly nice man who turns out to be a Bolton Wanderers fan and we later have a fruitful debate about Nat Lofthouse barging Harry Gregg into the net in the 1958 FA Cup Final so he understands completely.

It turns out things have taken a dramatic turn at Brentford since my previous visit to Griffin Park. Despite the geography teacher's fears about my shrewd spying mission, Brentford overcame Oldham in their FA Cup replay to embark on a glamorous, money-spinning Cup run. They beat the Premiership whipping boys Sunderland in the next round then flog the man who scored the goals to put them there, D.J. Campbell, to Birmingham City for £500,000. When they play at Charlton Athletic in the fifth round, Martin Allen comes up with another ruse to strengthen the ties between fans and club: he organises a £50-per-ticket raffle for a fan to win a place as the assistant manager for the day. The money raised pays for the team to stay in a posh hotel before the match and the winner, a chubby, well-spoken chap in a posh suit and club tie called Chris Swatton, gets to stay with them and take his place on the bench next to Mad Dog.

With Charlton two up, Allen pushes Swatton to the front of the technical area and the new assistant manager starts clapping, shouting and waving his fists at the players. The Brentford team can barely contain their mirth, stopping to point and snigger at the comical sight gesticulating at them, but while their backs are turned the unsporting Charlton sneaks break away to thump home a third goal. It must be the first time that Martin Allen has ever laughed when his team have conceded a goal. A gushing Swatton later says it's one of the best experiences of his life.

In the meantime Brentford have surged up the league, seemingly heading for the Championship, while those Bees United collecting boxes have done the trick, too, and enabled a supporters buy-out of the club. One of the first things they do is appoint a new chairman in celebrity fan Greg Dyke, he who invented Roland Rat and ran the BBC until that nasty business with Tony Blair and weapons of mass destruction.

This is splendid news. Greg Dyke is a big mate of mine. Well, he's not a *big* mate, exactly. Well, not so much a *mate* as an acquaintance: I used to know him a bit. My first job was as a cub reporter doing the usual round of magistrates courts and flower shows on the *Slough Evening Mail*, where one Greg Dyke was already something of a legend, racing around the place at a breathless pace, conducting three separate interviews at once and having them all written up and filed before he'd even put the phone down. The theory was that he somehow sucked in everybody else's energy and turned it into one bewildering ball of hyperactivity. It was like having your very own superhero around the place.

So calls are made, letters are written and I persuade Greg Dyke to buy me a cappuccino. As magnificently motormouthed as I remember him, he asks what I've been doing since those hazy, crazy days together on the *Slough Evening Mail* a million years ago and I give him a 30-second résumé and ask him what *he's* been doing. Well, you know, Greg, *apart* from inventing Roland Rat and running the BBC ... oh yes, you're running

Brentford now. 'Oh no, I'm just a figurehead,' he protests. 'They just got me in to open a few doors.'

But Brentford are flying now! You must have the Midas touch. 'Well, one of my ex-bosses once said to me, "Greg, I'll always put money into anything you're involved in." I said, "Why's that then?" and he said, "Because you're such a lucky bastard." So I join Brentford and immediately we win five games on the trot, including the FA Cup game against Sunderland. So at the moment the fans all love me because we win. In fact, a friend phoned me up after the fifth game and said, "Quit now." But then again, when Manchester United won the title seven times in nine years, the chairman Martin Edwards still got booed every time he set foot on the pitch. That's because he kept trying to sell the club. Fans don't like that. They like loyalty.'

Greg was on the board at Manchester United for four years before he was forced to relinquish the post to allow him to join the BBC. It didn't leave him with a very good impression of the inner workings of football and the word 'arseholes' regularly crops up as we talk. 'I sat on the board at Manchester United and thought if this is the best-run club in the country then God help us,' he says. 'I was the only director who didn't want to sell to Murdoch. I just thought, "What the fuck does *he* know about football?"' Greg has now fallen out of love with United because 'it's owned by these arseholes who don't give a fuck about football'.

Greg was brought up in Hayes just up the road from Brentford and well remembers Bill Dodgin Sr coming to the house to sign his brother to the club. 'He was about 16 and played for the A team for a couple of years and then left, but from that point we all became Brentford fans and I've stayed a fan more or less ever since.' The first thing he said to the other directors on becoming chairman was, 'Can we get rid of this ties bollocks?' He still has to wear a tie to get into the boardroom at away games, but he doesn't like it. 'The idea that you have to go to football on a Saturday afternoon wearing a tie is ludicrous.

When New Labour came in the first thing they did to get credibility was to wear suits and ties. Now the first thing that the New Conservatives are doing is taking them off!'

Brentford still has an £8 million or so debt and looks like losing £500,000 this season despite a good Cup run and the sale of D.J. Campbell to Birmingham for the same amount. 'No, it wasn't a hard decision to sell him,' says Greg. 'Here is a kid who was on £80 a week at Yeading, £800 a week at Brentford and now he's been offered £6,000 a week to go to Birmingham. How can we stand in his way?' The priority, he says, is a new stadium, and plans are well underway to build one. 'Well, our ground is crap, isn't it?' he says. 'It's like something out of the Dark Ages.' Well, yeah, but I find that quite endearing. It has, er … *roots*. 'Yeah, I love it too,' he says. 'Going down to get your Bovril …'

Bovril! Here speaks a true football man. I launch into my theory that the true soul of football is to be found in grounds that sell Bovril and Wagon Wheels. 'This is about you getting old and nostalgic,' he says. 'My kids have never had Bovril *or* Wagon Wheels at football matches. But I have. See, I'm 58 and I've had some big jobs at the BBC and the rest and I've had all the posh dinners and lunches and breakfast at the Savoy and all that, but now I really don't want any of these things. What I really want to do is go and *drink Bovril at Brentford*. I'm lucky I can mix in any strata, but what I love most is chatting to the working-class blokes at Brentford who tell me stories about when their dads used to come and watch the team. And I love the songs the fans sing. When Shrewsbury came here our fans all started singing, "You're Welsh, and you know you are." I just laugh out loud at some of the stuff they come out with.'

All the property developers infiltrating the game at the lower end to make a quick buck will never understand it, but football essentially is about romance. Greg Dyke recognises this better than most: 'When I was on the board at Manchester United my eldest son was in the middle of doing his finals at uni when United got to the Champions League final in Barcelona. He asked me, "Should I come to the match – I've got my finals the next day?" I said, "Let me tell you about life, son. When you're 30 nobody gives a fuck what degree you've got, but if you say you were in Barcelona the night that Manchester United won the European Champions League, they'll remember *that*!' Dyke Jr went to Barcelona with his dad.

So I take my seat in the Wendy House once again as Brentford tackle my old mates Bradford City at the ground that even their own chairman describes as 'crap'. It may be crap, but it's alive and vibrant – a far cry from the desultory scenario I found here four months ago. The players run out to a standing ovation and manager Martin Allen is greeted like a pop star as he walks to the dugout, shaking hands, waving at the crowd and acknowledging the huge reception all the way (although I note his taste in jumpers hasn't improved any). The crowd behind the goal maintains a constant barrage of songs and chants: 'Brentford Till I Die', 'You Are My Brentford', 'Bless 'Em All' and 'Hey Jude'.

Even when Michael Symes scores against the run of play for Bradford when the Bees defence fails to deal with a corner, it doesn't stop the party. 'That's it, we've got no chance of winning now,' says the most miserable man in the world next to me. But Lloyd Owusu strides through to grab the equaliser just before half-time and the players depart to loud applause.

The transformation in the atmosphere is amazing, and Greg Dyke's claims that Brentford are actually attracting new supporters from disillusioned Chelsea fans doesn't seem quite so ludicrous. Brentford pile on the pressure but the Bradford goal leads a charmed life. The geezer next to me tuts loudly at every miss and shouts 'chop chop' whenever Bradford get the ball, apparently in the belief that possession of the ball is a dastardly ploy to waste time. He is still certain Brentford will lose.

I think of Greg Dyke. I think of the Winstanleys, who have driven down from Scotland for the game as they always do. I think of our old greengrocer whose sole topic of conversation used to be the Bees. I think of the old bloke in the red bobble hat who lives in one of the terraced houses 50 yards away. I look at the miserable git next to me going 'chop chop' and I think of old

Harry Norris, who taught me that being a football fan was more about the suffering than the triumph and that there's no honour in the highs unless you've also lived through the lows. And I'm on my feet and screaming for Brentford to get the winner.

It doesn't happen. The match ends 1-1 and we shuffle out of the Wendy House in mild disappointment. But that's football for you. It will always find a way of letting you down. You are just thinking of the glory-glory lap of honour, and in comes football with its studs up to cut you down.

On the way out I stop at the snack bar for a comforting cup of Bovril. It's delicious.

Bibliography

John Aizlewood, *Playing at Home* (Orion)
Norman Barrett, *Daily Telegraph Football Chronicle* (Ted Smart)
Ian Black, *Two More Andy Gorams* (Black & White)
Tom Bower, *Broken Dreams* (Pocket Books)
Jack Bremner, *Shit Ground No Fans* (Bantam Press)
Niall Couper, *The Spirit of Wimbledon* (Cherry Red Books)
David Elleray, *The Man in the Middle* (Time Warner)
Four-Four-Two magazine (Haymarket Publishing)
Guinness Book of British Hit Singles (Guinness)
Robert Jeffery, *Pictorial History of English Football* (Parragon)
Stephen F. Kelly, *The Kop* (Virgin)
Stephen F. Kelly, *Graeme Souness: A Soccer Revolutionary* (Headline)
Keith Haynes & Phil Sumbler, *The Tony Ford Story* (Tempus)
Ian Lancashire, *A Swaying Mass of Humanity: Four Decades of County Song* (private)
Chris McLoughlin, *Spion Kop* (Sport Media)
News of the World Football Annual 2005-2006 (Invincible Press)
Playfair Football Annual 2005-2006 (Headline)
Mick Quinn with Oliver Harvey, *Who Ate All the Pies?* (Virgin)
Brian Scovell, *Football Gentry: The Cobbold Brothers* (Tempus)
John Tennant, *Football the Golden Age* (Cassell)
Adrian Thrills, *You're Not Singing Any More* (Ebury)
Stephen Walsh, *Voices of the Old Firm* (Mainstream)
Andrew Ward, *Football's Strangest Matches* (Past Times)